Anger and Racial Politics

Politicians, scholars, and pundits often disagree about whether race has been injected into a political campaign or policy debate. Some have suspected that race sometimes enters into politics even when political elites avoid using racial cues or racially coded language. *Anger and Racial Politics* provides a theoretical framework for understanding the emotional conditions under which this effect might happen. Antoine J. Banks asserts that making whites angry – no matter the basis for their anger – will make ideas about race more salient to them. He argues that anger, and not fear or other negative emotions, provides the foundation upon which contemporary white racial attitudes are structured. Drawing on a multi-method approach – lab and Internet survey experiments and nationally representative surveys – he demonstrates that anger plays an important role in enhancing the impact of race on whites' preferences for putting an end to affirmative action, repealing health care reform, hanging the Confederate flag high, and voting for Tea Party–backed candidates.

Antoine J. Banks is an assistant professor in the Department of Government and Politics at the University of Maryland, College Park. Banks earned a PhD in political science at the University of Michigan in 2009 and a BA in political science and African American studies at Hunter College, City University of New York. Banks specializes in American politics, with a focus on race and ethnic politics, political psychology, public opinion, and voting behavior. His current research interests center on two issues: emotion's importance in triggering the political impact of racial attitudes and emotions as a motivator for political action. His articles have appeared in peer-reviewed journals such as *American Journal of Political Science*, *Public Opinion Quarterly*, *Political Behavior*, and *Political Psychology*.

Anger and Racial Politics

The Emotional Foundation of
Racial Attitudes in America

ANTOINE J. BANKS
University of Maryland

CAMBRIDGE
UNIVERSITY PRESS

CAMBRIDGE
UNIVERSITY PRESS

32 Avenue of the Americas, New York NY 10013-2473, USA

Cambridge University Press is part of the University of Cambridge.

It furthers the University's mission by disseminating knowledge in the pursuit of education, learning and research at the highest international levels of excellence.

www.cambridge.org
Information on this title: www.cambridge.org/9781107629271

© Antoine J. Banks 2014

First published 2014
First paperback edition 2015

A catalogue record for this publication is available from the British Library

Library of Congress Cataloguing in Publication data
Banks, Antoine J., 1979–
Anger and racial politics : the emotional foundation of racial attitudes in America / Antoine J. Banks, University of Maryland
    pages cm
Includes bibliographical references and index.
ISBN 978-1-107-04983-3 (hardback)
1. United States – Race relations – Political aspects.   2. Race – Political aspects – United States.   3. Racism – Political aspects – United States.   4. Anger – Political aspects – United States.   5. Whites – United States – Attitudes. I. Title.
E185.615.B2846   2014
305.800973–dc23   2014001486

ISBN 978-1-107-04983-3 Hardback
ISBN 978-1-107-62927-1 Paperback

Contents

Acknowledgments

This book bears only my name, but many people have contributed to its completion. My thanks go, first and foremost, to my family because without their support and guidance this book would have never come to fruition. My grandmother, Regina Banks-Clark, has not only been my emotional backbone throughout the process, but has also given up many nights to serve as copy editor of several chapters. While I worked on this book, my mother, Juanita Banks, gave me the confidence to push through each difficult obstacle. I also wish to thank Karol Banks, my lovely wife, who keeps me calm and happy, and Jarred, Jourdan, and Blake, my children, who remind me that a larger purpose is always at hand. I am very grateful to all of them who have supported me through the bad times and enjoyed the good times with me. Much of the credit for my perseverance and completing this book goes to them.

I owe a great many intellectual debts. The most important are to Nicholas Valentino, Vincent Hutchings, Donald Kinder, John Jackson, and Norbert Schwarz, who guided me through the dissertation that was the early version of this book. I am especially grateful to Nick and Vince, who instilled in me that contributing to knowledge and good scholarship are what this enterprise is all about. I am honored to have learned from these two great scholars. The beginning stages of this project also grew through my interaction with fellow graduate students and excellent faculty members at the University of Michigan. They created an environment for me to express my ideas while providing sorely needed feedback. Their advice was invaluable, particularly that from Ted Brader, the late Hanes Walton Jr., Ismail White, Corrine McConnaughy, Nancy Burns, Robert Franzese, James Jackson, W. Russell Neuman, Dominick Wright, Tasha Philpot, Harwood McClerking, Anne Davis, Rosario Aguilar, Gaye Muderrisoglu, Irfan Nooruddin, Elizabeth Suhay, and Katie Drake. I am especially grateful to my good friend and fellow Michigan graduate, Eric Groenendyk, who never let me settle – always pushing me to think harder about the theory and its contribution.

Many people at the University of Maryland generously commented on chapters of this book. Most of all, I owe special thanks to Karen Kaufmann, who went beyond the call of duty. She read countless drafts of the manuscript, offering helpful suggestions and criticisms. James Gimpel and Eric Uslaner read an earlier version of this book, providing helpful comments for improvement. The book also greatly benefited from the comments of Brian McKenzie, Michael Hanmer, Daniel Corstange, Sarah Croco, Ian Ward, and Frances Lee. I also had the valuable opportunity of having a book conference. I thank Shanto Iyengar, Tali Mendelberg, and Kimberly Gross for attending. They read every word of the manuscript and offered great feedback. They also asked really hard questions, some of which I probably didn't want to hear, but in the process, they made it a much better book. As a result, I am eternally grateful to them.

I also had the pleasure of presenting parts of this book at academic conferences; the American Politics Workshop at Georgetown University; the Symposium on the Politics of Immigration, Race, and Ethnicity (SPIRE) at Rutgers University; and the Political Science department at Duke University. From these interactions, I especially wish to thank Leonie Huddy, Jamie Druckman, Richard Lau, D. Sunshine Hillygus, Hans Noel, Kerry Haynie, Jonathan Ladd, Christopher Johnston, Laia Balcells, Eric McDaniel, Christina Greer, Jennifer Wolak, George Marcus, and Michael MacKuen. The book also benefited tremendously from the comments of the three reviewers for Cambridge University Press, who posed tough questions and offered great advice, most of which I incorporated. I am also very grateful to Robert Dreesen at Cambridge University Press for his enthusiastic support of the book.

My gratitude also extends to a host of graduate and undergraduate research assistants. Sanata Sy-Sahande, Kerry Jones, Daniel Biggers,

Melissa Bell, Erin Byrd, Joanne Ibarra, Kerem Ozan Kalkan, and Hoyoun Kol all provided outstanding assistance. For financial support, I thank the University of Michigan and the University of Maryland, along with the National Science Foundation, for supporting my health care experiment via Time-Sharing Experiments for the Social Sciences (TESS). I also thank Wiley-Blackwell Publishers for permission to reprint materials originally published in "Emotional Substrates of White Racial Attitudes," *American Journal of Political Science* (with Nicholas Valentino) 56 (April 2012): 286–297; Oxford University Press for permission to reprint materials originally published in "Racialized Campaign Ads: The Emotional Content in Implicit Racial Appeals Primes White Racial Attitudes," *Public Opinion Quarterly* (with Melissa Bell) 77 (Summer 2013): 549–560; and Springer Press for permission to reprint materials originally published in "The Public's Anger: White Racial Attitudes and Opinions Toward Health Care Reform," *Political Behavior* (published online in 2013).

Introduction

In 1978, Howard Jarvis, a conservative politician, led what some considered "a second American Revolution" in California. At the time, inflation caused many Californians' home values to soar, raising property taxes to 52 percent above the national average (Sears and Citrin 1982). This increase in taxes ignited a tax revolt. An angry backlash against higher taxes emerged in the public. News accounts of the uprising described taxpayers as "mad as hell and aren't going to take it."[1] As a result, a referendum, Proposition 13, was put on the ballot. It was an amendment to the California constitution decreasing property taxes and requiring a two-thirds majority in both legislative houses to raise future state taxes. But soon after Proposition 13 passed by a two to one margin, Jarvis stated on *Meet the Press*:

I think welfare is a narcotic in this country. It will eventually destroy the country. To put welfare in the property tax is absolutely an abortion. A lot of people in this country are paying for welfare through property taxes when they don't have enough food to live on in their house. It should be that a guy can go home, shut the front door and tell the rest of the world to go to hell.[2]

No discussion of race took place during the tax revolt, so what impelled Jarvis to bring up his views about race? Sears and Citrin make a similar point, stating, "[s]ome scholars and many blacks had seen racism in the midst of a great many political issues that had little manifest racial content. The tax revolt appears to have been another one of them" (1982, 214). In fact, they find that racial prejudice had a more substantial impact on support for the tax revolt than did general conservatism and Republican Party identification.

Unfortunately, the tax revolt is not the only example of nonracial anger leading Americans to view politics via a racial lens. A more recent example is the collapse of the 2008 housing market, which contributed to a deep recession that included massive layoffs, home foreclosures, and contraction of the Gross Domestic Product (GDP). According to a 2009 *ABC News/Washington Post* poll, a majority of Americans opted for "angry" – angry about the role banks (70%), the Bush administration (58%), and large corporations (68%) played in the economic recession. But this nonracial anger about the financial meltdown soon turned into blaming blacks for the country's economic woes. For example, when asked who was to blame, Ann Coulter, a conservative pundit, forcefully responded: "[T]hey gave your mortgage to a less qualified minority."[3] Another ostensibly nonracial issue that has evoked strong feelings from a large percentage of Americans is Barack Obama and Democrats' proposal for comprehensive health care reform. In the summer and fall of 2009, we witnessed anger spilling out of town hall meetings on health care reform. Some politicians and pundits suggested that these emotionally charged public demonstrations against reform evoked racism.[4] Others strongly disagreed; they argued opposition to health care reform was simply about policy and had nothing to do with race.[5] All of these examples raise an important question. Can a seemingly nonracial stimulus (e.g., higher property taxes or health care reform) that evokes anger cause racism to play a more prominent role in American society?

Henri Tajfel, a renowned social psychologist, argued that, as humans, we strive for differentiation by dividing ourselves into us versus them to view the social world. Racial and ethnic prejudice is one consequence of this process. It is a phenomenon that dates back to the late medieval and early modern periods (Fredrickson 2002), and it has had a catastrophic impact on society – leading to mass genocide, extreme violence, and open forms of discrimination. Racial prejudice is an enduring problem of international and national importance, and scholars have made significant strides in understanding and combating this human problem. Even so, scholars have devoted little attention to understanding the circumstances that cause racism to have a greater impact on American society. Kinder and Kam agree, stating that "social scientists have been quite successful in developing and testing explanations [e.g., ethnocentrism], but much less successful in specifying the conditions under which those explanations apply" (2009, 35).

The primary purpose of this book is to examine whether the experience of *anger* increases the role of racial prejudice in people's political decision-making process. My main interest lies in the emotional circumstances that cause racism to have real consequences in American public opinion. On hot button political issues like affirmative action, busing, Confederate flag displays, and health care reform, or in presidential and congressional politics, we cannot fully understand the impact of racism in these domains without taking anger into account. My main theoretical argument is that anger, but not disgust or fear, is tightly linked to contemporary racism in the minds of many white Americans. In fact, I contend that anger and racial prejudice form such a strong bond that evoking anger should activate this racial belief system from memory. As a consequence, those holding strongly prejudiced views should be persuaded to more vehemently oppose racially redistributive policies and candidates perceived to help blacks.

The main contribution of this book – that anger is the dominant emotional underpinning of contemporary racism – suggests that racial thinking can enter into politics, even when political elites avoid using group cues (e.g., racial background). Subtle racial appeals like the "weekend passes" ad that showed a menacing photo of "Willie" Horton – an African American – have proved to be risky if the racial message is discovered, because the appeal loses its effectiveness. It seems we have gotten to the point where there is a strong norm of racial equality when it comes to elite discussions of race, which has driven overt racial appeals into hiding. If so, perhaps the apparent racialization of politics has decreased (Thernstrom and Thernstrom 1997). But the strong bond between anger and racial considerations suggests an alternative scenario. That is, the conditions under which racial thinking may be salient are more pervasive than scholars may have suspected. Unlike other negative emotions, anger is common in everyday life, so much so that people can become angry up to several times a day (Averill 1982). A similar effect occurs in the realm of politics. When asked how presidential candidates make them feel, people more often respond with anger than with fear (Valentino et al. 2011).[6] The sheer frequency with which people experience anger, in general and about politics, implies that race may be accessible and ready for use if a relevant judgment is called upon. Because today's battles of race are far less overt does not mean they are less racially potent. My theory of anger and race suggests that racial thinking is so ingrained in American society via emotions that race no longer needs to be salient for racial considerations to impact relevant political evaluations. As a result, scholars' neglect of the specific emotional underpinnings of contemporary racial attitudes has led us to underestimate the impact of racism on various political judgments.

For us to understand why anger and contemporary racism are so strongly linked, I turn to Gordon Willard Allport, a renowned professor of psychology at Harvard University. Allport's *The Nature of Prejudice* is widely considered the most influential book written on out-group prejudice. Driven by a strong moral conviction of justice and social concern, he established the theoretical framework for social scientists to understand prejudice. One of the most important aspects of racial and ethnic prejudice to Allport was the concept of *scapegoating*. He stated, "[S]capegoats need not be lily white in their innocence, they always attract more blame, more animosity, more stereotyped judgment than can be rationally justified" (1954, 245–246). With scapegoating, members of the in-group unfairly blame the out-group for causing the in-group's misfortunes. Other scholars, inspired by Allport, also recognized the importance of blame appraisals in prejudice. For example, Thomas Pettigrew's theory of "ultimate attribution error" posits that prejudiced individuals attribute the out-group's negative behavior to individualistic and dispositional causes (1979). Likewise, social dominance theory maintains that dispositional attributions, referred to as *legitimizing myths*, are used to justify group-based social inequality. Sidanius and Pratto state, "[w]hat all these ideas and doctrines have in common is the notion that each individual occupies that position along the social status that he or she has earned and therefore deserves" (1999, 46).

Allport's insight into the role of scapegoating (or blame attributions) in intergroup prejudice helps us explain that the Dutch strongly supported deporting immigrant groups such as Turks and Surinamers because they did not behave in accordance with the values of Northern Europeans (Pettigrew and Meertens 1995); that a majority of whites attribute America's racial problem to the notion that blacks fail to pull themselves up by their bootstraps (Kinder and Sanders 1996; Sears and Kinder 1971); that the Hindu-Muslim conflict in India stems, in part, from attributing the out-group's negative behaviors to its internal characteristics (Taylor and Jaggi 1974). Even prejudice toward more recent social groupings is centered on blame such as: people blaming obese people for being overweight and denigrating them for it (Crandall 1994; Oliver 2005) or healthy individuals holding AIDS victims responsible for their medical condition (Devine, Plant, and Harrison 1999). All of these studies clearly illustrate that across social groupings, and around the world, blame is a critical feature of out-group prejudice.

What can scapegoating teach us about the emotional underpinnings of out-group prejudice? When the in-group blames members of the out-group for their disadvantaged status, and they're provided with assistance to improve their social standing, it strikes a strong chord among prejudiced individuals. These individuals believe that they live life by a strict moral code – adhering to the rules and traditions that govern society – while the out-group does not. As a consequence, they view members of the out-group as blameworthy for their position in life. So when the out-group receives rights and resources from government, members of the in-group consider it unfair and unjust. My contention is that these individualistic attributions are strongly linked to feelings of anger (Lazarus 1991; Smith and Ellsworth 1985; Weiner 1986). So whenever blame dominates the discourse on out-group animosity, anger will be strongly attached to this belief system.

The arguments that I make here, and more fully in Chapter 1, are meant to be general in scope. My theory of anger and prejudice applies to out-groups generally, and is not limited to any particular group. That is, when people justify their dislike for out-groups (no matter the group) on the basis of perceived negative internal characteristics (e.g., lazy or untrustworthy) – basically undeserving – anger should be strongly linked to their beliefs. With that said, the majority of this book focuses on white Americans' antiblack attitudes. The reason for focusing on racial prejudice in the United States is because the debate on race, since the civil rights movement, has been infused with blame rhetoric. As a result, we would expect anger to be strongly attached to this belief system. Nonetheless, as a point of comparison, I also examine ethnocentrism, which differs from racial prejudice. It "is an attitude that divides the world into two opposing camps. From an ethnocentric point of view, groups are either 'friend' or they are 'foe.' Ethnocentrism is a general outlook on social difference, it is prejudice, broadly conceived" (Kinder and Kam 2009, 42). In Chapter 2, I investigate whether anger is also a condition under which ethnocentrism enters into people's opinions on matters of race and immigration.

Allport astutely recognized that emotion was an essential component of out-group prejudice. In his definition of prejudice, he included the concept of emotion – "[e]thnic prejudice is antipathy based upon faulty and inflexible generalization. It may be felt or expressed" (1954, 9). According to Allport, the prejudiced individual's insecurity to cope with his/her inner conflict leads to displacing anger and aggression upon the out-group (scapegoat). In fact, he suggested that anger and out-group prejudice coexist.

Throughout life the same tendency persists for anger to center upon available rather than upon logical objects. Everyday speech recognizes this displacement in a variety of phrases: to take it out on the dog: Don't take it out on me; whipping boy; scapegoat. While the full sequence is frustration-aggression displacement, current psychology speaks more simply of the "frustration-aggression hypothesis." The scapegoat theory of prejudice – probably the most popular theory – rests exclusively upon this hypothesis. (1954, 343)

Allport's approach to understanding prejudice was grounded in the personality of the individual – very similar to Adorno and his colleagues' (1950) authoritarian personality theory. Social identity theorists like Tajfel expanded on Allport's theory of prejudice and integrated it into a group-level process. Tajfel and his colleagues' work on in-group/out-group differentiation helps us understand how dispositional attributions aren't just the result of a personality flaw, but how members of the in-group justify their animosity and hatred toward other groups.

SOCIAL IDENTITY THEORY

Henri Tajfel and his Bristol colleagues questioned whether intergroup conflict was necessary for out-group discrimination and prejudice to occur. To test this proposition, they devised several ingenious laboratory experiments with the purpose of creating the most minimal conditions possible. To do so, the conflict of interest among groups, self-interest, and previous hostility were all eliminated.[7] Bristol teer aged boys were assigned to groups on a fairly trivial basis such as: estimating the number of dots shown in rapid sequence, preferring the painting of Klee to Kandinsky (abstract artists), or by the toss of a coin. Afterward, subjects were put into individual cubicles and given a task to allocate points worth money to other participants. They were also notified if the others involved were members" of their in-group (estimated the same number of dots, preferred the same painting, or received the same coin flip), members of the out-group, or anonymous individuals. Under these artificial conditions, participants overwhelmingly allocated points to favor their in-group. People favored their in-group even if it posed a loss to both groups, so they could maximize the differences in points between the in-group and the out-group. Remarkably, in the absence of intergroup conflict, cultural differences, or inequality in economic or political power, people acted in a biased fashion. What Tajfel and his colleagues discovered in these experiments was people's inclination to develop a psychological sense of distinctiveness from out-groups – no matter how arbitrary the criteria might be.

To explain these astonishing results, Tajfel argued that a basic function of human nature is to strive for a positive self-identity, and membership in social groups can greatly influence one's self-image. As a result, Tajfel created *social identity theory* (SIT) to explain in-group bias and out-group prejudice. He defines SIT as "that part of an individual's self-concept which derives from his knowledge of his membership of a social group (or groups) together with the value and emotional significance attached to that membership" (1981, 355). This process suggests that individuals tend to value their in-group more positively, and they maintain this positivity via out-group comparisons. Tajfel proffers that "the 'positive aspects of social identity' and the reinterpretation of attributes and engagement in social action only acquire meaning in relation to, or in comparisons, with other out-groups" (1981, 256). Individuals organize the world into a basic set of categories (e.g., racial background) with people falling into some categories and not into others. For that reason, people accentuate the similarities between themselves and their in-group and emphasize how they differ from out-groups. Consequently, their identity takes on an us versus them mentality.[8]

One way people justify their out-group prejudice, similar to scape-goating, is by using what Tajfel refers to as the *value preservation function*. We already know that people strive for group differentiation to positively enhance their self-image. Another proposition of SIT is that the in-group develops a value system that characterizes its members in a positive fashion such as hardworking, honest, or friendly. On the other hand, the out-group is not considered to possess these character-istics. As a consequence, when in-group bias and out-group prejudice occur, they are justified on these value differentials. These values pre-serve the positive image of in-group members and reinforce how the out-group differs. They develop a strong sense of moral superiority among in-group members. Brewer agrees:

To the extent that all groups discriminate between intragroup social behavior and intergroup behavior, it is in a sense universally true that "we" are more peaceful, friendly, and honest than "they." ... When the moral order is seen as absolute rather than relative, moral superiority is incompatible with tolerance for difference. To the extent that outgroups do not subscribe to the same moral rules, indifference is replaced by denigration and contempt. (1999, 435)

This lack of subscription by members of the out-group leads to blam-ing them for their misfortunes. The in-group believes that members of the out-group have control over adopting the values of the in-group, but they stubbornly choose not to. As a result, prejudice toward mem-bers of the out-group is justified on the basis that it's their own fault for not adhering to the values of the in-group. When these beliefs form the primary basis for disliking the out-group, I theorize, anger should be tightly linked to out-group prejudice.

One such example is white Americans' prejudice toward African Americans. Since the heyday of the civil rights movement, the sub-sequent racial debate has predominantly focused on whether blacks receive rights and resources that they do not deserve (Gilens 1999; Kinder and Sanders 1996; Schuman and Krysan 1999). A majority of whites consider issues such as affirmative action and welfare to exem-plify the unfair advantage the federal government gives to blacks. They believe discrimination is a thing of the past, and any shortcomings on the part of blacks are due to their lack of motivation. From this per-spective, if African Americans would adhere to American traditional values such as the Protestant work ethic, then America wouldn't have a race problem. Thus, the inequality between blacks and whites rests solely on the shoulders of blacks; they only have themselves to blame. According to Sears and Kinder's (1971) theory of symbolic racism, this belief system characterizes the white racist in American society today. So when the federal government provides assistance to blacks in the form of health care, housing, or education, it evokes a strong feeling of anger among many white Americans. This anger isn't fastened to one specific racial issue like affirmative action, but undergirds most race-based policies. The reason is that blame rhetoric has saturated the racial debate over the past forty years. As a result of blame's dominance in public discussions on race, anger and contemporary racism have been conjoined in the minds of many white Americans.

WHAT LIES AHEAD

This book begins in Chapter 1 by illustrating how the dominant emotional underpinning of racism has changed in American history from a feeling of disgust to one of anger. Old-fashioned racism, the racial belief system prevalent among white Americans up until the second half of the twentieth century, centered on the belief that blacks were a biologically inferior race. This earlier form of racism took on a different emotional character than racism as we think of it today. After discussing this change in the emotional narrative on race, I construct a theory of how anger and whites' contemporary racial attitudes form a strong bond in the minds of a large percentage of white Americans. Then, I propose that evoking anger may bring racial attitudes more easily to the top of the head, even when triggered by an event unrelated to race or politics. To build such a theory, I rely on the works of cognitive appraisal theories of emotion and emotional priming.

After the theoretical argument has been firmly established, Chapter 2 explores the emotional substrates of three explanations for whites' opposition to remedial racial policies: old-fashioned racism, symbolic racism, and race-neutral attitudes. My expectation is that in contemporary America, anger is strongly linked to, and can in fact trigger, symbolic racism while old-fashioned beliefs are rooted in and activated by feelings of disgust. Another expectation is that nonracial values are not activated by any of these negative emotions. To examine these propositions, I utilize two different methodological approaches. The first is an experiment on an adult national sample, and the second is the 1985 American National Election Study (ANES) pilot study. The first study experimentally induces disgust, anger, fear, or relaxation using an apolitical and nonracial task. This emotion induction procedure allows me to examine whether anger primes symbolic racism, disgust activates old-fashioned racism, and whether any of these negative emotions heighten race-neutral principles. Study 2 uses the 1985 ANES pilot study to examine the relationship between these specific emotions and the three attitude dimensions. Last, study 3 uses the 2008 ANES to investigate if anger matters most in triggering other forms of prejudice such as ethnocentrism. The chapter's findings show that anger is uniquely powerful at increasing opposition to racial policies among whites high in symbolic racism while disgust is mainly responsible for triggering old-fashioned beliefs. On the other hand, race-neutral principles are not activated by any of these negative emotions. A similar effect appears for ethnocentrism; that is, anger, as opposed to fear, increases the impact of this belief system on racial and immigration policy opinions.

In Chapter 3, I move from inducing general emotional states to generating emotion in the context of a racialized campaign ad. Scholars have argued that racial appeals powerfully evoke beliefs about race. A number of scholars and pundits have suggested that racial appeals are effective because they play to whites' racial fear. This chapter examines if anger, rather than fear, facilitates the racial priming effect. More specifically, I investigate how different emotional responses (i.e., anger and fear) to racial appeals affect white support for racial policy opinions. That is, do anger and fear, in the context of an implicit racial appeal, influence whites' views about race differently? Using an experiment that I conducted on a college student sample, I find that arousing anger from an implicit racial appeal, very similar to the "weekend passes" ad, boosts the effect of racial attitudes on racial policy preferences, relative to an implicit appeal that generates fear and the control group. The findings also show that an anger-laden appeal has no effect on self-reported political ideology. Furthermore, using the 1988 ANES, I demonstrate that when the "Willie" Horton story was implicit (not explicit) and most intense in media coverage, anger, not fear, increased the effect of symbolic racism on preference for George H. W. Bush.

Chapter 4 extends the impact of emotion to an ostensibly nonracial issue, such as the 2009–10 health care reform debate. Pundits and politicians vehemently debated whether race was implicated in the town hall meetings and public demonstrations against health care reform. Building on the previous chapters, I examine the extent to which nonracial and nonpolitical anger uniquely activates white racial attitudes and increases their effect on preferences for health care reform. Using a nationally representative experiment conducted over two waves, I induced several emotions to elicit anger, fear, enthusiasm, or relaxation. The results show that anger racially polarizes white support for health care reform. More specifically, anger pushes racial liberals to be more supportive of reform while it increases opposition among racial conservatives. On the other hand, anger does not produce a similar polarizing effect along the dimension of race-neutral political ideology.

When one thinks about the anger that engulfed the country during Barack Obama's first two years as president, one group immediately comes to mind – Tea Partiers. Their anger was most notable during the 2010 midterm elections, when Tea Party-backed Republican candidates' attacks on Obama and Democrats were often venomous, confrontational, and emotionally charged. Some groups like the National Association for the Advancement of Colored People (NAACP) accused Tea Party-backed candidates of igniting negative thoughts about race with their visceral rhetoric. Chapter 5 investigates whether anger enhances the impact of racial predispositions on support for Republican congressional candidates – when a Tea Party candidate is seeking office as opposed to when no such candidate is running for office. Using the 2010 ANES, I find that anger, as opposed to fear, augments the influence of racial considerations as criteria in evaluating congressional candidates – but only when a Tea Party candidate is on the ballot. Finally, I put all of these results together and discuss their implications in this book's concluding chapter. Here, I also explore how anger and out-group prejudice may operate politically in places other than the United States.

I

A Theory of Anger and Contemporary
White Racial Attitudes

As a child growing up in Alabama in the 1950s, John Lewis, who would go on to be a civil rights activist and represent Georgia in the U.S. House of Representatives, lived where the lines between blacks and whites were sharply drawn. Jim Crow, as an institution of discrimination, had a profound effect on Lewis. Later, when recalling his childhood in the Deep South, he stated, "I have a lot of memories about Troy that remain painfully strong. Like the washrooms at the bus station, the nice clean one marked 'WHITE,' and the dirty run-down one marked 'COLORED.' ... Then there was the public library, where I longed to go, but through whose doors I was not allowed to set foot" (1998, 48). At the time of Lewis's youth, segregation was the law of the land in the South. Segregationists believed wholeheartedly that blacks would debase the white race. To them, blacks were beastly, apelike, subhuman, and dirty – basically an inferior race (Fredrickson 1971). They were considered too foul to sit beside or eat next to, and any interracial contact was thought to contaminate the "purity" of the white race. This racist ideology was rooted in a strong feeling of disgust and justified a system that kept blacks and whites separated. But on May 20, 1961, Lewis and a courageous group of six black and six white freedom riders made news headlines by attempting to test segregated bus facilities in places like Montgomery, Alabama. The riders hoped to expose the evils of segregation and racial bigotry in the United States to the world.

Almost fifty years passed, and Congressman Lewis – a decorated hero and tested veteran of the civil rights movement – was back in the news, and not for proposing landmark legislation or securing electoral victory. Instead, on March 25, 2010, he and other members of the Congressional Black Caucus were victims of racial prejudice, but of a different kind than the one he faced as a child in Pike County, Alabama or traveling with his fellow freedom riders through the Deep South in the spring of 1961. Unlike the Southern whites whose faces cringed in disgust at the thought of blacks and whites intermingling, these were angry Tea Party protestors who had gathered in front of the U.S. Capitol building to rally against the passage of health care reform. When asked to describe the incident, Lewis responded: "[T]hey were just shouting.... [P]eople [were] being downright mean." As a civil rights activist with battle scars, he calmly stated, "It's okay, I've faced this before," but also mentioned that he hadn't "heard anything like this in forty, forty-five years. Since the march to [S]elma, really."[1]

These two stories of Congressman Lewis, and the emotional arc of racial history that connects them, make up the central thread of this book. Not only did the freedom rides, and the civil rights movement more broadly, shake the foundation of segregation by drawing national attention to Southern segregationists' hatred of blacks, they also displayed how emotionally charged the issue of race was in this country. The freedom rides were a response to the visceral disgust among white supremacists who loathed the idea of race mixing. Physical distance was the ideal of many Southern racists, because they believed "the Negro emitted a terrible stench" whose physical characteristics were "grotesque" (Wood 1968, 12). For many white racists, the Southern way of life of strict segregation was deemed necessary to protect them from the "mongrelization" of their race. For instance, a segregationist, repulsed by the freedom riders, wrote to the editor of the *Sun*, stating, "[T]his letter is to express my utter disgust with the recent actions taken by the Kennedy Administration in the Alabama Fiasco.... It is a shocking situation when the President of the United States lowers the dignity of his great office by allying himself personally with a group of agitators carrying a chip and daring anyone to knock it off."[2] These accounts of whites' strong displeasure with integration and the freedom riders put on display how emotionally charged racism was for many Americans.

Of course, just as important as the stories illustrating white supremacists' hatred of blacks were those showing whites and blacks coming together to stand up for racial equality. Some civil rights leaders considered whites who were sympathetic to the plight of blacks as complacent, insofar as they believed change was necessary but were unwilling to put themselves on the front line. The brave action of these six white freedom riders showed some whites were indeed committed to the struggle for blacks' civil rights. It also illustrated that whites were just as passionate as blacks about racial injustice. The feelings of disappointment, bitterness, frustration, anger, and anxiety that plagued the black community for generations were shared by these white freedom riders, because some witnessed institutional and individual racism up close for the first time. The freedom rides demonstrated that the fight for integration was an emotional one on both sides of the racial divide.

As legal segregation ended, a different kind of emotion began to shape the public policy debate on matters of race. After the civil rights era, the racial norm "of white supremacy was displaced by an ideology of racial equality" (Mendelberg 2001, 67). According to scholars, this change is attributable to leaders in the black community and the Democratic Party (during the civil rights movement) putting pressure on lawmakers to publicly disown the Southern philosophy of old-fashioned bigotry (Lee 2002; Mendelberg 2001). This pressure led to the landmark civil rights legislation requiring American citizens and institutions to behave in accordance with racial equality. As a result of these influences, the public discussion on race changed considerably. Now, feeling disgusted about blacks' beastly nature or genetic difference is inappropriate. With this change, the emotion overtaking many whites' opinions on race shifted from disgust to anger. While early race-based rhetoric focused on maintaining white purity via segregation, racial resistance in the contemporary era is characterized by claims that blacks gain an unfair and illegitimate advantage at the hand of the federal government. This latter sentiment is not rooted so much in disgust, but often it reflects a pervasive anger toward government giving blacks rights and resources they do not deserve.

One issue that illustrates this change in emotion is affirmative action. Supporters of affirmative action believe that remedial action is necessary to offset the deep stain of discrimination and continued racism prevalent in this country. On the other hand, opponents contend that it provides an unfair advantage to minorities by giving them preferential treatment in employment and educational opportunities (Gamson and Modigliani 1987). These strongly held and opposing views give us reason to suspect that contemporary racial issues like affirmative action stimulate strong emotions, especially anger. To determine how widespread anger toward affirmative action really is, Kuklinski and his colleagues (1997) developed an experimental technique to more accurately gauge what people really thought and felt about racially charged policies. This method is known as the *list experiment*. In this experiment, one-half of the subjects are presented with three statements (i.e., "the federal government increasing the tax on gasoline," "professional athletes getting million-dollar salaries," and "large corporations polluting the environment") and asked how many of these things make them angry (baseline condition). For the treatment condition, subjects are presented with the same three statements and an additional statement about "black leaders asking for affirmative action." By subtracting the number of angry responses in the treatment condition from those in the baseline condition, Kuklinski and his colleagues can determine the proportion of people who get angry at the mention of affirmative action. They find anger toward affirmative action is widespread among whites. Similarly, other research has found a strong relationship between anger and opinions toward affirmative action (Kinder and Sanders 1996; Sniderman, Crosby, and Howell 2000). These studies illustrate that the emotional reactions to racial issues retain a prominent place in American society.

While anger is strongly linked to explicit racial issues, it is also linked to implicit racial issues like welfare. Using the 1991 National Race and Politics Study, Federico (2005) finds that nearly all whites in the sample report feeling angry toward people who collect welfare.[3] Furthermore, he finds that whites who perceive blacks as lacking individual initiative are more likely to express anger toward a welfare recipient when that recipient is described as a "black man" as opposed to a "man."[4]

Recently, health care – another ostensibly nonracial issue – has become racialized. Tesler and Sears's (2010) spillover theory of racialization provides one explanation for why health care is racialized today. They argue that the racial evaluations associated with Barack Obama have spilled over to policies that he has taken a strong stance on – such as the 2010 health care reform bill. Skocpol and Williamson

(2012) offer another possible explanation for the racialization of health care. They argue that the political right, specifically the Tea Party, has framed the policy debate as unfairly favoring the poor and minority groups – seeing it as government redistribution at its worst – akin to welfare (Williamson, Skocpol, and Coggin 2011).

For example, in 2008, the United States was hit with an economic recession of a magnitude not experienced since the Great Depression. To stave off a depression and jump-start the economy, the federal government instituted a series of bailouts to banks and private industries. A substantial number of American citizens were angry about government bailouts and believed that excessive government spending got the country into this problem in the first place. As a result, in 2009, the conservative Tea Party movement emerged, distrusting government officials at all levels, but most notably the Obama administration. Tea Partiers insist that Obama's policies – like health care reform – help people they perceive as undeserving of governmental assistance. As a result, in the summer and fall of 2009, we witnessed the country immersed in an angry debate over health care reform. Thousands of protestors crowded in front of the U.S. Capitol waving incendiary signs like "We Are under Socialist Attack," "ObamaCare Makes Me Sick," and "Bury Obama Care with Kennedy," referring to the recent passing of longtime Massachusetts senator Ted Kennedy. Reporting for the Associated Press, Stephanie Condon wrote, "[T]hese people are angry ... angry about the possibility of losing health care benefits ... Angry at the thought of losing control over their future."[5] The Kaiser Family Foundation Health Tracking Poll measured people's emotional response to health care reform from September 2009 to February 2011. One of the survey questions asked respondents if they felt angry regarding "the health care reform law." As illustrated in Figure 1.1, more than a third of whites described feeling angry about reform. Knowing that conservatives had the strongest negative reaction to health care reform, one might suspect that anger over reform is conditional on partisanship. As expected, Figure 1.1 shows that a majority of Republicans were angry over health care reform, and that this anger continued until the 2010 midterm elections.[6]

It is clear that some of our most salient racial issues – past and present, explicit and implicit – stimulate strong emotions. And while emotions are commonly invoked in debates over race in American history,

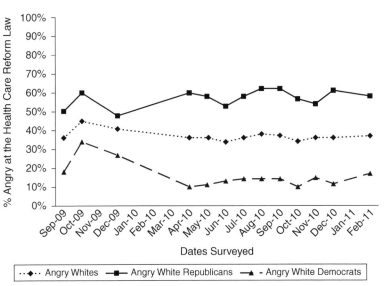

FIGURE 1.1. Percentage of total whites, white Republicans, and white Democrats angry about the Health Care Reform Law (from Sept. 2009 to Feb. 2011). *Source*: The Kaiser Family Foundation Health Tracking Poll.

their particular contribution to explaining racial attitudes, independent of cognitive forces, is rarely pursued. Scholars have devoted far more attention to the cognitive rather than the emotional elements of white racial attitudes, despite the fact that a plethora of reasons exists to suspect race relations in America are emotionally charged. The little attention scholars have given to studying the emotional aspect of racial attitudes has resulted in the opinion that "generalized anti-black affect" is an important part of racism (Bobo and Taun 2006; Kinder and Sanders 1996; Sears 1988; Sniderman et al. 2000). For example, Sears argues that antiblack affect is "experienced subjectively as fear, avoidance and a desire for distance, anger, distaste, disgust, contempt, apprehension, unease or dislike" (1988, 70).[7] On the other hand, as John Lewis's childhood experience with segregation demonstrated, the feeling of disgust, rather than a general negative feeling toward blacks, was strongly attached to the beliefs of white supremacists. And the same can be said for affirmative action, with anger playing a powerful role in shaping white opinion. Scholars not considering which emotions are most powerfully linked to white racial attitudes in a given time and context prohibits us from correctly understanding why whites oppose or support policies intended to reduce racial inequality. If we use the existing treatment of emotions in the racial politics literature, we would fail to understand the emotional circumstance that brought Jim Crow racists to protect the Southern way of life or the emotional condition that leads racial conservatives to oppose affirmative action.

This book attempts to fill this void. My main purpose is to explore how discrete emotions are connected to public opinion on matters of race. What is unknown at this point is whether some emotions as opposed to others have a distinct effect on the formation and application of racial attitudes, and whether emotions from stimuli that are apolitical or nonracial can make racial considerations more accessible in the minds of many white Americans. I argue that anger, and not fear or other negative emotions, provides the foundation on which contemporary white racial attitudes are structured. As I will demonstrate in the following chapters, the experience of anger in the context of modern American politics acts as a powerful force in priming thoughts about race among a large percentage of white Americans. I contend that this effect occurs because of the strong bond between anger and racial attitudes that develops over time. This book offers a theoretical account of the ways discrete emotions are tightly linked to specific group attitudes, along with empirical demonstrations that show how invoking an emotional reaction, independent of political and racial content, primes racial considerations in a wide array of public policy domains.

This book intends to show that today's subtle form of racism (alternatively referred to as *symbolic racism, modern racism,* or *racial resentment*) is indeed conceptually distinct from old-fashioned racism and race-neutral values. Scholars have questioned the evidence that has been marshaled to demonstrate that a new subtle form of racism exists, and that it is different from race-neutral values such as the proper size of government and individual initiative (Sniderman and Piazza 1993; Sniderman and Tetlock 1986). This book moves the debate forward by providing a robust theory that correctly predicts the emotional substrates across a range of political and group attitudes. My contention is that these different attitude dimensions have distinct emotional antecedents: old-fashioned beliefs about genetic racial differences are strongly linked to the emotion of disgust, while contemporary racism is rooted in anger. On the other hand, race-neutral principles are not strongly tied to any particular negative emotion.

COGNITIVE APPRAISAL THEORIES OF EMOTION

Before one can understand how specific emotions are woven into racial attitudes, it is important to know how an individual experiences a particular emotion. Cognitive appraisal theories of emotion help to clarify the unique causal antecedents and consequences of emotions. They distinguish emotions at a more fine-grained level than a simple valence approach does. Over the past twenty years, scholars have recognized that emotion and cognition are fundamentally linked (Brader 2005; Lazarus 1991; Lerner and Keltner 2001; Marcus, Neuman, and MacKuen 2000; Smith and Ellsworth 1985) and are not separate systems as earlier scholars proclaimed. From an appraisal theory framework, cognitive appraisals determine the broad contours of emotional experience (Lazarus 1991; Smith and Ellsworth 1985). That is, how people appraise their environment in relation to their personal well-being determines the type of emotion they experience (Lazarus 1991; Smith and Ellsworth 1985; Smith et al. 1993). This process involves two types of appraisals. Primary appraisals inform us of whether our environment is congruent with our goals. If so, positive emotions result. On the other hand, if circumstances are incongruent with our goals, negative emotions occur. Secondary appraisals identify coping strategies and future expectations and further differentiate emotions.

Smith and Ellsworth (1985) identify six appraisal dimensions that define the pattern underlying different emotional states: blame/responsibility, certainty, pleasantness, control, anticipated effort, and attentional activity. These cognitive dimensions determine whether an individual will experience anger as opposed to fear or hope as opposed to pride. For example, "the sensory pleasure of being stroked or stimulated sexually may lead to satisfaction when it is interpreted as signifying love or if there is willing participation, but to distress (e.g., anger, fear or despair) when it is deemed inappropriate and unwanted" (Lazarus 1991, 821). As a result, a given encounter appraised along these secondary dimensions (blame, credit, intentionality, and control)

can determine if the sexual act is wanted or unwanted and the resul-
tant emotion – an intense level of joy or a strong feeling of anger.

Appraisal theory suggests people experience anger toward others
when they feel threatened and are certain who is *responsible* or *blameworthy* for the offensive action; in other words, they place the blame
outside of themselves (i.e., external attribution of blame) (Lazarus
1991; Smith and Ellsworth 1985). Moreover, angry people perceive
themselves as having the ability to influence the likely outcome, so
coping potential and future expectations are considered bright (Averill
1983; Clore and Ceneterbar 2004; Lerner and Tiedens 2006). A pro-
totypical scenario for experiencing anger, in the case of race, is a
white applicant who has applied to law school and gets denied while
a black applicant perceived as less qualified gets in instead. This will
likely spur anger among many whites because it is clear to them that
blacks are to blame. A number of empirical studies have investigated
the experience of anger and its corresponding appraisals. Smith and
Ellsworth (1985) find that anger is strongly related to the appraisals
of other responsibility (or blame) and certainty. In the context of politics, Brader, Groenendyk, and Valentino (2011) show that threatening news that includes blame appraisals increases the likelihood of an
angry response, rather than a fearful one.

On the other hand, fear is experienced when a person negatively
evaluates an event that leads to threat and is uncertain of what hap-
pened and will happen in the future (Lazarus 1991; Lerner and Keltner
2001; Tiedens and Linton 2001). Lack of control is another important
attribute of fear: people believe that a situation is beyond their control (Smith and Ellsworth 1985). It is when one is threatened, uncertain of how to cope with the problem, and lacks control that fear is
more likely to be aroused. "[I]f we don't know what is going to happen or when, which is consistent with an existential threat, anxiety
is the likely emotion" (Lazarus 1991, 237). A story that often evokes
a fearful response in the context of race is when a white woman is
walking down a dark city street and an African American male slowly
approaches her.

The appraisal pattern of disgust also differs from anger. Perceptions
of physical contamination and repulsiveness are central to experiencing
disgust. In a sense, disgust helps protect the body from contaminated
and repulsive objects. Rozin and Fallon describe a disgust reaction

as "revulsion at the prospect of (oral) incorporation of an offensive object. The offensive objects are contaminants; that is, if they even briefly contact an acceptable food, they tend to render the food unacceptable" (1987, 23). Smith and Ellsworth find that disgust stems from "situations in which someone else did something physically repulsive that they wanted to shut out and get away from" (1985, 833). As discussed in depth in Chapter 2, this idea of contamination that is central to experiencing disgust most likely characterizes white old-fashioned racial beliefs of blacks' inherent biological inferiority.

Several studies using an appraisal theory framework have shown that the effects of anger diverge from other negative emotions (Huddy, Feldman, and Cassese 2007; Lerner and Keltner 2001; Lerner et al. 2003). For instance, Lerner and Keltner (2001) find that fear causes individuals to make more risk-averse choices while anger leads people to make more risk-seeking choices. The sense of uncertainty and lack of control that is associated with fear encourage pessimistic assessments, whereas the appraisals of certainty and control associated with anger produce more optimistic assessments. Similar effects have been shown to apply to terror-related events (Huddy et al. 2007; Lerner et al. 2003). For instance, Lerner and her colleagues (2003) find that people's anger over the September 11th attacks causes them to have a more optimistic view about future terrorist attacks while fear triggers a more pessimistic view about future attacks. They also find that these effects spillover to nonterror-related events like getting the flu and policy preferences, more generally.

Beyond risk perceptions, a substantial body of research has shown that the effects of anger differ from those of other negatively valenced emotions in terms of political participation (Valentino et al. 2011), punishment of criminals (Bang Peterson 2010), intergroup attitudes and action (DeSteno et al. 2004; Mackie et al. 2000), information seeking, (MacKuen et al. 2010; Valentino et al. 2009), and depth of processing (Tiedens and Linton 2001). Thus, this body of work strongly supports the proposition that the effects of anger differ from the effects of other negative emotions and are a robust finding that applies across multiple domains. In all, appraisal theory provides more than an ability to distinguish among emotions; it gives researchers a fuller understanding of what it means to experience a specific emotion and its likely consequences. Therefore, appraisal theory is especially useful for studying the emotional underpinnings of white racial attitudes because it offers a strong theoretical justification for my argument that specific emotions are powerfully linked to group attitudes.

BLAME APPRAISALS: LINKING ANGER TO CONTEMPORARY WHITE RACIAL ATTITUDES

Martin Luther King Jr. and many other members of the civil rights movement, through passive resistance, exposed how pervasive racial bigotry was in America, especially in places like Birmingham, Alabama, where police dogs, high-power water hoses, and club-wielding policemen set upon peaceful black protestors – at times in plain sight of television cameras, shocking most of the nation. Given that the country was witnessing widespread racial violence against blacks in the South, President Kennedy could no longer ignore the injustice directed toward African Americans and had to act, so on June 11, 1963, in an address to the nation, he stated, "[W]e are confronted primarily with a moral issue.... It is as old as the Scriptures and is as clear as the American Constitution. The heart of the question is whether all Americans are to be afforded equal rights and equal opportunities" (Salmond 1997, 115). Unfortunately, President Kennedy was unable to see his vision of racial equality become a reality, as he was assassinated shortly after giving this speech. But President Lyndon B. Johnson – Kennedy's vice president – withstanding intense opposition by Southern Democrats, was able to sign into law the Civil Rights Act of 1964 and the Voting Rights Act of 1965. Almost immediately following the passage of civil rights legislation, there was a precipitous decline in white support for overt discrimination, segregation, and the negative view of genetic difference between blacks and whites. The constant pressure from the black community via sit-ins, boycotts, freedom rides, and marches criticizing America's central political institutions, along with political leaders like Presidents Kennedy and Johnson pointing out the country's conspicuous moral defect, explains how whites were persuaded to abandon the ideology of white supremacy.[8] As a consequence, a majority of whites began to express support for racial egalitarianism in most spheres of life – education, employment, public accommodations, and housing (Schuman et al. 1997). Segregationist views of blacks as an inferior race no longer reflected the majority of whites' sentiments, at least publicly.

As civil disobedience dissipated in the mid-1960s and was replaced with race riots in American cities, a new racial conservative argument began to take shape. A transformation occurred. The public saw an end to peaceful sit-ins at lunch counters while singing "we shall overcome" and instead witnessed blacks violently protesting through the streets of cities like Newark, chanting, "burn, baby, burn." From blacks' standpoint, the civil rights movement did little to change their day-to-day conditions; they actually worsened – unemployment rates rose and housing and education conditions deteriorated (Ture and Hamilton 1992). Disillusioned with Gandhi's nonviolence strategy, blacks began to adopt a more militant philosophy of "black power" and "by any means necessary." Leaders of the more radical element of the civil rights movement like Malcolm X insisted, "if someone puts his hands on you ... send him to the cemetery." All of a sudden, riots became commonplace in the summers from 1964 to 1968. In addition, the assassination of Martin Luther King Jr. in 1968 contributed to large-scale urban uprisings in cities like Los Angeles, Newark, Detroit, Cleveland, New York, and Chicago (Sears and McConahay 1973). As a result of the riots, whites' sympathy for blacks started to wane and a massive backlash against civil rights progress began to materialize.

Before Watts, the typical picture looked something like this: neatly dressed blacks, petitioning peacefully for their basic rights, crouched on the ground, being pummeled with nightsticks and set upon by police dogs. After Watts, Americans were instead witness to pictures of mobs of young city blacks, hurling bricks at police cars, torching their own neighborhoods, and looting stores of all that they could carry. Such pictures invited the conclusion from whites that after all that had been done for blacks, after all that had been given to them, it was not enough. Blacks wanted more, they demanded more – and they took it. (Kinder and Sanders 1996, 104)

After the riots, the debate over race shifted from a battle over civil rights to a set of character attacks that focused on blacks' drug abuse, criminal activity, cheating the welfare system, gang violence, and sexual promiscuity. Kinder and Sanders in their telling book, *Divided by Color: Racial Politics and Democratic Ideals*, point out that for most whites the riots represented senseless violence and a deficiency in blacks' moral character. A new racial narrative had developed explaining the plight of black America. It focused heavily on an individualistic frame that held blacks responsible for their lower status in society because of their own moral failings. A quintessential example of this characterization is the highly vitriolic welfare debate. Within this debate the identity of the welfare queen emerged in which the public conflated most welfare recipients with single, poor, black mothers (Hancock 2004). Racial disparities in news coverage of poverty seemed to reinforce this notion that most people on welfare were black. Gilens (1999) in his content analysis of news coverage on poverty found that images of blacks were clearly overrepresented and that the tone of these stories was predominantly negative. Iyengar (1996) also showed that the contemporary debate on issues such as poverty was filled with attributions of blame and responsibility. According to his findings, when poverty was framed as episodic (focusing on specific instances), blacks, more than whites, were judged responsible for poverty (Iyengar 1990).[9] As the civil rights movement ended, fewer whites than before counted discrimination as a factor in blacks' disadvantages. Instead, many whites believed that the 1960s civil rights legislation had swept away any racial barriers that had previously impeded black progress. The dysfunctional character of blacks was now thought to be responsible for their disadvantaged status in society. Thus, a "blame the victim" mentality became the dominant racial narrative in debates on race.

With most whites losing interest in civil rights, the narrative that blacks were to blame for America's racial problems dominated how whites thought about race (Schuman and Krysan 1999). This point is made forcefully in Figure 1.2. The figure shows that, at the height of the civil rights movement, whites held blacks and whites equally responsible for black disadvantages in society. During the time of the riots, a dramatic shift occurred in white opinion as to who was to blame for blacks' lower status. Looking at Figure 1.2, we see that whites blaming whites decreased by 21 percent and holding blacks responsible increased by 21 percent from 1963 to 1968. This shift in blame attribution continued and widened slightly over time. By 1995, 80 percent of whites believed the lack of motivation on the part of blacks was responsible for their shortcomings in society. Thus, blame became a central tenet in whites' negative racial attitudes. The relative ease by which Americans attached themselves to the individualistic cultural

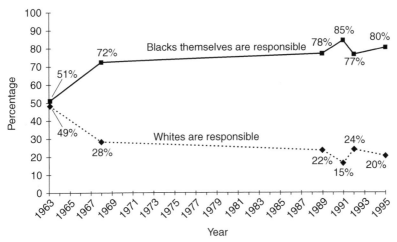

FIGURE 1.2. Responses to question attributing blame for blacks' disadvantage by year: whites aged twenty-one and older, Gallup surveys.
Source: Schuman and Krysan 1999, 851.

narrative when it came to blacks might not be surprising. For instance, as discussed in the introduction to this book, social identity theory contends that value differentials are used to explain intergroup behavior like in-group favoritism and out-group prejudice (Tajfel 1981). So when the out-group fails to subscribe to the values of the in-group, it is likely to foster out-group animosity. Members of the out-group are thought to be responsible for their own misfortunes because they fail to adopt the values of the in-group. Similarly, in the contemporary period of U.S. race relations, white Americans have used value differentials to express their dislike of black Americans.

Sears and Kinder (1971) recognized this transformation of white racial attitudes and proposed that a new subtle form of racism had emerged, which they referred to as *symbolic racism*. This form of racism was defined as a blend of antiblack affect and the perception that blacks violate core American values such as individualism. They proposed that today's form of racial prejudice is much more subtle – it doesn't reflect segregationists' views of blacks as beastly, backward, and barbarous – but is now intertwined with attributions of blame. As a result, those high in symbolic racism believe blacks' poor work ethic is to blame for the inequalities between blacks and whites. Kinder and

Sanders state, "[A] new form of prejudice has come to prominence.... At its center are the contentions that blacks do not try hard enough to overcome the difficulties they face and that they take what they have not earned" (1996, 105–106). In addition, blame is a main fixture of other concepts of contemporary racial prejudice like laissez-faire racism (Bobo and Kluegel 1997) and aversive racism (Gaertner and Dovidio 1986). Gordon Allport in his seminal work, *The Nature of Prejudice*, also recognized blame as a central canon of racism. He referred to it as a *scapegoat ideology* that gave racially prejudiced people a way to justify their racist thinking. Along the same lines, Gurin and her colleagues contend that the dominant group justifies its advantage over lower-status groups by blaming them for their failings (Gurin, Miller, and Gurin 1980; Miller et al. 1981).

With blame appraisals central to contemporary racism, anger forms a strong bond with this racial belief system. Prejudiced whites believe blacks lack the moral character to succeed and, because of this, rights and valuable resources from the federal government are unfairly redistributed to them. They see the real tragedy of racial inequality as blacks themselves. They believe abuse of the welfare system, explosion of criminal activity and drug abuse, preferential treatment in education and in the workplace, and dependency on government handouts exemplify blacks' moral failures. What makes a large percentage of whites angry is that they believe blacks are receiving illegitimate and unfair advantages. Seeing blacks continue to ask for assistance from the federal government while they are considered the ones to blame for their lower position in society evokes strong feelings of anger among many white Americans. Therefore, it is these appraisals common to anger more than those of other negative emotions (i.e., disgust and fear) that map onto the ways negative ideas about race are formed in the contemporary period.

Supporting this position, Eliot R. Smith states that the "racial resentment [or symbolic racism] items and the definition all involve appraisals of an outgroup as violating ingroup norms or obtaining illegitimate advantages, leading to the emotion of anger" (1993, 308–309). Work in psychology also finds that anger is a precursor to prejudiced beliefs and actions. In intergroup emotions theory, Mackie and colleagues (2000) find that people who possess a strong in-group identity and feel angry toward an out-group are more inclined than those who experience fear to take action against the group. Similarly, DeSteno, Dasgupta, Bartlett, and Cajdric (2004) demonstrate that anger, compared to sadness and a neutral state, is the primary ingredient in outgroup animosity.

Racially Liberal Whites

Most of the attention within the racial policy debate has focused on whites high in symbolic racism. Very little empirical attention has been devoted to understanding the beliefs of white racial liberals – let alone the emotional undertones of this belief system. Gary Orfield's work on racial liberalism suggests that the race riots of the mid-1960s took away the political advantage of racial liberals on the issue of race and gave it to racial conservatives. Black urban unrest made it extremely difficult for racial liberals to maintain the moral high ground of the civil rights movement and claim basic changes were still needed within the black community. According to Orfield, "the liberal view seemed weak and defensive in contrast to a clear and aggressive conservative defense of law and order, and of firm action against violence" (1988, 329). Conservative elites like George Wallace, Richard Nixon, and Ronald Reagan could now denounce government action on behalf of blacks as counterproductive. Proposals for civil rights and integration policies slowly eroded from the national dialogue on race, which signified that racial liberalism lost its intellectual and political capital (Jackson 1990). It appears that the loss of support for racial liberalism among many whites may be due, in part, to the urban riots that swept across the country in the mid-1960s.

Looking at those who score low in symbolic racism gives us one way to understand what racial liberalism means today. In contrast to those high in symbolic racism, those at the low end believe structural and individual discrimination are the main reasons behind the race problem in America. For racial liberals, the perceived notions in society that blacks are lazy, violent, and promiscuous are just used as smoke screens for racist whites to justify their opposition to policies designed to assist blacks. They think blacks are as hard working as whites and rightfully deserve help from the federal government.

The 2008 American National Election Study (ANES) shows that only a minority of white Americans is considered racially liberal.

Looking at those low in symbolic racism, only 37 percent of whites believe that past slavery and discrimination make it more difficult for blacks to succeed. A mere 20 percent of whites disagree with the statement that "if blacks would only try harder they could be just as well off as whites," and only 13 percent disagree with "the belief that blacks should overcome prejudice on their own without any special favors" and that "Irish, Italian, Jewish and many other minorities overcame prejudice and worked their way up. Blacks should do the same without any special favors." Overall, it seems that only a small percentage of whites believes that structural obstacles as opposed to individual failures are mainly responsible for black disadvantages in society.

For racial liberals, racial prejudice and discrimination – past and present – are to blame for why blacks have received less than they deserve. They view residential segregation, economic inequality, and health disparities between whites and blacks as examples of the continued racism blacks endure. Essentially, racial liberals differ from racial conservatives in where they attribute responsibility for America's racial problem. While whites high in symbolic racism find fault in the moral character of blacks, whites low in symbolic racism blame the discrimination and racism blacks have endured over generations. To them, the solution is more government assistance, not less. As a result, blame appraisals are also an important part of the belief system of white racial liberals. Given this, I contend that racially liberal attitudes are also strongly linked to feelings of anger.[10] Anger stems from what they see as a long history of racial bigotry that hasn't been eradicated. In their eyes, blacks are treated unfairly and deliberately excluded from rights and scarce resources. Therefore, I argue that anger not only undergirds the belief system of racial conservatives, but that of racial liberals as well. The next section discusses when this linkage might occur.

Racial Socialization

Research has shown that racial predispositions are learned at a fairly early age and reflect the norms and culture that dominate an individual's environment (Aboud 2005; Allport 1954; Epstein and Komorita 1966; Mosher and Scodel 1960; Sears 1988). Several socializing forces such as family, peers, self-esteem, and to some extent the media have been offered to explain why people develop racial prejudice or racially tolerant views. Allport (1954) argues that parental child-rearing practices – especially those that reinforce obedience or teach a hierarchical view of society – are strong determinants of a prejudiced belief system. Ward (1985), in a follow-up study of Robert Lane's (1962) sample of New Haven residents, finds that racially prejudiced parents transmit their underlying racial attitudes to their offspring. Other research has discovered that parental communication style, family income, and self-esteem play an important role in determining a person's level of racial tolerance (Owens and Dennis 1987; Zellman and Sears 1971). Several studies also demonstrate that the residues of preadult socialization are strong predictors of racial attitudes in adulthood (Miller and Sears 1986; Sears, Hensler, and Speer 1979), and that these beliefs remain relatively stable throughout a person's life span (Kinder and Sanders 1996). Therefore, several studies demonstrate that racial attitudes are acquired prior to adulthood, remain relatively stable, and are long-lasting.

An emotional experience is also fundamental to the racial socialization process. For instance, negative attitudes of Nazis and Communists were attributed to feelings about the group that were acquired in late childhood and early adolescence (Zellman and Sears 1971). Sears, Hensler, and Speer attest that the early socialization of racial attitudes is filled with emotional labels and reactions, and that these attitudes "respond in a highly affective way to symbols which resemble the attitude objects to which similar emotional responses were conditioned or associated in earlier life" (1979, 371). Perhaps parents pass on their negative feelings about race in the home after experiencing a threat-related event (Harding et al. 1969). So whites may be socialized from an early age to attribute certain emotional responses to blacks. If so, early adult socialization is one possible route for the link between anger and thoughts about race.

On the other hand, the lifelong openness model suggests another possible route for the link between anger and whites' racial attitudes. Under this model, racial predispositions "have an approximately uniform potential for change at all ages; it essentially asserts that age is irrelevant for attitude change" (Sears 1990, 77). In this case, social and political events in adulthood may also cause a person to develop an emotionally charged response to race (Searing, Wright, and Rabinowitz

1976). Thus, the feeling of anger could also attach itself to ideas about race later in life.

My theory of anger and contemporary racial attitudes does not make strong claims about when this link occurs, but I suspect that it is probably learned at a fairly young age. My contention is that experience and culture expose an individual to consistent blame appraisals regarding race; as a consequence, the emotion of anger becomes linked to this particular racial attitude dimension. Over continuous interactions between these cognitive and affective responses, the bond between anger and racial thinking coalesces. Then, simply experiencing anger should activate the corresponding racial attitude from memory and boost the impact of this belief system on relevant political judgments.

Emotional Priming: Activating Existing Racial Predispositions with Anger

To understand how and why emotions prime racial attitudes, I rely on emotional state dependent theory (Bower 1981; Bower and Forgas 2001; Forgas 1995). Gordon Bower, the architect of this theory, proposes a learning model in that information learned in one emotional state is more likely retrieved from memory when an individual is returned to that same emotional state. He offers an associative network theory to account for this effect. Under this theory, emotional nodes are connected with particular thoughts and objects in memory. For example, when a boss congratulates you on a good job and a feeling of pride results, the thought (boss's compliment) and emotion (pride) become fused together in memory. So afterward, future instances of pride should activate the corresponding thought: your boss's support. Bower and colleagues find evidence consistent with a mood-dependent retrieval effect for recall of word lists and autobiographical events.

Using an experimental approach, Bower (1981) had subjects record emotional events daily in a diary for a week. After a week, participants were randomly assigned to a pleasant or an unpleasant mood induction and then asked to recall events from their diary. People assigned to the pleasant condition recalled more of their pleasant experiences and participants in the unpleasant condition recalled more of their unpleasant experiences. These findings exhibited a mood-dependent retrieval effect; subjects recalled a greater amount of information that was emotionally congruent with the mood they were in during recall.

While most of the work on emotional priming examines the effect of general moods on memory, applying an appraisal theory framework to Bower's theory suggests specific emotions should bring emotionally congruent attitudes to the surface. It may be that an emotional node in an associative network framework is strongly linked to its appraisal themes. For instance, anger may be closely connected to blame appraisals in memory so that an angry state is more likely to activate thoughts and beliefs that involve attributions of responsibility for norm violations. This process suggests that discrete emotions and their appraisal themes have a recursive relationship, each causing the other (Lerner and Keltner 2001; Tiedens and Linton 2001). As a result, not only does blame produce anger, but one's anger leads one to make more blame attributions. For example, Goldberg, Lerner, and Tetlock (1999) randomly assigned participants to either an anger-laden video or a neutral video and found that the anger-filled clip led to a greater willingness to blame and punish individuals for wrongdoing. Similarly, Keltner and colleagues (1993) find that anger, relative to sadness and a neutral state, increases the likelihood of blaming others for a negative event and judging their actions as unfair. Other studies show similar results in that anger augments blame cognitions (Lerner, Goldberg, and Tetlock 1998).

My theory proposes that the linkage between anger and white racial attitudes develops over time. More than likely, the learning of racial predispositions (for both racial conservatives and racial liberals) takes place during an angry event or incident.[11] After these repeated experiences, anger becomes strongly linked to whites' racial predispositions. Once this linkage is firmly established, experiencing anger should activate the corresponding racial attitude from memory. If anger is strongly linked to racial schemas in memory for many whites, the emotion may bring the racial attitude more easily to the top of the head *even when triggered by an event unrelated to race or politics*. As a result, subsequent policy and candidate decisions should be more strongly predicted by the activated racial predisposition. The process by which anger can in fact trigger racial attitudes is depicted in Figure 1.3. A moderating effect best describes this process, in that racial attitudes can be activated from general experiences or episodes

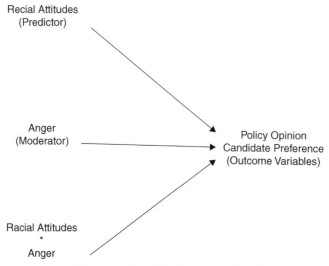

FIGURE 1.3. Moderator Model: The process by which anger and racial attitudes can affect policy and candidate preferences.

of anger, which then heighten the impact of these attitudes on relevant
policy and candidate opinions. The figure shows three causal paths
that can affect the outcome variable. It illustrates the impact of racial
attitudes as a predictor (path a), the impact of anger as a moderator
(path b), and the interaction of these two (path c). A moderating effect
is supported if the interaction (path c) is significant (Baron and Kenny
1986). That is, anger should increase the strength of the relationship
between racial attitudes (racial conservatives or racial liberals) and
support of or opposition to racial policies and candidates perceived as
racially sympathetic.

WHY NOT FEAR

An alternative perspective is that racial considerations are not driven
by anger but rather by fear of group competition. V. O. Key's (1949)
treatise on Southern politics sparked researchers' suspicion that fear
was fundamental to whites' perceptions of racial conflict. Pertaining to
attitudes, group position theory is also known for advancing this position. The group threat perspective contends that racism stems from
resource conflicts among groups, and that racial animus relies on the

social stratification system that distinguishes between dominant and subordinate groups (Blumer 1955, 1958; Bobo 1983, 2000; Bobo and Hutchings 1996; Kaufmann 2004). Under the group position model, there are four main components: (1) feelings of superiority, (2) belief that the subordinate race is intrinsically different and alien, (3) belief in a proprietary claim to certain areas of privilege and advantage, and (4) fear and suspicion that the subordinate race harbors designs on the prerogatives of the dominant race (Blumer 1958, 4). Research has found that perceiving blacks as competitors for jobs, promotions, and other valuable goods stimulates strong opposition to racial policies.

Based on group position theory, fear results from whites' perception that blacks intend to take away valuable and scarce resources. For example, Blumer states, "fear is an emotional recoil from the endangering of group position," and "[t]he remaining feeling essential to racial prejudice is a fear or apprehension that the subordinate racial group is threatening, or will threaten, the position of the dominant group" (1958, 4). Other theories of prejudice, like ethnocentrism, stipulate that a generalized fear of others underlies racial animus (Kam and Kinder 2007). Empirical evidence exists that supports fear as a feature of group threat attitudes. For instance, Stephen and colleagues (2002) find a correlation between intergroup anxiety and racial threat attitudes. Nonetheless, given the sizable economic and political disparities between the two groups, do blacks really pose a serious challenge to whites? In other words, does the position blacks hold in society make them a realistic threat to valuable and scarce resources?

One can use various indicators to gauge group competition – wealth, family income, education, and policy responsiveness, to name a few. If blacks were on relatively equal terms with whites in most economic and political spheres of life, then that would be a good indication that blacks are viable competition. The data, however, doesn't seem to support this. According to the 2009 American Community Survey, the white family median income was $54,535 in comparison to $34,445 for blacks. The gap is even more severe when looking at unemployment and poverty rates. Just more than 25 percent of blacks live below the poverty line as opposed to roughly 10 percent of whites. In terms of unemployment rates, The Bureau of Labor Statistics reported in July 2011 that blacks (15.9 percent) were almost twice as likely to be unemployed in comparison to whites (8.1 percent). Wealth, another barometer of potential competition, shows a chasm between blacks and whites. For example, in 2006, analysts found that the black-white median net worth ratio hovered around .10, "that is, blacks have control of ten cents for every dollar of net worth that whites possess" (Oliver and Shapiro 2006). The numbers are even more sobering in 2009. A Pew study showed that the median wealth of white households was now twenty times that of black households. These differences are not a product of the 2008 economic recession that resulted from the bubble bursting in the housing market, but instead reflect a long-term trend (Farley 1984; Sears et al. 2000). Blacks also lag far behind whites in terms of policy responsiveness. Griffin and Newman (2008), in their impressive book on race and representation, find that whites' policy preferences are more likely to be implemented than those of blacks or Latinos, even in districts where minorities make up a larger portion of the population.

In all, the numbers seem to show no real reason for whites to perceive blacks as genuine competitors for scarce goods and resources. Nevertheless, reality and perception are two different things and the latter does not necessarily have to follow the former. To determine if this is the case, I examined whites' level of perceived racial threat of blacks in the 2004 National Politics Survey (NPS). The survey includes two of the four group conflict attitude items. Among whites, only 13 percent believe that "more good jobs for African Americans means fewer good jobs for people like me" and "the more influence African Americans have in politics, the less influence people like me have in politics." These results indicate that only a small minority of whites perceives blacks as a competitive threat for resources. What about the threat of affirmative action? Does a majority of whites believe that blacks have an advantage over whites in entry into college or university? A 2005 Gallup Poll asked a national sample of adult Americans, "if two equally qualified students, one black and one white, applied to a major U.S. college or university, who do you think would have the better chance of being accepted to the college?" Half of the white respondents said each student had an equal chance of being accepted, while 24 percent said the black student had the advantage, and 21 percent said the white student had the advantage – numbers far from indicating whites are greatly concerned that affirmative action advantages blacks over whites.

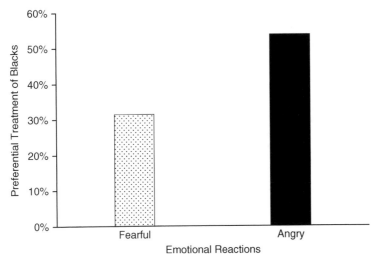

FIGURE 1.4. Whites' emotional reactions to affirmative action.
Source: 1985 ANES Pilot Study.

Perhaps when we look at whites' emotional reactions to affirmative action, a different picture will emerge – one with a high percentage of whites expressing fear. The 1985 American National Election Study (ANES) pilot study asked respondents how they felt about "preferential treatment of blacks." Figure 1.4 shows that 32 percent of white respondents express feeling fearful about affirmative action. Conversely, we see that 54 percent of whites report feeling angry about the policy (a difference of 22 percent). These results suggest that anger, more than fear, dominates how whites feel about policies like affirmative action designed to assist blacks.

Even so, scholars have examined whether anxiety heightens the use of racial attitudes when evaluating racial policies. In an experiment, Suthammanont and her colleagues (2010) randomly assigned subjects to either a threatening or a nonthreatening news story and afterward asked their support for several racial policy measures. They found that the threatening condition boosted the impact of symbolic racism on racial policy preferences – relative to the nonthreatening condition – and that anxiety mediated this effect. What remains unclear from their study, however, is whether the mediation effect is due to feelings of anxiety or anger. That is, their anxiety measure is a combination of self-reported feelings of anxiety and anger.

All in all, it appears that fear isn't the dominant emotional narrative on contemporary matters of race. This viewpoint doesn't mean that whites don't express fear when it comes to race. As we saw in the example of affirmative action, a minority of whites expressed feeling fearful about preferential treatment of blacks. Feelings of fear may also be present when whites avoid black areas of town because they think they may get assaulted, or when white women are wary of black men because they believe black men have an insatiable desire to take advantage of them. As a result, perhaps the effect of fear emerges in the domain of crime. Chapter 3 examines the link between racial crime and fear to see if in this domain, fear is linked to whites' racial attitudes. My contention is not that fear isn't present in the contemporary debate on race, but that it's not the dominant emotional force. The reason is that the appraisals central to fear – lack of control and uncertainty – don't largely map onto contemporary debates about race. As a result, my expectation is that fear will have a difficult time bringing negative thoughts about race to mind in the contemporary period. This doesn't mean that fear could never be linked to racial attitudes. When the racial debate is dominated by fear appraisals (i.e., uncertainty and lack of control), my suspicion is that fear should be linked to whites' racial attitudes.[12] Under this condition, fear should cause whites to oppose racial policies by making their racial attitudes more accessible in memory.

2

The Emotional Foundation of White Racial Attitudes

As the Jim Crow era ended, white support for racial equality in principle increased (Schuman et al. 1997). Most whites began to support blacks and whites attending the same schools, living in the same neighborhoods, and even in some respects getting married. But when asked to support government efforts to alleviate racial inequality, a different picture emerged – one that showed most whites were in opposition. This difference presented a dilemma. Despite the fact that a majority of white Americans accept racial equality, they are not inclined to support policies designed to reduce racial inequality.

Several explanations have been offered to explain the divergence in support for racial equality in principle and practice. One is that white opposition to racial policies derives from a new subtle form of racism. David Sears and Donald Kinder recognized that whites no longer opposed racially redistributive policies because they regarded blacks as biologically different from and inferior to whites. Instead, opposition was much more subtle and grounded in the beliefs that "blacks do not try hard enough to overcome the difficulties they face and that they take what they have not earned" (Kinder and Sanders 1996, 106). From this, they developed a new theory of racism. It acknowledges that old-fashioned racism has genuinely receded in both prevalence and influence. In its place, a new form of racism (symbolic racism) has emerged that is rooted in an organic synthesis of anti-black affect and the sense that blacks violate cherished American values such as individualism (Kinder and Sanders 1996; Sears and

Henry 2003). Scholars have shown that symbolic racism makes a substantial contribution to explaining racial policy opinions and vote preferences, over and above the impact of other explanations such as old-fashioned racism, race-neutral principles, and self-interest (Kinder and Sears 1981; McConahay 1986). For instance, utilizing the 1986, 1988, and 1992 American National Election Study (ANES), Kinder and Sanders (1996) found that whites' objection to racial policies was mostly an expression of symbolic racism, controlling for material threats to self-interest, American core values, and social and demographic variables.

An alternative explanation is the politics-centered approach (Sniderman, Crosby, and Howell 2000; Sniderman and Piazza 1993), which insists that Sears and Kinder overestimate the role of racial animus in society. Instead, Sniderman and colleagues argue that race-neutral principles regarding the proper size and role of government, political ideology, and individual effort mainly underlie opposition to racial policies. That is, the political parties present policy alternatives in a liberal-conservative framework across issues; this framework leads to a clash over the proper responsibilities of government and the appropriate obligations of citizens. As a result, opposition to racial policies does not stem primarily from racism, but that these government-sponsored programs are inefficient by wasting government resources and reward people's lack of individual effort. Their criticism of symbolic racism theory focuses on two related dimensions.

First, Sniderman and his colleagues challenge that a new form of racism has emerged in American society, and thus question whether old-fashioned racism and symbolic racism are truly distinct. They state, "Kinder not only claims that symbolic and old-fashioned racism are worth distinguishing; he claims that they have been proven to be different. We do not believe available data warrant this conclusion" (Sniderman and Tetlock 1986, 179). Nonetheless, scholars have provided evidence to demonstrate the distinctiveness of old-fashioned racism from symbolic racism. Using factor analysis, McConahay (1986) demonstrates that modern racism and old-fashioned racism load on two independent factors. Furthermore, Sears and colleagues (1997) show that symbolic racism and old-fashioned racism have distinguishable effects on racial policy opinion, with symbolic racism having the largest impact.

Yet skepticism persists because proving causal relationships with survey data is so challenging, especially because these multiple attitude dimensions are often quite highly correlated (Bobo 1988; Sidanius and Pratto 1999; Sniderman and Tetlock 1986). Sniderman and Tetlock state that "every observed cause of the one has also been found to be a cause of the other; and every observed consequence of one has been found to be a consequence of the other. Hence, it is prudent – indeed, necessary – to ask whether the two 'types' of racism differ" (1986, 180). One way to advance this debate is to theorize and empirically explore the conditions under which these particular attitude dimensions may become salient.

A second criticism voiced by Sniderman and colleagues is that measures of symbolic racism are contaminated with race-neutral principles. These nonracial values, not racism, are the major determinants of opposition to racially redistributive policies. Whites "endorse standing on your own two feet when it comes to whites as when it comes to blacks. There is no evidence at all of a racial double standard" (Sniderman et al. 2000, 247). Conservatives believe *everyone* should work hard, which explains why they score relatively highly on measures of symbolic racism.

The two criticisms of symbolic racism theory are at odds: the first says that symbolic racism is identical to old-fashioned racism; the second insists that the symbolic racism scale (but not old-fashioned racism) actually captures nonracial values such as support for small, efficient government and individual initiative. Studies testing these competing explanations remain inconclusive because all three dimensions – old-fashioned racism, symbolic racism, and race-neutral values – are correlated with each other and with racial policy opinions.[1] The debate, then, often reduces to proper measurement, model specification, or subjective characterizations of the explained variance of each dimension. This chapter intends to move this debate forward by theorizing about the emotional substrates of each attitude dimension. I move a step back in the causal chain to consider whether distinct emotional antecedents of these attitudinal dimensions exist. If, in fact, symbolic racism, old-fashioned racism, and nonracial values are strongly linked to specific emotions and can in fact be triggered by different emotions, the argument in favor of their distinct role in shaping racial policy opinions would be much more plausible.

EMOTIONS AND RACISM, FROM OLD TO NEW

During much of the eighteenth century, viewing blacks as geneti-
cally inferior to whites was an acceptable way of thinking and not
interpreted as racist until abolitionists began to attack the servitude
of blacks. As the attacks on slavery started to mount, these beliefs
developed into a full-born racist ideology – to justify keeping blacks
enslaved. When the institution of slavery ended, the means to control blacks and maintain racial oppression became a real concern for
Southern whites. Scientific arguments were engineered to provide cre-
dence to the doctrine of biological racism. One such argument relied
on Social Darwinism to support the theory that the races were innately
different. Under this theory, blacks were inferior to whites in ability
and intelligence, which resulted from Darwin's principle of "survival
of the fittest." Other white Americans didn't need anthropologists to
prove blacks' inferior status; they believed observable features like the
often highly exaggerated "Negro's black skin, kinky hair, flat nose,
large lips, narrow shins, and protruding heels" (Wood 1968, 10) were
enough.

The hallmark of old-fashioned racism, the belief system prevalent
in white America until the second half of the twentieth century, was
blacks' biological inferiority to whites (Kinder and Sanders 1996;
Sears 1988). Stereotypes of blacks as beastly, apelike, and subhuman
were often explicit in the public discussion of race during that era
(Mendelberg 2001). Myrdal captures these sentiments in describing
white, early twentieth-century racial attitudes: "the Negro was hea-
then and a barbarian, an outcast among the peoples of the earth, a
descendant of Noah's son Ham, cursed by God himself and doomed
to be a servant forever on account of an ancient sin" (1944, 85). Racist
whites believed blacks' perpetual servitude was ordained by God, and
they used the Old Testament story of Noah and the "curse of Canaan"
to justify blacks' basic inferiority. Under this belief system, blacks were
seen as a contaminated group, such that any interracial contact would
lead to the "mongrelization" of the white race.

Besides biologically based arguments, another element of this
racial belief system was blacks' moral inferiority (Fredrickson 1971).
Arguments about the uncivilized and backward moral character of
African Americans gained momentum after emancipation in order to

undermine black freedom. Blacks' presumed lack of moral character called into question their ability to function in society. High rates of poverty, criminality, and lack of intelligence were seen as evidence confirming blacks' nature as innately incapable of becoming self-sustaining citizens. Though a wide array of negative black stereotypes was common among whites during the post–Civil War period, such stereotypes carried a paternalistic dimension: blacks were inherently inferior and therefore needed to be kept separate from whites for their own good, not just for the good of whites (Blake and Dennis 1943; Karlins, Coffman, and Walters 1969; Katz and Braly 1933). These beliefs, grounded in blacks' genetic and moral deficiencies, led Gunnar Myrdal to suggest that the central emotional underpinning of racism at the time was disgust. "When one speaks about 'Americans' or 'Southerners,' the Negro is not counted in. When the 'public' is invited, he is not expected. Like the devil and all his synonyms and satellites, he is enticing at the same time that he is disgusting" (1944, 101).

Based on appraisal theories of emotion, the appraisals of physical contamination and revulsion are necessary to experience disgust (Lazarus 1991; Rozin and Fallon 1987). Disgust is an emotional reaction to a specific type of threat, one that might poison or contaminate the body. It may also be experienced from a moral transgression (Lazarus 1991). In fact, Cuddy, Fiske, and Glick (2007) provide preliminary evidence for the automatic linkage between negative group stereotypes and feelings of disgust. Because measures of old-fashioned racism are dominated by beliefs of biological difference, I suspect this belief system is strongly linked to feelings of disgust. For the small minority who still endorse these views, I expect this group's thoughts about race to be moved by disgust.

As discussed in Chapter 1, my reading of contemporary debates about race in America lead me to suspect that symbolic racism is linked more strongly to anger than to disgust or fear. While the belief that blacks are innately inferior has declined, many whites still suspect that blacks purposefully *choose* not to try as hard.[2] Mendelberg (2001) and Valentino and colleagues (2002) suggest a similar transformation has occurred in political communication: racial appeals that once argued blacks are biologically inferior have been replaced by those involving blacks' motivation and work ethic. If blacks are considered equal in ability, this perceived lack of motivation leads to blame. According to appraisal theories of emotion, this attribution is essential for anger. In other words, because symbolic racism is situated in the belief that blacks are to blame for their own disadvantages (Kinder and Sanders 1996; Sears and Kinder 1971), it should be strongly linked to anger. If blame rhetoric dominates contemporary racial debates, anger will become powerfully fused to the symbolic racism belief system. Subsequently, for those high in symbolic racism, the experience of anger may trigger negative thoughts about race that will subsequently boost opposition to racially redistributive policies.

Might a similar process cause anger to become linked to race-neutral values, such as preference for small government, individualism, or nonracial ideological identities? The politics-centered approach suggests people oppose racial policies such as affirmative action, not because the recipients are black, but because they require large and inefficient government bureaucracies or they undermine individual initiative. Violating these values via government policy could generate anger if people believe blacks are intentionally demanding unfair treatment in comparison to other groups. For example, Sniderman and his colleagues find that most white Americans are angry when they think about affirmative action. If these nonracial values drive resistance to racially redistributive policies, anger should also powerfully prime race-neutral principles and boost opposition to racial policies among those high on measures of that belief system. Such an outcome would leave me in an indeterminate position. I would still not know if symbolic racism and race-neutral values are distinct, because they would not have distinct emotional triggers.

Another expectation is that no one emotion dominates race-neutral principles. Principles such as smaller and efficient government or self-reported political ideology encompass a wide array of beliefs (Campbell et al. 1960; Converse 1964; McCloksy and Zaller 1984). Perhaps several emotions are linked to race-neutral principles, making it difficult for any one emotion to serve as a trigger. In this case, perhaps none of the emotions (i.e., anger, fear, and disgust) augment race-neutral principles.

As stances like group position theory and the power-threat hypothesis (Key 1949) suggest, the threat of resource redistribution from white to black communities may prompt fear among whites (Blumer 1958). If so, then *fear* may in fact be most powerfully linked, and therefore should activate symbolic racism. Because I do not see contemporary discussions of race as dominated by appraisals of fear, I suspect fear should not boost opposition to racial policies among those high in *any* of these racial belief systems.

My expectation is that the experience of anger, independent of racial or political content, may be enough to bring ideas about race to mind. In this chapter, I test whether experiencing *anger*, even when generated by a nonpolitical or nonracial stimulus, will boost opposition to racial policies among those high in symbolic racism. But my theory also suggests that anger should be linked to the beliefs of racial liberals. As a result, I examine if anger primes their racial belief system as well. If the politics-centered approach is correct, anger should also have this effect for those high in nonracial attitudes such as preference for small government, individual initiative, and political conservatism. Next, I examine whether disgust (but not other negative emotions) will lead whites high in old-fashioned racism to oppose racially redistributive policies. Finally, I test if those high in symbolic racism, old-fashioned racism, and race-neutral values are affected by fear. To test these hypotheses, I use an experiment to independently induce negative emotions using a nonpolitical and nonracial task. This study provides a precise test of the causal mechanism I believe is at work in priming particular belief systems during racial policy opinion formation.

EXPERIMENTAL TEST OF THE EFFECTS OF EMOTIONS ON RACIAL AND NONRACIAL ATTITUDES

I conducted an experiment through Polimetrix/YouGov, an Internet survey company, from April 21 to April 30, 2008. Polimetrix/YouGov uses a matching technique to draw its adult sample.[3] Respondents are matched to the national population on gender, age, race, education, party identification, and political interest. The total sample size was 243 whites.[4] There was substantial variation in age (26% were 18–34; 38% were 35–54; 36% were 55 and over), gender (48% female), and education (43% high school degree or less; 30% some college; 18% college graduate). An oversample of the South (128 respondents) was included to increase variation in old-fashioned racism, because this belief system is more prevalent in Southern states (Valentino and Sears 2005).[5] As a result of the oversample, the sample was more likely than

the nation to identify as Republican (49%) and conservative (49%).[6]
The random assignment of subjects to conditions was successful: no
significant differences appeared across cells of the design in the proportion of sociodemographic or partisan variables. As a result, any
differences in the poststimulus dependent measures can be attributed
to the manipulation and not to other factors.

The experiment was conducted in two waves. This is an important, though costly, design choice. Many similar studies measure the
primed dimension in the posttest, because researchers fear the pretest
measure may itself activate thoughts about the group, thus eliminating
any experimental effects. However, tapping racial attitudes in the posttest carries a different risk: that the stimulus itself will lead to changes
in the primed dimension – racial attitudes. A preferable design is to
measure the racial attitudes in a pretest far enough in advance that it is
unlikely to remain salient by the time the individual is exposed to the
stimulus in the second wave.[7] As a result, I measured attitudes a week
prior to exposure to the emotion induction task. The first wave consisted of racial and general attitudes measures, that is, symbolic racism, old-fashioned racism, and race-neutral values (including ideology,
individualism, and size of government). Seven days later, respondents
participated in the second wave, which consisted of the manipulation
followed by measures of racial policy opinions.

EXPERIMENTAL MANIPULATION

The experimental manipulation utilized two induction techniques common in psychological studies of emotion (Bower 1981; Ekman 1993;
Lerner and Keltner 2001; Valentino et al. 2008). Subjects were asked
to recall and focus on events, people, or occurrences that led them to
experience a given emotion, while viewing an image of a person with
a facial expression corresponding to that emotion.[8] The combination
of written and visual stimuli ensures respondents experience distinct
negative emotions (i.e., anger, disgust, and fear). Facial expressions
have been shown to trigger the same emotion in the viewer (Ekman
1993). Subjects were asked via the computer to respond to the following query[9]:

Here is a picture of someone who is (ANGRY/AFRAID/DISGUSTED). We
would like you to describe in general things that make you feel like the person

in the picture. It is okay if you don't remember all the details, just be specific about what exactly it is that makes you (ANGRY/AFRAID/DISGUSTED) and what it feels like to be (ANGRY/AFRIAD/DISGUSTED). Please describe the events that make you feel the MOST (ANGRY/AFRAID/DISGUSTED); these experiences could have occurred in the past or will happen in the future. If you can, write your description so that someone reading it might even feel (ANGRY/AFRAID/DISGUSTED).

The technique does not focus the respondent's attention on politics or race. It is, therefore, a precise test of the hypothesis that emotions themselves can activate specific group-based belief systems. Had I asked the respondent to focus on political objects that caused them to experience specific emotions, one concern would be that thoughts about those objects, not the emotions they cause, were responsible for the changes I observe in policy views. Response length to the emotional prompt was unrestricted, but subjects were told to take a few minutes to write down anything in general that made them feel the intended emotion. After the induction, subjects completed a posttest questionnaire that included a variety of policy opinion measures.

MANIPULATION CHECK: DID THE EMOTION INDUCTION EVOKE THE INTENDED EMOTION?

Before examining the results from the manipulation check, here are examples of what subjects wrote in response to the emotion induction task.

[Respondent in the Anger Condition]

I felt most angry when my mom was killed by a twenty-year-old kid while she was in the car with my dad. I was and still am very angry at the boy for speeding and killing the most beautiful woman in the world. Feeling angry makes your blood pressure rise and you get a knot in your throat, at least I do. Your voice gets louder and your face gets red. You may use your hands in gestures or stomp your feet. I was so very angry with this kid and he got away with it. He was not supposed to be driving. He had a restricted license; he should not have been driving – my mom should still be alive!!!

[Respondent in the Disgust Condition]

Things that make me disgusted: Bad smells, road kill, too much perfume on people, throw up, pedophiles, men who beat women, women who beat their children, or anyone who kills another in cold blood, wasteful killing of

animals, cruelty to animals, verbal abuse of children, people getting off on
technicalities for crimes. To be disgusted feels like your stomach is rolling and
your tongue wants out of your mouth. The event that made me the most disgusted was when I found out my sister was sexually [abused] by our father.
It ruined my life and stained all of my relationships with men. This is not an
event, but the verbal abuse that was inflicted on my sister and I by our mother,
but more than that, the fact that no one tried to help us, no school counselor
took an interest in why we were so unhappy and so insecure. None of the rela-
tives stepped in to stop her. Our own father did not step in to stop the verbal
abuse. But by far the most disgusting was finding a [friend's] horse with her
legs torn off because someone had [tossed] an old box spring into her pasture,
full well knowing that horses were in the pasture. This horse of course had to
be shot by the owners. I will never get that horse's visage out of my mind.

[Respondent in the Fear Condition]

I feel [afraid] when I see spiders. Ever since I was a kid but it's even worse now
that I am an adult. Big ones little ones it doesn't matter, they scare me. I even
have nightmares that I am laying in bed and there are spiders coming down on
top of me. I feel them crawling on me. I wake up [screaming]. I look for spiders every where I go. I know the places they like to hide, places other people
wouldn't even think of. I buy dozens of cans of spider spray and use them all
over my house but they still get in. Big ones like wolf spiders and those black
ones that look like mini tarantulas and jump around. I don't want to be so
[afraid] but I can't help it.

As you can see, subjects discussed events in their personal lives that
reflected the intended emotion. I conducted a manipulation check to
determine if the induction procedure operated as expected. Open-
ended responses to the induction task were double-coded by two
trained graduate students unaware of the hypotheses. They identified
the intensity of any negative emotions expressed in the responses.[10]
The results of the manipulation check are presented in Table 2.1. As
expected, participants in the anger condition expressed significantly
more intense anger than those in the control (relaxed) condition, but
did not express more fear or disgust. Correspondingly, respondents in
the fear condition expressed more fear, but not more anger or disgust
relative to those in the control condition. Participants in the disgust
condition expressed more disgust, but also slightly more anger than
those in the control condition. Eighty-eight percent of the time, coders
correctly identified the fear expression and 100 percent of the time

TABLE 2.1. *Manipulation Check*

	Intensity of Anger Expressed	Intensity of Fear Expressed	Intensity of Disgust Expressed
	B (s.e.)	B (s.e.)	B (s.e.)
Anger Condition	.51*** (.04)	01 (.03)	02 (.04)
Fear Condition	.03 (.04)	.48*** (.03)	.00 (.04)
Disgust Condition	.13*** (.04)	.01 (.03)	.44*** (.04)
Constant	01 (.03)	.00 (.02)	.01 (.02)
N	241	241	241

Notes: * $p \leq .1$; ** $p \leq .05$; *** $p \leq .001$ (all by two-tailed test). Entries are unstandardized OLS regression coefficients and the standard errors are in parentheses.

correctly identified the anger and disgust expressions.[11] These results indicate that the induction performed as intended. The slightly over-lapping experience of anger and disgust is not surprising, given how often these emotions co-occur in real life. This result provides a more conservative test of my hypotheses about the distinctive links between each emotion and various attitude dimensions.

CAN EMOTIONS PRIME RACIAL AND NONRACIAL ATTITUDES?

Does the experience of anger significantly boost opposition to racial policies among those high in symbolic racism? To find out, I regressed racial policy opinions on emotion dummies (*Anger*, *Disgust*, and *Fear*), *Symbolic Racism*, and the interaction between the two, controlling for *Ideology*, *Education*, *Income*, *South*, *Political discussion*, and *Age*.[12] To measure symbolic racism, I used Kinder and Sanders's (1996) four-item ANES battery: 1. "Over the past few years, blacks have got-ten less than they deserve." 2. "Government officials usually pay less attention to a request or complaint from a black person than from a white person." 3. "It's really a matter of some people not trying hard enough; if blacks would only try harder they could be just as well off as whites." 4. "Generations of slavery and discrimination have created conditions that make it difficult for blacks to work their way out of the lower class."[13] I created a scale of *racial policy opinions* covering a broad spectrum of economic and symbolic remedies to eliminate racial inequalities by summing responses to five items. The items include support for *affirmative action, busing, government assistance to blacks, Confederate flag displays,* and official observance of the *Martin Luther King Jr. Holiday.*[14]

My main expectation is that the interaction between the anger condition and symbolic racism in an OLS regression model should be positive and significant. Column 1 of Table 2.2 shows evidence consistent with this prediction. The interaction between the anger condition and symbolic racism is in the expected direction and is substantively large. The main effect of anger (racial liberals) is negative as expected. Although this coefficient just misses reaching statistical significance ($p \leq .16$), it is in the right direction. On the other hand, neither the fear condition nor the disgust condition significantly boost symbolic racism's impact on racial policy opinions.[15] Figure 2.1 illustrates the marginal effect of each emotion condition on racial policy opinions across levels of symbolic racism. The figure displays a 95 percent confidence interval, in dotted lines, around the marginal effect of the anger condition in the solid black line. As I predict, as symbolic racism increases, the anger condition increasingly boosts opposition to racial policies such as affirmative action. The marginal effect of the fear condition, in long dashes, and the disgust condition, in short dashes, is flat across levels of symbolic racism. At high levels of symbolic racism, the anger condition produces significantly higher levels of opposition to racial policies than do the other emotions.

As we move to old-fashioned racism, what emotion activates this racial belief system? My prediction is that the disgust condition (and not anger or fear) should boost opposition to racial policies among those high in *old-fashioned racism.* I measured old-fashioned racism with a scale based on three items: 1. "On average blacks have worse jobs, income, and housing than white people. Do you think these differences are because most blacks have less in-born ability to learn?" 2. "Blacks come from a less able race and this explains why blacks are

TABLE 2.2. *The Priming Effect of Emotion for Racial and Nonracial Attitudes on Racial Policy Opinions*

	Racial Policies	Racial Policies	Racial Policies	Racial Policies	Racial Policies
	B (s.e.)	B (s.e.)	B (s.e.)	B (s.e.)	B (s.e.)
Anger Condition *Symbolic Racism	.32** (.14)			.29** (.14)	.32* (.16)
Disgust Condition *Symbolic Racism	.08 (.13)			.08 (.14)	.03 (.17)
Fear Condition *Symbolic Racism	.09 (.12)			.06 (.13)	.10 (.17)
Anger Condition *Old-Fashioned Racism		.57** (.27)		.38 (.24)	
Disgust Condition *Old-Fashioned Racism		.49** (.24)		.40* (.21)	
Fear Condition *Old-Fashioned Racism		.35 (.31)		.17 (.27)	
Anger Condition *Limited Government			-.09 (.12)		-.02 (.13)
Disgust Condition *Limited Government			.07 (.15)		.12 (.15)
Fear Condition *Limited Government			.03 (.12)		-.04 (.14)
Anger Condition	-.15 (.10)	.06 (.05)	.15* (.08)	-.17 (.10)	-.14 (.11)
Disgust Condition	-.07 (.10)	-.04 (.05)	-.03 (.09)	-.10 (.10)	-.10 (.10)
Fear Condition	-.04 (.09)	.00 (.05)	-.01 (.08)	-.03 (.09)	-.03 (.09)
Symbolic Racism	.37*** (.09)			.35*** (.10)	.36*** (.16)
Old-Fashioned Racism		-.03 (.16)		-.03 (.14)	
Limited Government			.23** (.10)		.10 (.11)
Ideology	.17*** (.05)	.31*** (.05)	.19** (.08)	.14** (.05)	.10 (.07)

(continued)

TABLE 2.2. *(continued)*

	Racial Policies	Racial Policies	Racial Policies	Racial Policies	Racial Policies
	B (s.e.)	B (s.e.)	B (s.e.)	B (s.e.)	B (s.e.)
Education	−.05 (.05)	−.15** (.06)	−.13** (.06)	−.08 (.05)	−.06 (.05)
Income	−.07 (.05)	.03 (.06)	−.06 (.06)	−.03 (.06)	−.08 (.05)
Age	.002** (.001)	.001 (.001)	.002* (.001)	.002** (.001)	.002** (.001)
South	.03 (.03)	.07** (.03)	.06** (.03)	.03 (.03)	.03 (.03)
Political Discussion	−.02 (.15)	−.10 (.17)	−.01 (.17)	−.03 (.15)	.02 (.15)
Constant	.19** (.08)	.38*** (.07)	.34*** (.08)	.24** (.09)	.20** (.09)
R^2	.54	.39	.38	.58	.56
N	181	172	184	163	176

Notes: * $p \leq .1$; ** $p \leq .05$; *** $p \leq .001$ (all by two-tailed test). Entries are unstandardized OLS regression coefficients and the standard errors are in parentheses. Variables are coded 0 to 1, where higher values indicate more opposition to racial policies.

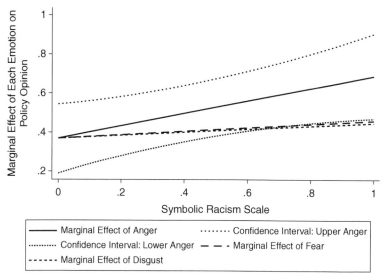

FIGURE 2.1. Marginal effect of each emotion on racial policy opinion as symbolic racism changes.

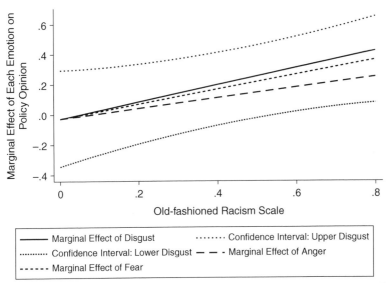

FIGURE 2.2. Marginal effect of each emotion on racial policy opinion as old-fashioned racism changes.

not as well off as whites in America." and 3. "How strongly would you object if a member of your family had a close relationship with a black person?" Column 2 of Table 2.2 displays a significant interaction between the disgust condition and old-fashioned racism on the racial policy index. Contrary to my expectation, the impact of old-fashioned racism on racial policy opinions was also significantly higher for those in the anger condition compared to those in the control group. In fact, the interaction between old-fashioned racism and the anger condition was slightly, though not significantly, stronger than that for old-fashioned racism and the disgust condition. Thus, both the anger and disgust conditions seem to trigger old-fashioned racism. To show this more clearly, Figure 2.2 displays these interactions visually and shows that the effects of the anger and disgust conditions are larger than that of the fear condition, but these differences are not as large or statistically distinct. However, as old-fashioned racism increases, both the anger and disgust conditions boost opposition to racial policies. That is, at very high levels of old-fashioned racism, both the anger and disgust groups boost opposition significantly more than that in the (relaxed) control group.

Now we turn to race-neutral principles. Perhaps anger is also the emotional underpinning of race-neutral attitudes like preference for *limited government*. If this value represents the primary driver of racial policy opinions, anger should also move opinions among those high on this dimension. The results in column 3 provide no support for this expectation. None of the interactions are substantively large or statistically significant on racial policy opinions.

Researchers have found symbolic racism and old-fashioned racism both to be driven by internal attributions (Huddy and Feldman 2009). As a result, to further assess distinctions between symbolic racism and old-fashioned racism, I ran an omnibus model including both sets of interactions described earlier. I estimated the interaction of each emotion with symbolic racism and old-fashioned racism simultaneously. The results are reported in column 4. They show that symbolic racism still interacts only with the anger condition while the disgust condition now interacts significantly only with old-fashioned racism.[16] In other words, the anger condition significantly moved opinions among those high in symbolic racism, while the disgust condition moved those high in old-fashioned racism.[17]

In addition to studies finding a link between symbolic racism and old-fashioned racism, they have also shown that symbolic racism and race-neutral principles are correlated with each other. Furthermore, Sniderman and his colleagues (2000) contend that symbolic racism is simply measuring race-neutral principles – like limited government, individual initiative, and race-neutral ideological beliefs – and not contemporary racism. To ensure distinctions between symbolic racism and race-neutral attitudes, I ran a model that includes both sets of interactions. The results for symbolic racism and limited government are in column 5. The column shows that the anger condition still primes the beliefs of those high in symbolic racism while it has no effect on those who prefer small government. In Table 2.3, I replicated these analyses for two other race-neutral dimensions: nonracial liberal-conservative ideology and individualism. Again, I find that the anger condition only interacts with symbolic racism, and it has no effect on nonracial conservative ideology or the value of individual initiative.

TABLE 2.3. *The Priming Effect of Emotion for Symbolic Racism, Individualism, and Ideology on Racial Policy Opinions*

	Racial Policies	Racial Policies
	B (s.e.)	B (s.e.)
Anger Condition *Symbolic Racism	.33** (.15)	.39** (.15)
Disgust Condition *Symbolic Racism	.11 (.15)	.14 (.16)
Fear Condition *Symbolic Racism	.14 (.14)	.18 (.15)
Anger Condition *Individualism	−.20 (.25)	
Disgust Condition *Individualism	−.08 (.27)	
Fear Condition *Individualism	−.21 (.25)	
Anger Condition *Ideology		−.15 (.14)
Disgust Condition *Ideology		−.11 (.14)
Fear Condition *Ideology		−.16 (.15)
Anger Condition	−.02 (.18)	−.11 (.11)
Disgust Condition	−.03 (.18)	−.04 (.10)
Fear Condition	.07 (.16)	−.01 (.09)
Symbolic Racism	.42*** (.10)	.31** (.10)
Individualism	.18 (.16)	
Ideology		.27** (.10)
Education	−.05 (.05)	−.04 (.05)
Income	−.07 (.06)	−.06 (.05)
Age	.003** (.001)	.002** (.001)

(continued)

TABLE 2.3. (*continued*)

	Racial Policies	Racial Policies
	B (s.e.)	B (s.e.)
South	.03 (.03)	.03 (.03)
Political Discussion	−.03 (.16)	−.02 (.15)
Constant	.12** (.12)	.18** (.08)
R^2	.52	.55
N	181	181

Notes: * $p \leq .1$; ** $p \leq .05$; *** $p \leq .001$ (all by two-tailed test). Entries are unstandardized OLS regression coefficients and the standard errors are in parentheses. Variables are coded 0 to 1, where higher values indicate more opposition to racial policies.

Perhaps anger doesn't only alter opinions on policies designed to assist blacks, but also affects emotionally charged nonracial policies. This proposition would suggest that the anger effect is not only about race. To determine if this is so, I examine people's opinions on the Iraq War. Research shows that the public has strong emotional reactions to foreign policy matters like terrorism and war (Berinsky 2009; Merolla and Zechmeister 2009). However, Table 2.4 shows that none of the emotion conditions boost the effect of racial or nonracial attitudes on support for the Iraq War.

In sum, the experimental results show that the anger condition activates symbolic racism.[18] Experiencing anger, independent of thoughts about race or politics, powerfully boosted the impact of symbolic racism on racial policy opinions. These results demonstrate that subtle racial appeals or racially coded language aren't the only means of bringing negative ideas about race to mind. Because today's subtle form of racism is so ingrained in our society through anger, general states of anger are enough for racial predispositions to have a powerful impact on policy opinions. The disgust condition primed old-fashioned racism, as originally predicted, but the anger condition also activated this belief system. The fear condition did not activate racial thinking of any kind. Moreover, none of the emotion conditions had an effect on race-neutral considerations.

TABLE 2.4. *The Priming Effect of Emotion for Racial and Nonracial Attitudes on Support for the Iraq War*

	Iraq War
	B (s.e.)
Anger Condition *Symbolic Racism	−.08 (.24)
Disgust Condition *Symbolic Racism	.16 (.24)
Fear Condition *Symbolic Racism	.04 (.22)
Anger Condition *Ideology	−.01 (.21)
Disgust Condition *Ideology	.01 (.21)
Fear Condition *Ideology	.00 (.21)
Anger Condition	−.01 (.17)
Disgust Condition	−.15 (.16)
Fear Condition	−.04 (.15)
Symbolic Racism	.17 (.16)
Ideology	.88*** (.15)
Education	−.12* (.07)
Income	.19** (.08)
Age	−.003** (.001)
South	.04 (.04)
Political Discussion	−.23 (.21)
Constant	−.06 (.13)
R^2	.56
N	225

Notes: * $p \leq .1$; ** $p \leq .05$; *** $p \leq .001$ (all by two-tailed test). Entries are unstandardized OLS regression coefficients and the standard errors are in parentheses. Variables are coded 0 to 1, where higher values indicate more support for the Iraq War.

OPEN-ENDED RESPONSES: RACIAL THINKING ACROSS
EXPERIMENTAL CONDITIONS

The results presented thus far show that specific emotions (i.e., anger
and disgust) can boost the effect of racial attitudes on racial policy
opinions. This test, however, does not allow me to determine if race
is more accessible when respondents are induced to feel certain emotional states. One approach to testing cognitive accessibility is to use a
lexical task (Fazio 1990; Nelson et al. 1997; Valentino, Hutchings, and
White 2002). With this task, subjects are presented with a race prime
and then given race-related words (e.g., black), non-race words (e.g.,
green), and nonsense letters (e.g., camjl) and asked to discriminate
between real words and nonsense words as quickly as possible. The
general expectation is that subjects receiving the race prime should
take less time identifying the race-related words. Another approach to
testing the accessibility of race is to look at respondents' open-ended
answers to the emotion induction task. Looking at their responses to
see if race was mentioned would give me some indication that race was
salient. My expectation is that respondents in the anger and disgust
conditions should be more likely to mention race in their open-ended
responses than those in the control and fear conditions.

To determine references to race, I had two trained research assistants coding for whether several race-related terms like *blacks*, *race*,
racial prejudice, *Barack Obama*, *affirmative action*, *welfare*, or *crime*
were mentioned.[19] Additionally, for a comparison group, they also
coded for whether subjects mentioned gender or class in their open-
ended responses.[20] Because the emotion induction task does not
ask respondents to focus on politics or race, my expectation is that
most subjects should have not mentioned race at all. Indeed, only
13 percent of subjects mentioned race in their responses, while an
even smaller percentage of respondents mentioned class (3%) or
gender (7%).

Figure 2.3 shows the percentage of respondents who mention race,
gender, or class across experimental conditions. It indicates that the anger
and disgust conditions have the most mentions of race in the emotion
induction task. Specifically, people in the anger condition mentioned race
about 26 percent of the time; it was mentioned 22 percent of the time
in the disgust condition. On the other hand, 7 percent of respondents

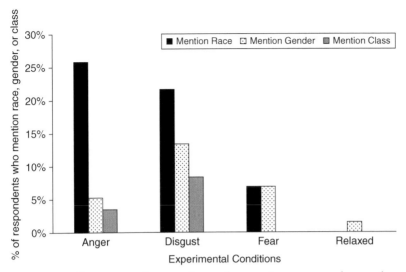

FIGURE 2.3. Percentage of respondents who mention race, gender, or class across experimental conditions.

mentioned race in the fear condition, and no mention of race took place in the relaxed condition. The figure shows that the anger condition causes subjects to discuss race at a significantly greater rate than those in the control condition and fear condition. A similar pattern emerges when comparing the disgust group to the control and fear groups.[21] Moreover, respondents are more likely to mention race than gender or class in the anger and disgust conditions. These results corroborate my previous findings; they demonstrate that the anger and disgust conditions make race more accessible in memory than the fear and control conditions.

However, are whites high in symbolic racism more likely to mention race than those at the middle of the scale or low in symbolic racism? Figure 2.4 shows that 50 percent of white racial liberals in the anger condition reference race. On the other hand, whites who are race neutral (at the midpoint) don't mention race at all. For racially resentful whites, 24 percent of them mention race. Based on my theory of anger and race, these results are what we would expect: thoughts about race at the top of the head among racial liberals and racial conservatives. But why do we see racial liberals mentioning race at a higher rate than racial conservatives? A possible explanation is that racial liberals feel free to give a racial response because their racial attitudes don't violate

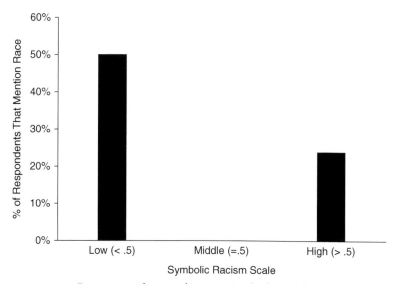

FIGURE 2.4. Percentage of respondents scoring high, middle, and low in symbolic racism who mention race in the anger condition.

the racial norm. For instance, here is an example of a racial liberal responding to the induction task in the anger condition:

I get very angry when I hear people discriminating against someone because of their race or because they are gay. It makes me very angry when I know someone is cheating. I get angry when I hear people put others down when they have no idea why they are doing something. Too many people think they are better than anyone else. I really get angry when I hear about child molesters and wife beaters.

We see that this person is angry about racial discrimination and other things. His/her response is not violating the norm of racial equality, but is in fact in line with it. Therefore, racial liberals mention race at higher rates than racial conservatives because their response is considered socially acceptable. Conversely, racial conservatives are concerned about being perceived as racists, so they are more likely to withhold mentioning race (Gaertner and Dovidio 1986; Mendelberg 2001).

While the experimental results strongly support my main expectations, I still must be cautious in generalizing these effects to the national population. The main threat to external validity in the experiment is the realism of my manipulation: I directly induced emotions to maximize the distinctiveness of my respondents' reactions. As a consequence, I now turn to a survey-based test. I utilize the 1985 ANES pilot study to test whether a significant relationship can be produced between particular emotions and predispositions (racial attitudes and race neutral principle) in a nationally representative sample tapping emotional reactions to several political attitude objects. This survey is useful because it contains emotion measures for disgust, anger, and fear as well as for symbolic racism and old-fashioned racism. For the survey-based test, I have two predictions. Anger, but not fear or disgust, toward several political objects is significantly correlated with symbolic racism. Disgust toward several political objects is significantly correlated with old-fashioned racism.

SURVEY DATA: RELATIONSHIP BETWEEN SPECIFIC EMOTIONS AND RACIAL AND NONRACIAL ATTITUDES

Here I examine multivariate correlations between specific emotions and the three belief systems examined previously: symbolic racism, old-fashioned racism, and race-neutral values. If my hypotheses are correct, correlations should be larger between anger and symbolic racism than with old-fashioned racism or race-neutral values. I also expect disgust to correlate most strongly with old-fashioned racism, not race-neutral values or symbolic racism. The 1985 ANES pilot study is a subsample of 429 participants from the 1984 ANES, a probability sample of Americans of voting age including 392 whites. The study contained various questions about emotional reactions to affirmative action and race relations as well as to both the Democratic and Republican presidential candidates Reagan and Mondale.[22] These measures are very different from the induction used in Study 1. I constructed scales of emotional states out of *all* the available emotion items across a wide range of targets to make the most conservative test possible: mean levels of anger across a variety of topics should be more highly correlated with symbolic racism than will mean levels of other emotions. On the other hand, I expect disgust (across this range of targets) should be more closely linked to old-fashioned racism, and fear should be linked to neither. Finally, race-neutral values (i.e., preference for limited government and self-identified political ideology)

TABLE 2.5. *Multivariate Relationship between Emotions, Racial and Nonracial Attitudes*

	Symbolic Racism	Old-Fashioned Racism	Limited Government	Ideology
	B (s.e.)	B (s.e.)	B (s.e.)	B (s.e.)
Anger	.22*** (.07)	.06 (.07)	.09 (.06)	.02 (.08)
Fear	.04 (.07)	-.01 (.08)	.02 (.07)	.16** (.08)
Disgust	-.01 (.06)	.00 (.07)	.01 (.06)	-.06 (.07)
Education	-.08 (.06)	-.25*** (.06)	.10** (.05)	-.03 (.06)
Ideology	.02 (.05)	.06 (.06)	.14*** (.05)	
Party Identification	.10** (.05)	-.02 (.05)	.08* (.04)	.32*** (.05)
Gender	.05 (.03)	.02 (.03)	-.01 (.03)	.02 (.03)
Age	.000 (.001)	.004*** (.001)	.002** (.001)	.002** (.001)
South	-.01 (.03)	.08** (.04)	.03 (.03)	-.03 (.04)
Constant	.41*** (.06)	.19** (.06)	.20*** (.06)	.35*** (.07)
R²	.11	.17	.15	.17
N	264	275	258	282

Notes: * $p \le .1$; ** $p \le .05$; *** $p \le .001$ (all by two-tailed test). Entries are unstandardized OLS regression coefficients and the standard errors are in parentheses.
Source: 1985 ANES pilot study.

should not be strongly correlated with any of these emotions. Note that if these emotion measures merely tap partisan affect, they should cancel each other when I combine evaluations of opposing parties. The strength of this test comes from taking the average emotional reaction to all targets, not simply emotional reactions to an individual's preferred candidate or party.[23]

Looking at column 1 of Table 2.5, my expectation finds support. *Anger* is significantly linked to *Symbolic Racism*, controlling for *Fear, Disgust, Ideology, Party Identification, Southern residence, Education,*

Age, and *Gender.* The link between anger and symbolic racism is larger and statistically distinguishable from that of fear (F, 1 255, 3.12, p<.10 by a two tailed test) and disgust (F, 1, 255 4.08, p<.05). Neither disgust nor fear is significantly linked to symbolic racism. Contrary to my previous finding, however, column 2 displays no significant link between disgust and old-fashioned racism. Consistent with my expectation, column 3 shows that preference for *Limited government* is not correlated with anger, disgust, or fear. In terms of political ideology, anger and disgust are not correlated with this belief system while fear is positively related to the liberal-conservative scale.[24]

In sum, the survey results parallel several of the experimental findings: feelings of anger, but not fear or disgust, are uniquely correlated with symbolic racism. Race-neutral principles like preference for limited government and political ideology are unrelated to the anger dimension, demonstrating the link between anger and contemporary racism is particularly powerful. On the other hand, contrary to my expectation, I find no correlation between reported feelings of disgust and old-fashioned racism.

EMOTIONS AND ETHNOCENTRISM

In the introduction, I argued that anger is linked to out-group prejudice in general and is not limited to a specific group. Perhaps whites are not the only group to justify their animosity toward blacks on the basis of value differentials (e.g., hard work); other groups may express their dislike for blacks based on similar differentials. Latino Americans and Asian Americans may also believe blacks are to blame for their lower status in society. In fact, Sears and his colleagues find that symbolic racism not only captures whites' racial animosity toward blacks, but also other racial and ethnic groups' negative attitudes about blacks (Sears, Haley, and Henry 2008; Tesler and Sears 2010). The same might be said of blacks and whites' views about immigration; they may believe Latinos (or Asians) are in the United States illegally and do not deserve rights and resources from the federal government. Perhaps the common thread is that members of the in-group use the perceived negative characteristics (e.g., lazy, violent, and untrustworthy) of the out-group (and how they differ from their in-group) as a way to justify their out-group prejudice. If members of the out-group are perceived as not subscribing to the values of the in-group, then they are blamed for their negative circumstances. As a consequence, I would expect anger to activate other forms of prejudice – not just prejudice toward a specific group – but prejudice broadly conceived or what scholars have referred to as *ethnocentrism*.

Kinder and Kam have reignited scholars' interest in the concept of ethnocentrism. To them, "[e]thnocentrism is a mental habit. It is a predisposition to divide the human world into in-groups and out-groups. Members of in-groups (until they prove otherwise) are assumed to be virtuous: friendly, cooperative, safe, and more. Members of out-groups (until they prove otherwise) are assumed to be the opposite: unfriendly, uncooperative, unworthy of trust, dangerous, and more" (2009, 8). They demonstrate that ethnocentrism plays an important role in Americans' views on a wide range of political issues like foreign policy, immigration, gay rights, social welfare, and affirmative action. Although ethnocentrism is important in American public opinion, it is not always salient in people's minds. Certain conditions give rise to ethnocentric thinking. Kinder and Kam argue that when politics is framed as us versus them or a conflict among groups, ethnocentrism should become important in people's political decision making. Specifically, "[c]onflict framed as a struggle between two groups – one side, malicious and brutal, bent on stealing or ruining; the other side, nobly determined to protect what is rightfully theirs – is just the sort of thing to set ethnocentrism to work" (2009, 41). This conflict between groups is likely to stir up strong emotions. As a result, do certain emotions activate ethnocentric thinking? My expectation is that anger, but not fear, should enhance the effect of ethnocentrism on policies that are framed in clear adversarial terms like racial and immigration policies.

I use the 2008 American National Election Study (ANES) to test this proposition. The 2008 ANES is a representative sample of American adult citizens.[25] A benefit of using the ANES is that it includes Kinder and Kam's ethnocentrism measure.[26] Because my interest is in whether emotions heighten ethnocentric thinking, I focus on the measure that captures the emotional aspect of ethnocentrism – the feeling thermometer scale. The thermometer scale asks respondents how they feel about groups in society in addition to political leaders. The question is usually posed as the following:

I'd like to get your feelings toward some of our political leaders and other people who are in the news these days.

I'll read the name of a person and I'd like you to rate that person using something we call the feeling thermometer. Ratings between 50 degrees and 100 degrees mean that you feel favorable and warm toward the person. Ratings between 0 degrees and 50 degrees mean that you don't feel favorable toward the person and that you don't care too much for that person. You would rate the person at the 50 degree mark if you don't feel particularly warm or cold toward the person.

After respondents answer questions about political leaders, they are asked to apply the feeling thermometer scale to various groups in society. To measure ethnocentrism, I use the feeling thermometer ratings of blacks, whites, Hispanic Americans, and Asian Americans. I created a measure of ethnocentrism by taking the average of the three out-group thermometers (e.g., whites, blacks, and Hispanic Americans) and subtracting it from the in-group thermometer (e.g., Asian Americans).[27] Consistent with Kinder and Kam's measure, the distribution of ethnocentrism shows that Americans on balance are ethnocentric.

I measure people's emotional states by using several emotion items in the 2008 ANES. Respondents are asked how they feel (angry/afraid) about a wide range of political targets such as Barack Obama, John McCain, and George W. Bush. Responses are summed to create mean level measures of *anger* and *fear*.[28]

I use two questions to measure racial policy opinions: (1) Some people say that because of past discrimination, blacks should be given preference in hiring and promotion. Others say that such preference in hiring and promotion of blacks is wrong because it gives blacks advantages they haven't earned. What about your opinion – are you for or against preferential hiring and promotion of blacks? (2) Some people feel that the government in Washington should make every effort to improve the social and economic position of blacks. Others feel that the government should not make any special effort to help blacks because they should help themselves. And, of course, some other people have opinions somewhere in between.... Where would you place yourself on this scale, or haven't you thought much about this? I summed the two items to create an *opposition to racial policy* index.[29]

The 2008 ANES asked four questions on immigration: (1) whether the number of immigrants from foreign countries who are permitted to come to the United States should be increased, decreased, or kept about the same; (2) whether federal spending on tightening border security to prevent illegal immigration should be increased, decreased, or kept about the same; (3) how likely it is that recent immigration levels will take away jobs from people already here – extremely likely, very likely, somewhat likely, or not at all likely; (4) whether controlling and reducing illegal immigration should be a very important foreign policy goal, a somewhat important foreign policy goal, or not an important foreign policy goal at all. I summed the four items to create an *opposition to immigration policy* index.[30]

To test my predictions, I regressed *Racial Policy Opinions* on *Anger* and *Fear*, *Ethnocentrism*, and the interaction between the two, controlling for *Ideology*, *Authoritarianism*, *Male*, *Education*, *Income*, *Assessment of Economic Condition*, and *South*. Table 2.6 presents the results of the OLS regression model. The first column shows that anger significantly boosts the effect of ethnocentrism on racial policy opinions. On the other hand, fear has no effect on ethnocentrism. For people who are less ethnocentric (or see out-groups as more virtuous than their in-group), anger makes them more supportive of racial policies. It is important to point out that absent anger and fear, ethnocentrism does not have an effect on racial policy opinions. In other words, only when anger is experienced does ethnocentric thinking play an important role in opinions on matters of race. Figure 2.5 visually shows these results. We see that as ethnocentrism increases, anger enhances opposition to policies like affirmative action. The figure also indicates that anger produces significantly higher levels of opposition to racial policies than fear (starting at .4 of the ethnocentrism scale). Moreover, we see that anger increases support for racial policies among the least ethnocentric. Conversely, the marginal effect of fear, the long dashed line, is flat across levels of ethnocentrism.

A similar pattern of results appears in column 2 for opinions about immigration. Column 2 shows that anger significantly increases opposition to immigration policies among those scoring high in ethnocentrism.[31] On the other hand, ethnocentrism is unaffected by fear. We also see that ethnocentrism increases opposition to immigration among those who didn't experience either anger or fear. Figure 2.6 displays these results visually and shows a pattern that resembles the previous

TABLE 2.6. *The Effect of Emotion for Ethnocentrism on Racial and Immigration Policy Opinions*

	Opposition to Racial Policies (Blacks are Excluded)	Opposition to Immigration Policies (Hispanics are Excluded)
	B (s.e.)	B (s.e.)
Anger*Ethnocentrism	.63**	.42**
	(.24)	(.21)
Fear*Ethnocentrism	.11	.06
	(.19)	(.21)
Anger	−.12**	−.04
	(.05)	(.04)
Fear	.01	−.04
	(.04)	(.04)
Ethnocentrism	−.09	.13**
	(.06)	(.05)
Ideology	.10***	.06**
	(.02)	(.01)
Authoritarianism	.04	.17***
	(.03)	(.03)
Male	.02	.00
	(.01)	(.01)
Income	.15***	.11***
	(.03)	(.03)
Education	.01	−.18***
	(.04)	(.03)
South	.07***	.02
	(.01)	(.01)
Assessment of the Economic Conditions	.02	.08***
	(.02)	(.02)
Constant	.53***	.51***
	(.04)	(.04)
R^2	.16	.26
N	1235	1315

Notes: * $p \leq .1$; ** $p \leq .05$; *** $p \leq .001$ (all by two-tailed test). Entries are unstandardized OLS regression coefficients and the standard errors are in parentheses.

figure. As people are more ethnocentric, anger increases opposition to immigration policies while the effect of fear is flat. All in all, these results indicate that anger is not just the emotional underpinning of antiblack attitudes, but of out-group prejudice more broadly.

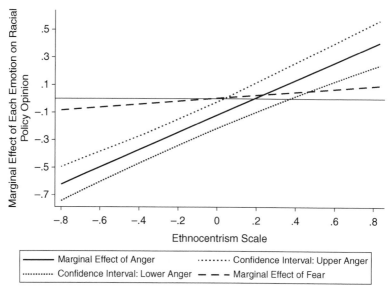

FIGURE 2.5. Marginal effect of each emotion on racial policy opinion as ethnocentrism changes.

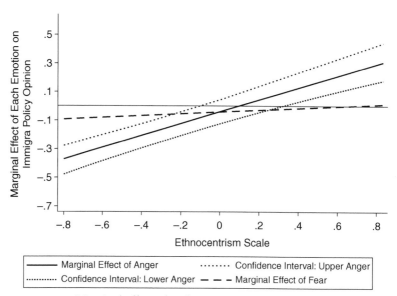

FIGURE 2.6. Marginal effect of each emotion on immigration policy opinion as ethnocentrism changes.

CONCLUSION

Many white Americans support racial equality in principle but oppose policies designed to bring it about. What explains this contradiction? The racial policy opinion literature has long returned a contested answer: people are motivated either by racial bias or by race-neutral views of how government works best. Much of the debate has focused on measurement difficulties: What do contemporary measures of racial animus such as symbolic racism really capture? Sears and Kinder have strongly contended that such measures capture today's subtle form of racism. Sniderman and colleagues have vehemently disagreed – arguing they reflect nothing more than race-neutral ideological principles. Their distinction has enormous implications for understanding how prevalent racism is in American society.

One purpose of this chapter was to show that symbolic racism has a different emotional underpinning than race-neutral principles. My prediction was that symbolic racism would be linked to and activated primarily by anger. On the other hand, none of the negative emotions should be strongly associated with race-neutral attitudes (i.e., limited government, individualism, and race-neutral ideological beliefs) – making it very difficult for any of these emotions to trigger this belief system. This chapter provided strong evidence in support of these expectations. The results support the argument that symbolic racism and race-neutral principles are indeed distinct, both conceptually and in their effect on racial policy opinion. The fact that they have distinct emotional antecedents indicates that symbolic racism is not, then, simply a substitute for nonracial values.

This chapter also set out to demonstrate that a new subtle form of racism does exist, in that symbolic racism is conceptually and empirically distinct from old-fashioned racism. To demonstrate this, my goal was to explore the emotional conditions under which these specific attitude dimensions would be activated. The experimental results showed that both the disgust condition *and* the anger condition triggered opposition to racial policies among those high in old-fashioned racism. Given my interpretations of the kinds of attributions that might have dominated whites' thoughts about race when belief in biological differences was dominant, this is puzzling. One explanation is that anger appraisals have found their way into the old-fashioned racism only recently. If so, an expectation would be that both the anger and disgust conditions should boost opposition to racial redistribution among those high in old-fashioned racism. While those high in old-fashioned racism may have once experienced disgust at the thought of racial intermixing, for example, they may now feel a mix of anger and disgust about the "unfair demands" made by blacks embodied by policies such as affirmative action. In fact, when symbolic racism and old-fashioned racism were simultaneously included in the model, the disgust condition uniquely activated old-fashioned beliefs. In consequence, this result indicates that old-fashioned racism is mostly rooted in disgust when symbolic racism is taken into account.

Another purpose of this chapter was to examine if anger is linked to out-group prejudice more broadly. The 2008 ANES results demonstrate that anger enhances the effect of ethnocentrism on racial and immigration policy opinions across a large group of Americans. On the other hand, fear does not boost the impact of ethnocentrism on policy opinions. Therefore, we see that anger not only has a strong connection with symbolic racism but also ethnocentrism – a general form of prejudice.

One implication of these findings is that group cues do not have to be salient for racial considerations to impact racial policy preferences. Because race is such a strong part of American society via emotions, it simply takes evoking certain emotional states to prime one's thoughts about race. Subtle racial campaign ads like the "weekend passes" ad from the 1988 presidential election are not the only paths for racism to rear its ugly head. Simply experiencing anger or disgust in general provides another avenue for racial bigotry to have a larger impact on public opinion. All in all, these results suggest that the conditions under which racism will impact one's political judgment are more pervasive than scholars might have imagined.

Does knowing that anger and racial prejudice form such a strong bond help us solve America's problem of racism? Perhaps the solution is as simple as that Myrdal suggested in his pathbreaking treatise on race more than sixty years ago. "The simple fact is that an educational offensive against racial intolerance, going deeper than the reiteration of the 'glittering generalities' in the nation's political creed, has never seriously been attempted in America" (1944, 49). Americans have had difficulty pinpointing the type of education that is needed to reduce racial prejudice. In fact, some scholars have shown that racism hasn't declined over time like Myrdal predicted, but remains just as much of a significant force (Kinder and Drake 2009). By identifying the emotional substrate of contemporary racism, we can pinpoint the direction where policy makers and educators should concentrate their educational energies. The main focus should be on dislodging the link between anger and people's thoughts about race, and it should start with removing the blame rhetoric from the dialogue on race. This approach is potentially one viable way to reduce racism in America.

APPENDIX

Index/Scale Construction

Anger, *Fear*, and *Disgust* (Study 1) are dummy variables, where 1=treatment condition and 0=control ("relaxed") condition.

The prompt for the *Relaxed* condition stated, "Now we would like you to describe in general things that make you feel **RELAXED**. It is okay if you don't remember all the details, just be specific about what exactly it is that makes you **RELAXED** and what it feels like to be **RELAXED**. Please describe the events that make you feel the **MOST RELAXED**; these experiences could have occurred in the past or will happen in the future. If you can, write your description so that someone reading it might even feel **RELAXED**."

Anger and Disgust (Study 2) are both the sum of four measures recoded onto a 0 to 1 scale, where 0=not angry/disgusted and 1=angry/disgusted. Four items were additively scaled for each emotion. The specific items are 1) Think about changes over the past twenty years in relation between blacks and whites in this country. Have these changes ever made you feel angry/disgusted? 2) Has preferential treatment of blacks ever made you feel angry/disgusted? 3) Think about Walter Mondale. Now, has Mondale (because of the kind of person he is, or because of something he has done) ever made you feel angry/disgusted? 4) Think about Ronald Reagan. Now, has Reagan (because of the kind of person he is, or because of something he has done) ever made you feel angry/disgusted? (*Anger* Mean=.42, S.D.=.27, Min=0, Max=1) (*Disgust* Mean =.42, S.D.=.29, Min=0, Max=1).

Fear (Study 2) comprised eight measures (combination of uneasy and afraid) and was recoded onto a 0 to 1 scale, where 0=not fearful and 1=fearful. Eight items were additively scaled. Response options for each question were "yes" or "no." The specific items are 1) Think about changes over the past twenty years in relations between blacks and whites in this country. Have these changes ever made you feel *afraid/uneasy*? 2) Has preferential treatment of blacks ever made you feel *afraid/uneasy*? 3) Think about Walter Mondale. Now, has Mondale (because of the kind of person he is, or because of something he has done) ever made you feel *afraid/uneasy*? 4) Think about Ronald Reagan. Now, has Reagan (because of the kind of person he is, or because of something he has done) ever made you feel *afraid/uneasy*? (Mean=.30 S.D.=.23, Min=0, Max=1).

Old-fashioned racism (Study 2) consists of three measures and was coded onto a 0 to 1 scale, where the higher values correspond to endorsement of old-fashioned racism. Three items were additively scaled. Response options for the first two questions ranged from "strongly agree" to "strongly disagree." The specific items are 1) In past studies, we have asked people why they think white people seem to get more of the good things in life in America – such as better jobs and more money – than black people do. Here is a reason given by both blacks and whites. Please tell me whether you agree or disagree. The differences are brought about by God; God made the races different as part of His divine plan. 2) Blacks come from a less able race and this explains why blacks are not as well off as whites in America. 3) Suppose there is a community-wide vote on a general housing issue. There are two possible laws to vote for. One law says that homeowners can decide for themselves who to sell their house to, even if they prefer not to sell to blacks. The second law says that homeowners cannot refuse to sell to someone because of their race or color. Which law do you support? (Mean=.35, S.D.=.27, Min=0, Max=1).

Ideology is coded onto a 0 to 1 scale, where the higher values correspond to identifying as strongly conservative. The measures were based on a two-item skip pattern. (1) "We hear a lot of talk these days about liberals and conservatives. On a seven-point scale, where 1 is very liberal and 7 is very conservative, where would you place yourself on this scale, or haven't you thought much about this?" (2) If respondent enters 8 "haven't thought much about this," then they get: "If you had to choose, would you consider yourself a liberal, a moderate, or a conservative?" (Study 1 Mean=.57, S.D.=.28, Min=0, Max=1) (Study 2 Mean=.65, S.D.=.30, Min=0, Max=1) (Study 3 Mean=.57, S.D.=47, Min=0, Max=1).

Limited government (Study 1) consisted of two items, coded onto a 0 to 1 scale, where 0=increase government spending and 1=reduce government spending. Two items were additively scaled. (1) "Some people think the government should provide fewer services in order to reduce spending. These people are at point 1 of the scale. Other people feel it is important for the government to provide more services even if it means an increase in taxes. These people are at point 7 of the scale. Where would you place yourself on this scale, or haven't you thought much about this?" (2) "Some people think the government should provide fewer services, even in areas such as health and education, in order to reduce spending. These people are at point 1 of the scale. Other people feel it is important for the government to provide many more services even if it means an increase in spending. These people are at point 7 of the scale. Where would you place yourself on this scale, or haven't you thought much about this?" (Mean=.57, S.D.=30, Min=0, Max=1).

Limited government (Study 2) consisted of one item, coded onto a 0 to 1 scale, where 0=increase government spending and 1= reduce government spending. The following item was used: "Some people think the government should provide fewer services, even in areas such as health and education, in order to reduce spending. These people are at point 1 of the scale. Other people feel it is important for the government to provide many more services even if it means an increase in spending. These people are at point 7 of the scale. Where would you place yourself on this scale, or haven't you thought much about this?" (Mean = .50, S.D. = .25, Min = 0, Max = 1).

Individualism consisted of five items, coded onto a 0 to 1 scale, where 0=doesn't value hard work and 1= values hard work. Respondents were asked if they agree or disagree with the following items: (1) "Most people who do not get ahead should not blame the system. They have only themselves to blame." (2) "Any person who is willing to work hard has a good chance of succeeding." (3) "Even if people try hard they often cannot reach their goals." (4) "Hard work offers little guarantee of success." (5) If people work hard they usually get what they want." (Mean=.68, S.D.=.15, Min=0, Max=1).

Racial Policy Opinions ranges from 0 to 1, where the higher value corresponds with the conservative response. The measure is a combination of *Affirmative Action, Government assistance to blacks, Confederate Flag, Busing,* and *Martin Luther King Jr. holiday.* (Mean =.64, S.D.=.23, Min=0, Max=1).

Affirmative action is comprised of two items. The items are (1) "What do you think the chances are these days that a white person won't get a job or promotion while an equally or less qualified black person gets one instead?" (2) "What do you think the chances are these days that a white person won't get admitted to a college or university program while an equally or less qualified black person gets admitted instead?" The response options were "very likely," "somewhat likely," "not very likely."

Government assistance to blacks is based on the following item: "Some people think that blacks have been discriminated against for so long that the government has a special obligation to help improve their living standards. Others believe that the government should not be giving special treatment to blacks. Where would you place yourself on this scale, or haven't you thought much about this?" The scale ranged from 1 to 7, where 1 = I strongly agree the government is obligated to help blacks and 7 = I strongly agree that government shouldn't give preferential treatment.

Confederate flag is based on the following item: "The Confederate flag is a symbol of prejudice." Response options ranged from "strongly agree" to "strongly disagree."

Busing comprised of one item. The following item was used: "There is much discussion about the best way to deal with racial problems. Some people think achieving racial integration of schools is so important that it justifies busing children to schools out of their own neighborhood. Others think letting children go to their neighborhood schools is so important that they oppose busing. Where would you put yourself on this scale, or haven't you thought much about this?" The scale ranged from 1 to 7, where 1=Bus to achieve integration and 7=Keep children in neighborhood schools.

Martin Luther King Jr. holiday is based on the following item: "It is important that the celebration of Martin Luther King Jr.'s birthday is a national holiday." Response options ranged from 1= "extremely important" to 4= "not important."

Gender is a dummy variable, where o=female and 1=male. (Study 2 Mean=.45, S.D.=.50, Min=0, Max=1) (Study 3 Mean=.43, S.D.=.50, Min=0, Max=1).

South is a dummy variable, where o=non-Southern resident and 1=Southern resident. The Southern states are Alabama, Arkansas, Delaware, Washington DC, Florida, Georgia, Kentucky, Louisiana, Maryland, Mississippi, North Carolina, Oklahoma, South Carolina, Tennessee, Texas, Virginia, and West Virginia. (Study 1 Mean=.51, S.D.=.50, Min=0, Max=1) (Study 2 Mean=.27, S.D.=45, Min=0, Max=1) (Study 3 Mean=.47, S.D.=.50, Min=0, Max=1).

Education is coded onto a o to 1 scale, where the higher value corresponds to postgraduate degree. (Study 1 Mean=.43, S.D.=.28, Min=0, Max=1) (Study 2 ANES Mean=.36, S.D.=.29, Min=0, Max=1) (Study 3 Mean=.56, S.D.=.22, Min=0, Max=1).

Age is a continuous variable and ranges from eighteen to eighty-three years old. (Mean=47, S.D.=18, Min=17, Max=92).

Income is coded onto a o to 1 scale, where the higher value corresponds to highest income bracket. (Study 1 Mean=.57, S.D.=.28, Min=0, Max=1) (Study 3 Mean=.55, S.D.=25, Min=0, Max=1).

Party identification is measured with the standard seven-point party identification scale. This measure is captured with a three-item, skip pattern design: (1) "Generally speaking, do you usually think of yourself as a Republican, a Democrat, and Independent, or what?" (2) [If R answers Rep or Dem] "Would you call your-self a strong Republican/Democrat or a not very strong Republican/Democrat?" [3] [If R answers Independent] "Do you think of yourself as closer to the Republican Party or the Democratic Party? The variable is coded onto a o to 1 scale, where the highest value equals strong Republican. (Mean=.48, S.D.=.35, Min=0, Max=1).

Political Discussion is a measure of several political topics respondents mention in their open-ended responses to the emotion inductions. I had two research assistants code whether respondents mentioned six political and racial issues: war, terrorism, economy (inflation, jobs, unemployment, recession, etc.), education, civil rights (voting rights, free speech, and freedom of religion), environment, and affirmative action. The Cronbach's alpha (.84) reveals a high level of reliability across the two coders (Mean=.04, S.D.=.09, Min=0, Max=.5).

Assessment of Economic Conditions is coded onto a 0 to 1 scale, where the higher values correspond to the respondent thinking he/she is worse off than a year ago. The measures were based on a two-item skip pattern. 1) "We are interested in how people are getting along financially these days. Would you say that you are better off or worse off than you were a year ago?" 2) If respondent has been better off in last year /If respondent has been worse off in last year, they get either "much better or somewhat better? /much worse or somewhat worse?" (Mean=.57, S.D.=.32, Min=0, Max=1).

Authoritarianism consists of four items and is coded onto a 0 to 1 scale, where the higher values correspond to endorsement of authoritarianism. The four items were additively scaled. The question states: "Although there are a number of qualities that people feel that children should have, every person thinks that some are more important than others. I am going to read you pairs of desirable qualities. Please tell me which one you think is more important for a child to have." The qualities are: 1) Independence or Respect for Elders; 2) Curiosity or Good Manners; 3) Obedience or Self-Reliance; 4) Being Considerate or Well-behaved. (Mean=.67, S.D.=.27, Min=0, Max=1).

Facial Expressions Used in Emotion Induction Task

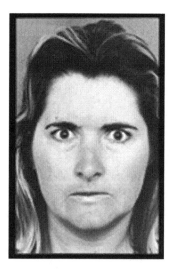

Anger Expression

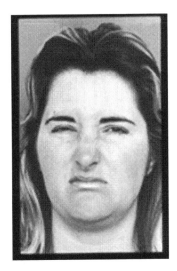

Disgust Expression

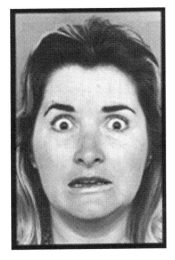

Fear Expression

3

The Emotional Content in Racialized Campaign Ads Primes White Racial Attitudes

"I'm sitting there, somewhat relieved that the numbers had come down," he recalled, "but still somewhat perplexed about not having one silver bullet issue, and trying to figure out whether the pledge would work better or the furlough.... This one woman starts talking to the other woman.... And one of them said, 'I just read this thing in *Reader's Digest* that you would not believe.' And the other woman said, 'What?' And she said, 'This criminal furlough thing that Michael Dukakis did is the most amazing thing I've ever seen.' So I just turned around and said, 'My God! What in the world are you all talking about?' And I threw in a few little things to spice up the cake. I said, 'You've got to be kidding.' One of the guys speaks ups and says, 'That's the dumbest shit I've ever heard about in my life. That son of a bitch.'"

–Lee Atwater

What did Lee Atwater recognize sitting at Brown's Chinese restaurant to convince him he had his silver bullet issue? One answer scholars have given is that the furlough program enabled Bush and his team to communicate race under cover. William Horton, a black man, was convicted of murder and sentenced to life in prison. While on furlough from a Massachusetts prison, Horton escaped, assaulted a white couple, and raped a woman. Supporters of George H. W. Bush, specifically the National Security Political Action Committee (NSPAC), aired what is known as the "weekend passes" ad, which included a menacing photo of Horton and stated that Dukakis gave Horton "free weekend passes" that allowed him to terrorize a white couple. Scholars have argued that it is the subtlety of this appeal that makes it effective at priming racial considerations (Hurwitz and Peffley 2005; Mendelberg 2001; Valentino et al. 2002). Yet, equally important, which Atwater also recognized in his ad hoc focus group, was people's emotional response to the Horton story. "Atwater recalled, 'Eureka!' I don't care what pundits ever say ... this thing has got a life of its own. I had never seen such passion evoked" (Germond and Witcover 1989, 164).

While some scholars emphasize the importance of implicit racial messaging, others contend that subtle racial appeals don't matter at all in people's decision making. Abigail Thernstrom (1987), for example, maintains that subtle racial appeals risk race not being recognized at all, and therefore make them ineffective at influencing whites' political opinions. On the whole, the dominant approach to studying the effects of subtle racial appeals has been zero-sum; that is, they either affect people's policy and candidate positions or not. What the literature has not considered are the conditions under which implicit racial appeals might be effective or ineffective. In this chapter, I argue that it's not just the subtle nature of these appeals that makes them effective, but also the specific emotion that they generate.

In Chapter 2, I demonstrated that inducing anger rather than fear, independent of racial or political content, powerfully primes symbolic racism. Some scholars, however, might argue that the situation where race is most likely to be invoked is within a racial context. One such context is political campaigns where candidates have implanted racial messages with the intention of appealing to whites' racial sentiment. Perhaps, in these circumstances, fear as opposed to anger triggers a racial response. Kathleen Hall Jamieson, in her analysis of racialized campaign ads, would seem to suggest so, claiming that the "weekend passes" ad attempted to "play to whispered fears, prejudices privately held but publicly denied" (1992, 84). Mayer agrees: "[B]ut Bush didn't have to mention that Horton was black, because the other components of the Horton campaign were doing such a marvelous job of appealing to white fear" (2002, 219). Surprising, we know very little of how emotions from racial appeals influence people's opinions on matters of race. My theoretical contention is that anger and racial attitudes are strongly linked in memory, which leads me to suspect that an angry reaction, rather than a fearful one, to an implicit racial appeal is more likely to evoke a racial response. Thus, in terms of the Horton story, it was not the fear of blacks terrorizing whites that made the ad effective. Instead, whites' anger over undeserving black criminals receiving free weekend passes made the Horton appeal effective. But before I turn to why implicit racial appeals are more effective under specific emotional states, it's important to understand the long history of candidates inserting race into political campaigns.

RACIAL CAMPAIGN APPEALS: FROM EXPLICIT TO IMPLICIT

Our country's first experience with racial appeals was very explicit in nature; they drew on blacks' genetic inferiority and advocated for a political system that sustained racial inequality. One such example is the 1864 presidential election pitting Abraham Lincoln (Republican) against George McClellan (Democrat). Before the Civil War, there was little reason and benefit in launching a campaign against blacks. The racial norm among many Democrats and Republicans was that blacks were an inferior race destined for a life of slavery. Thus, on the issue of race, there was not much difference between the political parties. However, the ominous implications of emancipation became a major force in dividing the parties on the race question (black freedom), which turned into an important campaign issue. With black freedom potentially on the horizon, the Democratic press and elites started a fierce miscegenation campaign against Abraham Lincoln. They claimed Lincoln not only supported black freedom, but openly endorsed inter-racial marriage. In a campaign pamphlet entitled "Miscegenation or the Millennium of Abolitionism," a political caricature depicted Lincoln entertaining several interracial couples while in the backdrop whites chauffeured blacks around on horseback (Wood 1968).

Republicans, upset with the Democrats' smear campaign, decided to counterattack, accusing Democrats of being the real friends of "Negros." They argued that Democrats were the ones who really wanted to make blacks and whites equals. For instance, "a political cartoonist for Harper's Weekly asserted in 1862 that the southern sla-veowner was the greatest 'Nigger worshipper' of all: he sent his son to war, but fearing financial loss he kept his field hands at home" (Wood 1968, 31). Republicans supported blacks' right to citizenship, but by no means full racial equality. In some cases, they even proposed cre-ating a separate colony for blacks. Mendelberg states, "Republicans advocated colonization (the removal of blacks) in a deliberate way, to counter the charge of pro-black advocacy and demonstrate their conformity to the norm of racial inequality" (2001, 37). Although the two parties converged on their explicitly racist appeals, they diverged on whether blacks should be taken out of bondage and incorporated into the American political system. In the end, Lincoln won the election quite handily, which suggested that the war and the South's secession were more important in voters' decision making than the idea of miscegenation.

Throughout the late nineteenth and early twentieth century, explicit racial appeals continued to dominate how political campaigns communicated race to the American public. Campaigns continued to use derogatory images and statements of blacks – highlighting to whites what they thought was the obvious – the physical, mental, and behavioral differences between the races. As support for overt discrimination declined in the 1960s and conflicted with the norm of racial equality, the use of explicit racial appeals by politicians declined as well. Mendelberg argues that during the middle of the twentieth century racial communication changed. "Politicians now appeal to race under cover. What created this historical break, in part, was the shift in attitudes about racial equality – more precisely, the repudiation of racism" (2001, 67). The landmark civil rights legislation of the 1960s shifted the racial norm from racial inequality to racial equality. Despite this shift, political candidates developed new ways of packaging prejudice. They used racially coded language like law and order, states' rights, and urban unrest to appear nonracial, but still convey a racial message (Esdall and Esdall 1991). These subtle racial appeals were especially evident in the 1968 presidential election.

Most political aficionados consider the 1968 presidential election the most racially charged in American history. The country had been immersed in race riots that broke out in cities everywhere for four straight summers. Martin Luther King Jr., the beloved leader of the civil rights movement, was assassinated six months before the election. Robert F. Kennedy, the Democratic presidential primary candidate and civil rights activist, was assassinated two months later. And a staunch segregationist, George Wallace, entered the race as a third party candidate. The Vietnam War and urban unrest were the most important issues of the campaign. Many whites felt that the large scale of violence by blacks was inexplicable, especially after all that had been done for them on the part of civil rights. The riots created a massive white backlash against civil rights initiatives and a demand for a tougher stance on law and order. George Wallace tried to capitalize on this violence and the racial resentment it spurred. Before running for president in 1968, he was mostly known for his 1963 gubernatorial inaugural address in which he stated, "segregation today, segregation tomorrow, segregation forever!" But by the 1968 presidential campaign, he proclaimed himself a changed man and repudiated anyone linking him to racism. But some remained suspicious, like one Alabama senator who stated, "[h]e can use all the other issues – law and order, running your own schools, protecting property rights – and never mention race. But people will know he's telling them. 'A nigger's trying to get your job, trying to move into your neighborhood'" (Rosenstone, Behr, and Lazarus 1984, 111). On the other hand, many voters considered Hubert Humphrey – the Democratic candidate – too far to the left on the issue of race and unable to solve America's current racial problem.

Richard Nixon's campaign strategy tried be a calming influence during the tumultuous time of Vietnam and race riots. He struck hard on the issue of law and order, but managed to present himself as an alternative to Wallace's more aggressive approach. Nixon's strategy was simple: to use television as his means of communicating to the American public. And via this medium, he inserted very subtle racial cues to play to white voters' racial sentiment. For example, in one campaign ad, he showed a white woman walking down a dark and lonely New York City street. At the same time, the narrator described how a violent crime was committed in America every sixty seconds. "Watching it, you were sure the woman would not make it to the end of the commercial without being mugged" (McGinniss 1969, 112). To Nixon, the ad served its purpose; it conveyed a racial message under cover. With appeals like this, Nixon situated himself as the best choice to calm the country's racial unrest. Voters had three options: "a candidate who sympathized with rioters because there weren't enough swimming pools in the inner city, an extremist candidate who wanted to put a bullet in the brain of every rioter, and a soothing candidate who promised tough but measured action" (Mayer 2002, 89). In the end, Nixon won a plurality of the vote and demonstrated that an implicit racial strategy could prove successful.

The 1988 presidential campaign with the "Willie" Horton story is the quintessential example of playing the race card. George H. W. Bush used the furlough program to attack Michael Dukakis and to portray him as sympathetic to black criminals.[1] Throughout the campaign, Bush and his supporters succeeded at turning Horton into a symbol of terror and crime. One way, already described, was the "weekend passes" ad, and another way was the "revolving door" ad. The "revolving door" ad was effective because it made people believe the furlough program was unique to Massachusetts. It also contained a very subtle reference to race: showing a black inmate – that looked similar to Horton – staring into the camera while the narrator said, "His revolving door prison policies gave weekend furloughs to first degree murderers not eligible for parole. While out, many committed other crimes like kidnapping and rape and many are still at large. Now Michael Dukakis says he wants to do for America what he has done for Massachusetts. America can't afford that risk." Despite Bush trailing Dukakis by as much as seventeen points in the polls over the summer, he managed to pull ahead and win quite decisively in November. Years later, journalists and politicians attributed Bush's victory to his campaign's ability to make Horton appear as the Democratic vice presidential nominee.

In addition to presidential campaigns, subtle racial appeals have also been used in congressional campaigns. Many pundits and political commentators considered the 2006 Tennessee senatorial race between Harold Ford Jr. (Democrat) and Bob Corker (Republican) particularly nasty and racially charged. Mr. Ford, if elected, would have been the first black senator to represent the South since Reconstruction. The Republican National Committee (RNC) aired a racially tinged campaign ad that attacked Ford, with the hope of mobilizing racially conservative Tennesseans to the ballot box. The ad features an attractive white woman, shoulders bare, winking while saying, "I met Harold at a playboy party" and "Harold call me." The NAACP called it "a powerful innuendo that plays to pre-existing prejudices about African American men and white women" (Johnson 2006). At the time, Ford was a thirty-six-year-old bachelor, and the possibility of him frolicking with white women seemed incomprehensible and played to an age-old stereotype of African American men's sexual proclivity for white women (Fredrickson 1971). In fact, Berinsky and his colleagues (2011) demonstrate that when a campaign message ties Barack Obama to a sex scandal with two white women, politically interested and racially resentful whites are more likely to perceive him as "liberal" compared to the same message about John Edwards. Furthermore, among the same group of whites, the scandal penalizes Obama's overall candidate evaluations. Ford losing the election, despite receiving 48 percent of the vote, demonstrates how subtle racial cues that include sexual accusations involving white women can be detrimental to African American candidates.

THE RACIAL PRIMING EFFECT

Tali Mendelberg, in her pathbreaking book *The Race Card: Campaign Strategy, Implicit Messages, and the Norm of Equality*, gives the most thorough description of how racial considerations come into play when racial discretion is used. Her theory of racial priming contends that, despite whites' commitment to the norm of racial equality, a significant number of whites oppose policies and candidates intended to reduce racial inequalities, which are shaped by their negative racial attitudes. She further proposes that implicit racial appeals are effective because on the surface, they seem to be about something other than race. An implicit racial appeal appears in a nonracial manner; it omits racial nouns or adjectives such as *black* or *racial* and instead consists of negative images of blacks or racial code words like *inner city*. Mendelberg argues that the appeal's implicitness makes it effective because whites do not consciously believe they are violating the norm of racial equality. Thus, they place greater weight on their racial predispositions when making political decisions that have a racial association such as affirmative action or government aid to blacks. On the other hand, she argues that an explicit racial appeal no longer shapes racially conservative whites' opinions because it is seen as violating the racial norm. In this case, whites reject explicit racial appeals because they are concerned with being perceived as racist.

A substantial body of research has supported the racial priming effect, showing that implicit appeals are most effective at priming racial predispositions (Hurwitz and Peffley 2005; Mendelberg 1997, 2001; Nelson and Kinder 1996; Valentino 1999; Valentino et al. 2002; White 2007).[2] For instance, Mendelberg's study on welfare demonstrates the power of implicit appeals over explicit and counter-stereotypical appeals in activating racial predispositions. Using fictitious news stories about Michigan's gubernatorial race, she presented subjects with a conservative argument that welfare recipients are an unfair burden on government and society. Her experimental manipulation varied the type of racial appeal. The explicit appeal contained a visual and verbal reference to blacks while the implicit appeal consisted of a visual but no verbal reference to blacks and the counter-stereotypical appeal had a visual reference of whites but no verbal reference. She found that the implicit appeal primed negative racial predispositions while the explicit and counter-stereotypical appeals neutralized this effect. Hurwitz and Peffley (2005) found a similar effect for racially coded words. In their experiment, individuals were asked whether they supported funding for prisons to lock up "violent criminals" or "violent inner city criminals." Respondents that received the racially coded question were more likely to use their racial attitudes to explain their preferences for punitive policies than those who received the nonracial question.

In this chapter, my contention is that a particular emotion facilitates the racial priming effect. As it stands in the literature, a political appeal wherein a message's racial content is unrecognized by the audience allows the cue to effectively activate whites' negative racial predispositions. But when whites are aware of the racial content of the message, they withhold their racial response. Thus, the ambiguity of the racial message – unclear whether it's about race – is essential to facilitate racial thinking (Gaertner and Dovidio 1986). Mendelberg states, "[a]mbiguity about the racial nature of a candidate's message may lead voters to increase their reliance on racial predispositions" (2001, 126). Although an ambiguous message allows whites to oppose racial policies or candidates without being perceived as racist, it is still unclear why an implicit appeal uniquely activates racial predispositions. Under these circumstances, couldn't an implicit racial appeal have a similar effect on nonracial predispositions? Given this, it seems that we are still unclear about the mechanism that activates racial predispositions and neutralizes nonracial predispositions. My theory of emotion and race would suspect that anger resulting from implicit appeals plays an important role in uniquely bringing thoughts about race to mind.

As discussed in Chapter 1, Bower and Forgas's (2001) theory of emotional priming provides a role for emotions to contribute to the racial priming process. This theory relies on state-dependent memory – events or information learned in one emotional state are more easily recalled when a person is put back into that same emotional state. Because my argument is that anger and white racial attitudes are strongly linked, an anger-laden implicit appeal should activate this racial belief system from memory.[3] That is, an angry reaction to racial code words such as *inner city* or an image of a black male linked to crime should make racial predispositions more accessible in memory. And with these attitudes at the top of the head, they should be a stronger predictor of relevant policy and candidate preferences. Initially, the racial priming hypothesis was developed to explain the factors that heightened the beliefs of racial conservatives. My theory of anger and race suggests that implicit appeals should also activate the belief systems of racial liberals. This effect occurs because anger is also tightly linked to whites' beliefs at the lower end of the symbolic racism scale. Thus, racial conservatives are not the only ones who associate anger with race; racial liberals are also angry, but about the continued racism and discrimination that blacks have endured over the years. Some empirical evidence from the racial priming literature supports this argument. For instance, Hurwitz and Peffley (2005) found that implicit appeals not only activated racial conservative beliefs, but racial liberal beliefs as well. And in some cases, Mendelberg (1997) found that exposure to the Horton story moved racial liberals to be more supportive of racial policies.

On the other hand, counter to pundits and scholars' speculation about the role of racial fear, I don't expect a fearful reaction to implicit appeals to activate racial predispositions from memory. As I argued in Chapter 1, fear appraisals do not dominate contemporary discussions on race, and because of this, fear and racial attitudes shouldn't form a strong bond in the minds of many white Americans. As a result, I expect that fear-inducing racial stimuli should have a difficult time bringing ideas about race to mind. Additionally, I don't expect anger or fear generated from an implicit appeal to bring race-neutral attitudes to bear on policy or candidate preferences. The reason is that race-neutral attitudes like self-reported political ideology include an array of beliefs. McClosky and Zaller capture this point well when describing ideologues: "They are usually described as liberal if they seek to advance such ideas as equality, aid to the disadvantaged, tolerance of dissenters, and social reform; and as conservative if they place particular emphasis on order, stability, the needs of business, differential economic rewards, and defense of status quo" (1984, 189). Because race-neutral ideological orientations encompass several beliefs, they are not likely to form a strong bond with any particular emotion. As a consequence, it will be extremely difficult for any one emotion to activate this belief system.

In terms of explicit racial appeals, my expectation is that anger resulting from these appeals should have little impact on racial attitudes. Consistent with the racial priming theory, whites should control their racial response when an appeal is unambiguously perceived as racial – even if it arouses anger – because they want to abide by the norm of racial equality. Mendelberg states, "People follow a norm not because they fear the arm of the law or physical punishment but because they wish to avoid social censure or the pangs of conscience" (2001, 17). Whites' concern over being perceived as racist forces them to withhold giving greater emphasis to racial considerations – even if they experience anger.

Indirect evidence from the racial priming literature seems to support my argument that anger in the context of an implicit appeal activates racial predispositions. Valentino, Hutchings, and White (2002) find that certain racial cues make negative racial predispositions more accessible in memory – heightening their effect on preference for George W. Bush. Their study shows that an implicit racial cue's most powerful effect emerges when the ad focuses on undeserving blacks. I think that anger underlies this effect because blacks getting something they are thought not to deserve triggers anger among many white Americans (Kinder and Sanders 1996; Sniderman et al. 2000).

My main hypothesis is that the relationship between racial predispositions and racial policy opinions is enhanced as a function of experiencing anger generated by an implicit appeal. That is, experiencing anger from an implicit appeal should increase opposition to racial policies among those high in symbolic racism and boost support among those low in symbolic racism. Conversely, my expectation is that racial attitudes should not be affected by an implicit appeal that provokes fear. Furthermore, I predict that race-neutral principles like political ideology should not be affected by either an anger-laden or a fear-laden implicit appeal. To test these hypotheses, I conduct an experiment on a predominantly college student sample to independently arouse anger and fear from an implicit racial campaign advertisement.

CRIME EXPERIMENT: AN EXPERIMENTAL TEST OF AN
ANGER-LADEN AND A FEAR-LADEN IMPLICIT APPEAL

I conducted an experiment at the University of Maryland from October 19 to November 20, 2009. The total sample size was one hundred thirteen and included eighty-five whites. I recruited subjects by posting signs in university buildings and asking students in government courses to participate in a study on current events. The sample reflects one of convenience – undergraduate students – and is not representative of the U.S. population as a whole. I obtained good variation on gender (47% male), but liberals were overrepresented in the sample (65%). The random assignment of subjects to conditions was successful: no significant differences appeared across cells of the design in the proportion of sociodemographic or partisan variables.

Like the emotion induction experiment discussed in Chapter 2, the crime experiment was conducted over two waves.[4] The first wave took place in several classrooms and included a pretest questionnaire of racial and general attitude measures such as symbolic racism, political ideology, and sociodemographic measures.[5] Subjects were paid three dollars for participating in the first wave. Several days later, respondents were contacted via e-mail to participate in the second wave and told they would receive five dollars for watching ads on current events.[6] Once at the lab, a graduate research assistant randomly assigned subjects to one of several advertising conditions. To minimize interviewer bias, subjects solely interacted with the computer throughout the study. After completing a practice question, respondents received instructions via the computer to put on a pair of headphones and watch an advertisement. Respondents in the treatment groups viewed a political advertisement while subjects in the control group viewed a product advertisement.[7] Subsequently following the ad, subjects answered a posttest questionnaire that included racial policy opinion measures. Afterward, respondents were debriefed and paid for their participation.

EXPERIMENTAL MANIPULATION

Most studies validating racial priming effects use news stories as their stimulus in various forms (Gilliam and Iyengar 2000; Mendelberg 1997, 2001; Valentino 1999; White 2007). Instead, I chose to use political ads because research has shown that music and sound effects from an ad can arouse distinct emotional responses (Brader 2006). The critical feature of my stimulus is to keep subtle racial cues constant and only manipulate information and sound that trigger anger and fear. Achieving this control entails building ads from the bottom up. My goal was to purposefully create an ad that mimicked the "weekend passes" ad in several respects. The ad pits two white candidates against one another on the issue of crime during a mayoral election – with the sponsoring candidate, Andrew Fellows, appearing tougher on crime in comparison to the opposing candidate, Brian Alexander.[8] Using a crime-related ad provides a very conservative test of my hypotheses. If racial fear is going to have an effect, it is most likely when the ad centers on crime. However, if I am able to show that anger, and not fear, generated from such an appeal amplifies racial thinking, then this would be strong evidence in support of my theory.

Table 3.1 presents a detailed description of the two treatment conditions. Except for sound, the first half of the ad for the treatment groups is identical. The ad begins contrasting the candidates on crime, with onscreen text stating, "Andrew Fellows is tough on crime" and "Brian Alexander is soft on crime." Following this, the text reads: "Fellows wants to increase the number of police officers" and "Alexander as city council member voted to cut the police force to balance the budget." Next, the words "more criminals" move slowly across the screen. The implicit racial cue appears after with an image of three young black males, and a newspaper quote follows stating, "[w]ho last month assaulted a man and woman in College Park, sending them to the hospital." In the second part of the ad, I manipulate the text to induce an angry or fearful response. Knowing appraisals distinguish people's emotional experiences, I insert the appraisals of control/lack of control, uncertainty, and blame into the ads (Lerner and Keltner 2001; Lerner and Tiedens 2006; Smith and Ellsworth 1985).

For the anger condition, the second half of the ad begins with text stating "time to take control"; then, a jail cell slams shut. In sequence,

TABLE 3.1. *Content of the Implicit Racial Advertisement Manipulation*

Anger Ad	Fear Ad
Andrew Fellows tough on crime. [*Enter image of Andrew Fellows*] Brian Alexander soft on crime. [*Enter image of Brian Alexander*] Andrew Fellows supports increasing the number of police officers in College Park. As city council member Brian Alexander voted to cut the number of police officers on the street.	Andrew Fellows tough on crime. [*Enter image of Andrew Fellows*] Brian Alexander soft on crime. [*Enter image of Brian Alexander*] Andrew Fellows supports increasing the number of police officers in College Park. As city council member Brian Alexander voted to cut the number of police officers on the street.
More Criminals. Like Allen Jenkins, Will Andrews and Mike Harrison... [*The image of three young African-American males flashes on the screen*] "who last month assaulted a man and woman in College Park sending them to the hospital" –*Gazette*.	More Criminals. Like Allen Jenkins, Will Andrews and Mike Harrison... [*The image of three young African-American males flashes on the screen*] "who last month assaulted a man and woman in College Park sending them to the hospital" –*Gazette*.
Time to take control [*The image of a jail door slamming shut flashes on the screen*] Brian Alexander = Higher Crime **Brian Alexander is to blame!** **People Are Angry!** Aren't you?	**Losing control** [*The image of a jail door opening flashes on the screen*] Brian Alexander = Higher Crime **Too much uncertainty with Brian Alexander!** **People Are Afraid!** Aren't you?

Note: Text in bold represents the differences between the ads.

the text then reads "Brian Alexander = Higher Crime"; "Brian Alexander is to Blame!"; "People are Angry"; and "Aren't You?" In the fear condition, the text reads "Losing Control," which is followed by the opening of a jail cell. Subsequently, the text states "Brian Alexander = Higher Crime"; "Too Much Uncertainty With Brain Alexander!"; "People are Afraid"; and "Aren't You?" I also manipulate the ad's sound effects, expecting it leads to different emotional responses. In the fear condition, the ad consists of police sirens playing in the background – fading in and out as text appears on the screen. In contrast, the anger condition includes a low thumping sound effect as text appears on the screen.[9]

THE EFFECTS OF IMPLICIT APPEALS

As in Chapter 2, I first conducted a manipulation check to test whether the ads produced the intended emotion. After viewing the ad, subjects were asked an open-ended question – how did the advertisement make you feel?[10] The open-ended responses were double-coded by two trained research assistants. They identified the intensity of any negative emotions expressed in the responses.[11] As expected, participants in the anger condition expressed significantly more intense anger relative to subjects in the control condition (β=.44 p $\geq$ .001) and to respondents in the fear condition (β=.34 p $\geq$ .001). They also expressed some fear (β=.19 p $\geq$ .05) relative to the control condition. In the fear condition, respondents expressed an intense amount of fear (β=.57 p $\geq$ .001) relative to the control group, but they did not express anger. Moreover, subjects in the fear condition expressed significantly more fear (β=.38 p $\geq$ .001) relative to people in the anger condition.[12] I expected some bleeding over of emotions. A discussion of crime rates does carry some previous emotional attachment, particularly fear (Tyler and Weber 1982). Albeit, I believe this effect provides a harder test of the anger hypothesis.

My expectation is that an implicit appeal that generates anger should boost the effect of racial attitudes on racial policy opinions. Three racial policy opinions are examined: *Government assistance to blacks*, our official observance of the *Martin Luther King Jr. Holiday*, and *Reparations for blacks*. A scale of racial policy opinions is created summing responses to all three items.[13] Similar to Chapter 2, these measures are used because they cover a broad spectrum of economic and symbolic remedies to eliminate racial inequalities.

My main prediction is that the anger appeal will significantly boost opposition to racial policies among those high in symbolic racism and increase support for these policies among those low in symbolic racism. Thus, I expect a positive interactive effect between the anger condition and symbolic racism. Moreover, the effect of the anger condition on opposition to racial policies among racial liberals should be negative. In my model, I regressed *Racial Policy Opinions* on emotion conditions

(*Anger* and *Fear*), *Symbolic Racism*, and the interaction between the two, controlling for *Gender* and *Age*.[14] Table 3.2 shows evidence consistent with my expectations. The coefficient for the anger condition and symbolic racism is positive, substantively large (four times the size of the interactive effect of fear and symbolic racism), and statistically significant.[15] Looking at the effect of the anger condition, I find a negative and statistically significant coefficient – demonstrating that the anger condition pushes those low in symbolic racism to be more supportive of racial policies. Looking at row 2, we see that the interaction between the fear condition and symbolic racism is insignificant.[16] I also substituted the fear condition as the baseline condition and found that the interaction between the anger condition and symbolic racism remained positive and statistically significant. Furthermore, the effect of the anger condition (racial liberals) on opposition to racial policies was still negative and significant. These results show that the anger condition not only boosts the effect of racial attitudes on racial policy opinion relative to the control condition, but also when compared to the fear condition.[17] To be confident that anger was priming racial attitudes, I reran the model but excluded respondents in the anger condition who expressed fear. I found that the interactive effect between the anger condition and symbolic racism was even larger when these respondents were dropped from the analysis.[18]

Figure 3.1 visually illustrates the results in column 1. It shows the marginal effect of each emotion condition on racial policy opinions as symbolic racism changes. The figure displays a 95 percent confidence interval, in dotted lines, around the marginal effect of the anger condition in the solid line. As I suspect, the marginal effect of the anger condition on racial policy opinion increases as symbolic racism increases. The marginal effect of the fear condition, in the long-dash black line, is relatively flat across levels of symbolic racism. The figure also indicates that at higher levels of the symbolic racism scale (starting at .7), the anger appeal produces significantly higher levels of opposition to racial policies in comparison to the fear appeal. Conversely, among those low in symbolic racism, the effect of the anger appeal doesn't differ from the fear appeal.

As pointed out earlier in this chapter, the racial priming literature is unclear about the precise mechanism that causes implicit appeals to uniquely prime racial predispositions. My position is that it is anger

TABLE 3.2. *The Effect of an Emotional Implicit Appeal on Racial Policy Opinions Via Symbolic Racism And Political Ideology*

	Opposition to Racial Policies	Opposition to Racial Policies	Opposition to Racial Policies
	B (s.e.)	B (s.e.)	B (s.e.)
Anger Condition*Symbolic Racism	.48** (.23)		.58* (.31)
Fear Condition*Symbolic Racism	.10 (.22)		.24 (.29)
Anger Condition*Ideology		.01 (.22)	−.13 (.25)
Fear Condition*Ideology		−.13 (.23)	−.19 (.25)
Anger Condition	−.21* (.12)	−.04 (.09)	−.22* (.12)
Fear Condition	−.05 (.11)	.02 (.09)	−.05 (.11)
Symbolic Racism	.46** (.15)		.35 (.22)
Ideology		.34** (.17)	.14 (.20)
Gender	−.04 (.04)	−.01 (.05)	−.05 (.04)
Age	.002 (.008)	.002 (.009)	.002 (.008)
Constant	.26 (.17)	.37* (.20)	.26* (.17)
R²	.40	.14	.41
N	80	80	80

Notes: * p ≤ .1 (two-tailed test); ** p ≤ .05 (two-tailed test); *** p ≤ .001 (two-tailed test). Entries are unstandardized OLS regression coefficients and the standard errors are in parentheses. All variables are coded 0 to 1, except for Age. Higher values indicate more opposition to racial policies. For gender, 1=male and 0=female. Age ranges from eighteen to thirty-eight years old.

from implicit appeals that primes thoughts about race and not general ideological orientations. And this effect occurs because anger is strongly linked to racial attitudes and not race-neutral principles. If this proposition is correct, anger from an implicit appeal should have no effect on race-neutral principles. In column 2, I regressed *Racial*

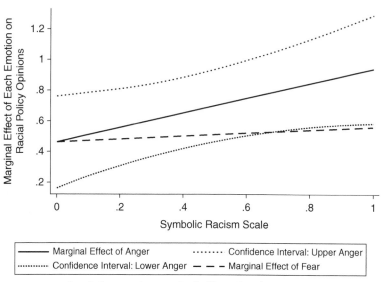

FIGURE 3.1. Implicit appeals: marginal effect of each emotion on racial policy opinions as symbolic racism changes.

Policy Opinions on emotion dummies (*Anger* and *Fear*), *Political Ideology*, and the interaction between the two, controlling for *Gender* and *Age*. The results show that neither the anger appeal nor the fear appeal has a significant effect on self-reported political ideology.

However, to ensure distinctions between racial attitudes and race-neutral principles, I ran another model that includes both sets of interactions. This new model estimates the interaction of each treatment condition with symbolic racism and political ideology simultaneously. Column 3 shows that the interaction between the anger condition and symbolic racism is still positive and statistically significant while the effect of the anger condition (racial liberals) is still negative and significant.[19] On the other hand, the interactive effect of the anger condition and self-reported political ideology is in the wrong direction and insignificant.

In summary, the crime experiment showed that an anger-laden implicit appeal was most effective at conjuring up racial thinking. In contrast, fear generated from an implicit appeal didn't activate whites' racial predispositions. The experiment also demonstrated that anger was the causal mechanism that leads subtle racial appeals to call attention to some predispositions (racial) while ignoring others (race neutral). Although my experimental findings support my theoretical expectations, I now turn to a survey-based test to see if these effects diminish when a subtle racial appeal is pointed out by elites to have racial connotations – therefore making it explicitly about race. I utilize the 1988 ANES to test whether anger experienced when the Horton appeal was implicit rather than explicit increases support for George H. W. Bush among racial prejudiced whites.

BUSH VERSUS DUKAKIS: THE 1988 AMERICAN NATIONAL ELECTION STUDY

Bush and his campaign staff first launched the Horton story to the American public in early June. At the time, most pundits, reporters, and politicians considered the story to be about crime and didn't suspect any racial meaning. Not until October 21 did critics like Jesse Jackson denounce the "weekend passes" and "revolving door" ads as racist. After that, the Horton story went from an implicit racial appeal to being explicitly about race. Not only did the racial style of the Horton message vary throughout the campaign, but also the intensity of the story. For instance, Mendelberg's content analysis of the 1988 campaign revealed a stark difference in media coverage of Horton during the implicit phase of the campaign. She found that newspaper coverage of the Horton story dramatically increased from September to October by 24 percent. Television news coverage produced an even more substantial difference – a jump of 50 percent. Because of this variation in media coverage of Horton, Mendelberg separated the implicit phase into low-exposure (September 6–October 2) and high-exposure (October 3–October 20) phases. She found this difference in coverage mattered in how much of an influence race had on vote choice. In fact, she found the largest effect of symbolic racism on preference for Bush in the high-exposure implicit phase. Because the intensity of Horton coverage mattered greatly, I take this into consideration when examining the impact of emotion and racial attitudes on support for Bush.

The 1988 ANES is a probability sample of Americans of voting age, containing 1,698 whites. One advantage of using the 1988 ANES preelection survey is that it interviewed American citizens from September 6 to November 6. This survey gives me the opportunity to examine whether there is a discernible difference in the effects of anger in the high-exposure implicit phase versus the low exposure implicit phase and explicit phase of the campaign. My prediction is that anger and not fear – during the high-exposure implicit phase – should boost the impact of symbolic racism on preferences for Bush. Conversely, I also expect this effect to disappear among comparable angry whites interviewed during the low-exposure implicit phase and explicit phase.[20] The reason that anger should not enhance symbolic racism during the low-exposure implicit phase is because fewer people were aware of the Horton story at the time. Thus, my three main predictions are: (1) Anger experienced during the high-exposure implicit phase should increase support for Bush among those high in symbolic racism; (2) anger experienced during the low-exposure implicit phase and explicit phase should have no effect on symbolic racism; (3) fear from neither the implicit nor the explicit phases should affect symbolic racism.

In terms of the emotion measures, the 1988 ANES unfortunately does not ask respondents how they feel about Horton. However, I believe the emotion measures of Dukakis capture in some respect people's feelings toward Horton.[21] When Jamieson's focus group members were asked to recall what they remembered about the 1988 presidential election, one recollection consistently appeared across participants – they could recall "Willie" Horton. Such recognition signified the Horton story permeated throughout the campaign. For instance, Jamieson states, "William Horton and Michael Dukakis are now twined in our memory" (1992, 16). Because feelings toward Dukakis are linked to feelings toward Horton, I think the emotion measures of Dukakis are a good indication of how people feel about the Horton story.

Consistent with Mendelberg's index of intensity in Horton coverage, I created three phases: people interviewed during the low-exposure implicit phase, high-exposure implicit phase, and explicit phase. The survey dates for respondents ranged from: September 6–October 2 (low-exposure implicit phase), October 3–October 20 (high-exposure implicit phase), and October 21–November 6 (explicit phase).[22]

My main prediction is that anger toward Dukakis should increase support for Bush among whites high in symbolic racism, but only during the high-exposure implicit phase and not the other phases of the campaign. In my model, I regressed *Vote Choice* on emotion dummies (*Anger* and *Fear* toward Dukakis), *Symbolic Racism*, and the interaction between the two, controlling for *Party Identification, Ideology, Income, Education, South, Gender, Attention to the Campaign, and Age*.[23] Table 3.3 shows the effect of symbolic racism on vote choice conditional on anger and fear in each of the three phases. Column 1 shows the results for the low-exposure implicit phase. For this phase, we see that the interactions between anger and symbolic racism and fear and symbolic racism are insignificant. Turning to the high-exposure implicit phase in column 2, I find that the interactive effect of anger and symbolic racism is substantively large and statistically significant.[24] On the other hand, the interaction between fear and symbolic racism is in the wrong direction and insignificant.[25] Furthermore, I find that the interactive effect of anger and symbolic racism is statistically larger than that of fear.[26] Moving to the explicit phase in column 3, we find none of the interactions are statistically significant.[27] In all, Table 3.3 demonstrated that when the Horton appeal was implicit and at its height in media coverage, anger toward Dukakis, rather than fear, boosted the impact of symbolic racism on preference for Bush.[28]

Figure 3.2 visually shows the high-exposure implicit phase effects in column 2 of Table 3.3. The figure shows that the marginal effect of anger (solid line) on preference for Bush increases as symbolic racism increases, whereas the marginal effect of fear on preference for Bush decreases as symbolic racism increases. We also see that the effect of anger is statistically different from fear at high levels of symbolic racism.

Overall, the findings from the 1988 ANES support my hypotheses. I found that anger toward Dukakis increased support for Bush among whites high in symbolic racism, but only in the high-exposure implicit phase, and not in the other phases of the campaign. On the other hand, fear of Dukakis did not boost the effect of symbolic racism on vote choice across any of the three phases. Consistent with the crime experiment, these results indicate that an implicit racial appeal is most effective when an angry response is generated.[29] Moreover, the survey results show that when elites point out the racial content of the Horton story – making it explicit – the ability of anger to activate racial prejudice is neutralized.

TABLE 3.3. *The Impact of Emotion and Symbolic Racism on Preference for Bush During the Implicit and Explicit Phases of the 1988 Presidential Campaign*

	Vote Choice: Bush	Vote Choice: Bush	Vote Choice: Bush
	B (s.e.)	B (s.e.)	B (s.e.)
	Low-Exposure Implicit Phase	High-Exposure Implicit Phase	Explicit Phase
Anger*Symbolic Racism	−.14 (.14)	.33** (.15)	.03 (.18)
Fear*Symbolic Racism	.17 (.17)	−.14 (.17)	−.04 (.20)
Anger	.15 (.09)	−.11 (.10)	.06 (.12)
Fear	.04 (.11)	.18 (.12)	.10 (.14)
Symbolic Racism	.15* (.09)	.01 (.10)	.07 (.12)
Party Identification	.75*** (.05)	.62*** (.05)	.76*** (.05)
Ideology	.05 (.07)	.28*** (.08)	.05 (.09)
Income	.06 (.06)	.00 (.07)	.05 (.08)
Education	−.02 (.06)	−.03 (.07)	.04 (.08)
Age	−.001 (.001)	−.001 (.001)	−.001 (.001)
Gender	.02 (.03)	−.02 (.04)	.04 (.04)
South	.05 (.03)	.04 (.04)	.07* (.04)
Attention to the Campaign	−.07 (.08)	−.11 (.08)	−.14 (.09)
Constant	.00 (.09)	.12 (.10)	.09 (.11)
R^2	.53	.60	.68
N	397	285	174

Notes: * $p \le .1$ (two-tailed test); ** $p \le .05$ (two-tailed test); *** $p \le .001$ (two tailed test). Entries are unstandardized OLS regression coefficients and the standard errors are in parentheses. The dependent variable is the five-point vote choice item, running from strong support for Dukakis to strong support for Bush, where the higher value indicates strong preference for Bush. All variables are coded on a 0 to 1 scale, except for Age.

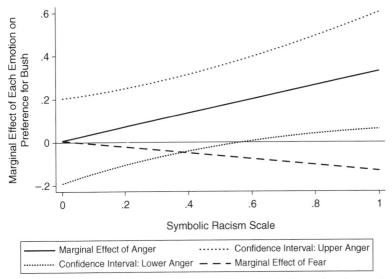

FIGURE 3.2. High-exposure implicit phase: marginal effect of each emotion on preference for Bush as symbolic racism changes.

CONCLUSION

What is the mechanism that causes implicit racial appeals to uniquely bring thoughts about race to mind? Put differently, what aspect of the Horton appeal activated racist sentiment but left general conservatism dormant? The existing literature does not provide a clear answer to this crucial question. But my theory of anger and race offers one answer. My theoretical argument is that anger is strongly tied to racial attitudes and not race-neutral principles, which would suggest that it is the anger from implicit appeals that causes racial predispositions, and not race-neutral predispositions, to dominate whites' opinions on matters of race.

Conversely, some scholars contend that if any emotion contributes to the racial priming effect, it must be fear. Most observers of the 1988 presidential election believed that Michael Dukakis lost, in part, because of the Bush campaign's ability to ignite whites' racial fears. Reeves states, "[t]he Horton furlough campaign tactic was meant to stir and arouse racial anxieties of white southerners" (1997, 16). The results from this chapter suggest otherwise. They show that an encoded racial appeal's power derives from an angry, rather than a fearful, response.

For instance, in the crime experiment, I found that an anger-laden implicit appeal primed whites' racial attitudes and boosted their effect on racial policy preferences. To be more exact, the implicit racial cue that generated anger drew out symbolic racism and increased opposition to racial policies. The anger condition not only boosted the impact of symbolic racism relative to the control condition, but also had a similar effect when compared to the fear condition. The experimental findings also revealed that the anger-laden appeal caused whites low in symbolic racism to be more supportive of racial policies, relative to the control group. These findings indicate that anger from an implicit appeal activates both racial conservatives and racial liberals' beliefs – pushing the two groups in opposite directions in their support for racial policies. In the case of race-neutral principles, neither the anger-laden appeal nor the fear-laden appeal had an effect on this belief system. This result demonstrates that anger facilitates the racial priming effect and is the reason implicit appeals only bring to mind thoughts about race and not race-neutral conservative beliefs.

On the other hand, an implicit appeal that generated fear did not prime racial attitudes. This null finding does not support the racial fear hypothesis. Most people would suspect that fear would have its biggest effect on racial attitudes when the ad focuses on black criminals. But the experimental findings showed that a campaign appeal that focused on black criminals was most effective when it aroused anger. Consequently, these findings reveal that there are circumstances in which a subtle racial appeal is ineffective at priming racial considerations. This has important implications for understanding when political campaigns will be effective at evoking race. The type of emotion experienced from racialized campaign appeals is important in determining when race will enter into political campaigns. Knowing this allows us to better understand the conditions when race will be used to explain opposition or support for policies or candidates intending to reduce racial inequality.

Because the crime experiment was unable to speak to how emotions would interact with explicit racial appeals, I also examined the 1988 ANES. Here I found evidence that corroborated my experimental results. Specifically, when the Horton story was implicit and the media coverage was most intense, anger toward Dukakis enhanced the effect of symbolic racism on support for Bush. Conversely, when

Jesse Jackson brought to the public's attention the racial content of the Horton story (making it explicit), the effectiveness of anger on racial prejudice waned. Additionally, no matter if the Horton story was implicitly or explicitly about race, fear of Dukakis did not increase support for Bush among racially prejudiced whites. There is good reason to suppose that the emotion measures toward Dukakis underestimated the actual impact anger had on symbolic racism during the 1988 presidential campaign. Yet, even with these indirect emotion measures of Horton, we were still able to discern a sizable effect of anger on symbolic racism.

Overall, this chapter shows that subtle racial messages like the Horton appeal are most effective when they trigger anger. Many white Americans believed it was unfair that "Willie" Horton, a convicted murder not eligible for parole, was given free weekend passes to terrorize a white couple. This feeling of racial anger, not racial fear as many scholars and pundits have speculated, motivated racially prejudiced whites to support Bush.

APPENDIX: SCALE/INDEX CONSTRUCTION

Crime Experiment

Independent Variables
Anger and *Fear* are dummy variables, where 1=if they were in the treatment condition and 0=if they were in the control condition.

Symbolic Racism consists of four measures and was recoded onto a 0 to 1 scale, where the higher values correspond to endorsement of symbolic racism. Four items were additively scaled. Response options for each question ranged from "strongly agree" to "strongly disagree." The specific items are: (1) Over the past few years, blacks have gotten less than they deserve. (2) Irish, Italian, Jewish and many other minorities overcame prejudice and worked their way up. Blacks should do the same without any special favors. (3) It's really a matter of some people not trying hard enough; if blacks would only try harder they could be just as well off as whites. (4) Generations of slavery and discrimination have created conditions that make it difficult for blacks to work their way out of the lower class. I decided to omit two items used in the past for symbolic racism, because of their manifest policy content. Don't knows were coded into the middle of the scale, because of the relatively small sample size. Running the model with "don't knows" as missing does not change the magnitude and direction of the coefficients. (Mean=.47, S.D.=.22, Min=0, Max=1).

Gender is a dummy variable, where 0=female and 1=male. (Mean=.48, S.D.=.50, Min=0, Max=1).

Age is a continuous variable and ranges from eighteen to thirty-eight years old. (Mean=20, S.D.=2)

Dependent Variable

Racial Policy Opinions ranges from 0 to 1, where the higher value corresponds with the more conservative response (Mean=.50, S.D.=.19, Min=0, Max=1). The measure is a combination of *Government assistance to blacks*, *Reparations for blacks*, and *Martin Luther King Jr. Holiday* and ranges from 0 to 1, where the higher value corresponds to opposition to racial policies. Don't knows were coded into the middle of the scale; nevertheless, the results remain essentially the same with running the model with don't knows as missing. For government assistance to blacks the following item was used: "Some people think that blacks have been discriminated against for so long that the government has a special obligation to help improve their living standards. Others believe that the government should not be giving special treatment to blacks." The scale ranged from 1 to 7, where 1 = I strongly agree the government is obligated to help blacks and 7 = I strongly agree that government shouldn't give preferential treatment. The *Martin Luther King Jr. Holiday* item was "It is important that the celebration of Martin Luther King Jr.'s birthday is a national holiday." Response options ranged from 1 = "extremely important" to 4 = "not important." The *Reparations for blacks* item was "Because of slavery and state-sponsored segregation, the government in Washington should provide blacks with reparations." Response options ranged from "strongly agree" to "strongly disagree."

The 1988 American National Election Study

Independent Variables

Anger and Fear (Study 2) are two measures recoded onto a 0 to 1 scale, where 0=not angry/afraid and 1=angry/ afraid. The specific items are:

(1) "Think about Michael Dukakis. Now, has Dukakis (because of the kind of person he is, or because of something he has done) ever made you feel angry/afraid?" (Anger Mean=.31, S.D.=.45 Min=0, Max=1) (Fear Mean=.24, S.D.=.42, Min=0, Max=1).

Symbolic Racism is the same measure as in Study 1 (Mean=.63, S.D.=.22, Min=0, Max=1).

Ideology is coded onto a 0 to 1 scale, where the higher values correspond to identifying as strongly conservative. The measures were based on a two-item skip pattern. (1) "We hear a lot of talk these days about liberals and conservatives. On a seven-point scale, where 1 is very liberal and 7 is very conservative, where would you place yourself on this scale, or haven't you thought much about this?" (2) If respondent enters 8 "haven't thought much about this," then they get: "If you had to choose, would you consider yourself a liberal, a moderate or a conservative?"(Mean=.58, S.D.=.22, Min=0, Max=1).

Gender is a dummy variable, where 0=female and 1=male. (Mean=,44, S.D.=.50, Min=0, Max=1).

South is a dummy variable, where 0=non-Southern resident and 1=Southern resident. The Southern states are Alabama, Arkansas, Delaware, Washington DC, Florida, Georgia, Kentucky, Louisiana, Maryland, Mississippi, North Carolina, Oklahoma, South Carolina, Tennessee, Texas, Virginia, and West Virginia. (Mean=.31, S.D.=.46, Min=0, Max=1).

Education is coded onto a 0 to 1 scale, where the higher value corresponds to a postgraduate degree. (Mean=.45, S.D.=.28, Min=0, Max=1).

Age is a continuous variable and ranges from seventeen to ninety-eight years old. (Mean=46, S.D.=18).

Income is coded onto a 0 to 1 scale, where the higher value corresponds to the highest income bracket.

Party identification is measured with the standard seven-point party identification scale. This measure is captured with a three-item, skip pattern design: (1) "Generally speaking, do you usually think of yourself as a Republican, a Democrat, an Independent, or what?" (2) [If R answers Rep or Dem] "Would you call yourself a strong Republican/Democrat or a not very strong Republican/Democrat?" [3] [If R answers Independent] "Do you think of yourself as closer to the Republican Party or the Democratic Party? The variable is coded onto a 0 to 1 scale, where the highest value equals strong Republican. (Mean=.51, S.D.=.34, Min=0, Max=1).

Attention to the Campaign is a combination of four variables coded onto a 0 to 1 scale; higher values indicate respondents paid more attention to the campaign. The specific items were: (1) "How much attention did you pay to news on TV about the campaign for president – a great deal, quite a bit, some, very little, or none?"(2) "How much attention did you pay to magazine articles about the campaign for president – a great deal, quite a bit, some, very little, or none?" (3) "Did you listen to any speeches or discussion about the campaign on the radio – yes or no?" (4) Some people don't pay much attention to political campaigns. How about you? Would you say that you have been very much interested, somewhat interested, or not much interested in the political campaigns so far this year?" (Mean=.40, S.D.=22, Min=0, Max=1).

Crime is measured by a dummy variable where 0=no mention of crime and 1=mention of crime. The specific question asked: "Is there anything in particular about Mr. Dukakis that might make you want to vote against him?" Codes 968, 969, 970, 971, 972, 974, 975, 976, 977, 978, 1042 from the open-ended responses were coded as 1, whereas all else was coded as 0. (Mean=.11, S.D.=.32, Min=0, Max=1).

National Security is measured by a dummy variable where 0=no mention of national security and 1=mention of national security. The specific question asked: "Is there anything in particular about Mr. Dukakis that might make you want to vote against him?" Codes 1184, 1107, 1185, 1186, 1101, 1103 from the open-ended responses were coded as 1, whereas all else was coded as 0.

Economy is measured by a dummy variable where 0=no mention of economy and 1=mention of economy. The specific question asked: "Is there anything in particular about Mr. Dukakis that might make you want to vote against him?" Codes 901, 902, 903, 904, 907, 930, 935, 937 from the open-ended responses were coded as 1, whereas all else was coded as 0.

Dependent Variable

Vote Choice is recoded on a 0 to 1 scale. There are five categories for this variable: 1=strong preference for Bush, .75=some preference for

Bush, .5=they support another candidate or are unsure who to support .25=some preference for Dukakis, and o=strong preference for Dukakis. The specific items were "Who do you think you will vote for in the election?" and "Would you say that your preference for this presidential candidate is strong or not strong?" Several versions of this variable were tested, including one that discarded subjects who did not support either Bush or Dukakis. Results were identical with this alternative specification. (Mean=.56, S.D.=39, Min=0, Max=1).

TABLE 3A. *The Impact of Emotion and Symbolic Racism and Political Ideology on Preference for Bush During the High-Exposure Implicit Phase of the 1988 Presidential Campaign*

	Vote Choice: Bush
	B **(s.e.)**
	High-Exposure Implicit Phase
Anger*Symbolic Racism	.39** (.16)
Fear*Symbolic Racism	−.16 (.17)
Anger*Ideology	−.24 (.16)
Fear*Ideology	.09 (.16)
Anger	.00 (.12)
Fear	.13 (.15)
Symbolic Racism	−.02 (.10)
Party Identification	.62*** (.05)
Ideology	.34*** (.10)
Income	−.01 (.07)

(continued)

TABLE 3A. *(continued)*

	Vote Choice: Bush
	B **(s.e.)**
	High-Exposure Implicit Phase
Education	−.03 (.07)
Age	−.001 (.001)
Gender	−.01 (.04)
South	.05 (.04)
Attention to the Campaign	−.11 (.08)
Constant	.10 (.10)
R^2	.61
N	285

Notes: * p ≤ .1 (two-tailed test); ** p ≤ .05 (two-tailed test); *** p ≤ .001 (two-tailed test). Entries are unstandardized OLS regression coefficients and the standard errors are in parentheses.

4

The Public's Anger: Racial Polarization and Opinions about Health Care Reform

The previous two chapters demonstrated that evoking anger in general and from a racialized campaign ad in particular can significantly affect support for racial policies by activating thoughts about race. This finding is consistent with other work that demonstrates campaign messages can powerfully alter which considerations are made salient when making political evaluations (Druckman 2004; Iyengar and Kinder 1987; Krosnick and Kinder 1990).[1] Thus far, my focus has been predominantly on race-specific issues. This chapter extends my examination of the effects of anger to policies that on the surface seem to lay outside the domain of race. One such issue is the 2009–10 health care reform debate over what was later referred to as the Patient Protection and Affordable Care Act. This act was intended to lower the total health care cost for millions of Americans.

Key benefits included expanding Medicaid and Medicare; not allowing private insurers to drop people with preexisting medical conditions; and young adults remaining on their parents' insurance plans until age twenty-six (Jacobs and Skocpol 2010). This seemingly nonracial issue, however, became racialized via a combination of forces: a black president as the face of the policy, and how opponents framed the issue. Tesler and Sears (2010) argue that the racial symbolism associated with Barack Obama, as the first black president of the United States, has led racial evaluations associated with him to spillover to policies he is strongly attached to, such as health care policy. Another force that has contributed to the racialization of health care reform is that opponents have framed the issue as penalizing hardworking Americans and benefiting undeserving freeloaders (Skocpol and Williamson 2012). This opposition was strongest from the political right, most notably Tea Partiers, who argued that the policy unfairly benefited the poor and minorities. With health care reform framed by opponents as government redistribution – similar to welfare – it might not be surprising that race would enter into people's health care policy decisions. This chapter examines whether the ability of anger to prime racial considerations in the context of racial policy opinions is portable to an ostensibly nonracial issue like the 2009–10 health care reform debate.

In addition to this chapter shifting the focus to an implicitly racial issue, it also examines whether anger has contributed to the racial polarization of health care reform opinions. Research in political science has indicated that the attitudes of Americans are more polarized than they have been in a long time (Abramowitz and Saunders 2008).[2] Some scholars argue that this increase in polarization is, in part, a response to the strong divisions among Democratic and Republican elites, and that this division has mostly affected strong partisans who are politically engaged (Layman and Carsey 2002) – the electorate that is often paying the most attention to politics (Zaller 1992). Recently, research has demonstrated that public opinion on health care reform is more polarized along racial lines than along nonracial ideological lines (Tesler and Sears 2010). For instance, Tesler (2012) finds that when health care reform is framed as part of Obama's reform plan, racial attitudes have a much stronger effect on health care policy opinions than do race-neutral principles. What remains unclear is why support for health care reform is more divided by racial attitudes than nonracial attitudes. Put differently, what is the mechanism that polarizes health care opinions on racial grounds but not on race-neutral ideological grounds? Consistent with my theory of anger and racial attitudes, I argue that anger helps explain why we see opinions on health care polarized more along racial lines than along nonracial ideological lines.

THE 2009–2010 HEALTH CARE REFORM DEBATE

During Barack Obama's run to be the forty-fourth president of the United States, he expressed a strong commitment to comprehensive health care reform. For instance, on March 24, 2007, at a health care forum in Las Vegas, he pledged, "I will judge my first term as president based on the fact on whether we have delivered the kind of health care that every American deserves and that our system can afford."[3] Once elected as president, Obama continued his charge for reform by pressuring Congress to take immediate action on health care. His main priorities in reforming health care were to lower the skyrocketing health care costs for lower- and middle-class Americans and to prevent private insurers from dropping people with preexisting medical conditions. In spite of Obama's urging, Republican members of Congress threatened to stymie any type of reform. They were not alone. Groups like health insurance companies that might see their profit margins shrink also fought reforming the health care system. Opponents claimed that reforming the system would strain a fragile economy – by increasing taxes and raising the United States' federal deficit – already considered out of control by many. As the bill made its way through the halls of Congress, an intense battle ensued among opponents fighting to kill the bill and supporters fighting for its survival. This clash was most notable during the 2009 August congressional recess.

As members of Congress returned to their districts and states trying to sell health care reform, some met a barrage of criticism from hostile protestors. One criticism by opponents of health care reform was that it would extend the federal government's reach too far by forcing citizens to have health insurance – claiming this mandate is akin to socialism. Critics also charged that it would provide health coverage to illegal immigrants. Some went even further and suggested that it would create "death panels" allowing the government to "pull the plug on grandma" at any time (Seelye 2009). Former Pennsylvania Senator Arlen Specter at a town hall forum on health care faced these types of criticisms up close when an angry protestor yelled out, "[O]ne day, God's gonna stand before you and he's gonna judge you and the rest of your damn cronies up on the Hill, and then you can get your just deserts."[4] Congressman Dingell (D) also experienced an angry backlash while trying to sell the president's health care agenda in his district of Romulus, Michigan. Seething protestors in the crowd interrupted the congressman at every turn, shouting, "Fascists' America" and "Socialized Medicine." Rather than discouraging this type of behavior, leaders within the Republican Party seemed to be the catalyst behind it. For example, during Obama's speech to a joint session of Congress, South Carolina Republican congressman Joe Wilson shouted, "You lie!" when the president said health legislation would not mandate coverage for illegal immigrants.

At the time, national polls captured much of the public's visceral anger about "ObamaCare," as opponents called it. For example, a Pew research poll, conducted in August 2009, found that 40 percent of Americans were angry and disappointed with the health care reform bill. Higher levels of anger emerged among Tea Party supporters. Based on a CBS/NY *Times* poll, when given a chance to describe their frustration at the president and Congress, 53 percent opted for angry – angry about health care reform and government spending.[5] To display their anger at the president and members of Congress, Tea Partiers traveled to Washington DC to protest against "ObamaCare." They gathered in front of the U. S. Capitol building chanting, "Liar, Liar, Liar!" while waving incendiary signs like "Parasite in Chief" and "God Heals, ObamaCare Steals!" Some scholars and politicians suggested that anger over government spending was not the only reason for people's opposition.

According to Tesler and Sears, some people opposed health care reform because it was part of a black president's policy agenda. "[T]he symbolism of Barack Obama as the first black president, at least one year into his tenure in the White House, still appeared to make racial attitudes one of the most important determinants of how the American public responded to him" (2010, 159). Former president Jimmy Carter agreed, claiming that opposition to Obama and his policies, such as health care reform, was partly grounded in racism.[6] In fact, in an interview with Brian Williams on NBC *Nightly News*, Carter stated, "racism ... still exists and I think it is going to bubble up to the surface because of a belief among many white people ... that African Americans are not qualified to lead this great country." We saw this racism exhibited in offensive signs protestors held up at town hall meetings and public demonstrations against health care reform. For example, at a rally one sign portrayed Obama as a witch doctor wearing a feather headdress and a bone through his nose with the words "Obama Care" underneath the image.[7] Besides waving racially offensive signs, some opponents expressed their opposition by screaming racial epithets at members of Congress. At the end of a rally protesting health care reform in front of the U.S. Capitol building, a confrontation ensued between Tea Partiers and members of Congress. News accounts of the confrontation reported that Tea Party protestors shouted antigay remarks to Rep. Barney Frank (D-MA) and hurled racial slurs at Rep. James Clyburn (D-SC), a member of the Congressional Black Caucus (CBC), and called fellow member Rep. John Lewis (D-GA) the "N" word. Recalling his clash with Tea Partiers, Clyburn stated, "I have heard things today that I have not heard since March 15, 1960, when I was marching to get off the back of the bus."[8]

Obama's strong stance on health care reform might not be the only reason racism was implicated in discussions over health care reform. Research has shown that when an issue is framed as the federal government giving handouts to undeserving individuals, people's opinions become colored with racial animosity. One example is welfare. Scholars, including Martin Gilens (1999), have argued that opposition to policies like the food stamp program is the result of some Americans' perception that welfare recipients take advantage of the system by choosing not to work when they can. Because the public thinks that most people on welfare are black – and incorrectly I might point out – scholars have found that racial attitudes tend to dominate their policy opinions (Gilens 1995; Winter 2006). Skocpol and Williamson (2012) suggest that the health care debate has produced similar appraisals and is viewed by opponents as another instance of government redistributing resources from hardworking American citizens to undeserving freeloaders. During a town hall meeting in Congressman Norm Dicks's district of Washington State, a protestor criticized the reform plan by saying, "If you believe that it is absolutely moral to take my money and give it to someone else based on their supposed needs … then you come and take this twenty dollars and use it as a down payment on this health care plan" (Zernike 2010, 84). This opponent's criticism of health care reform supports Skocpol and Williamson's view that opposition to reform stems from people's unwillingness to redistribute resources to those perceived as lazy and undeserving. With whites usually considering the less fortunate to be disproportionately minorities, one would expect negative racial attitudes to be a strong predictor of health care reform opinions. Several scholars have found support for this proposition – demonstrating that racism has a powerful impact on opposition to health care reform (Henderson and Hillygus 2011; Knowles et al. 2010; Tesler 2012; Tesler and Sears 2010).

On the other hand, former Republican National Committee (RNC) chairman Michael Steele strongly disagreed with Carter and others' accusation that racism was behind opposition to Obama's health care reform plan – saying it had nothing to do with race and was strictly about policy (Phillips 2009). Others like Abigail Thernstrom (2010) agreed, arguing that the public's anger merely reflected an expression of conservative principles and had nothing to do with racism. From her perspective, opponents like the Tea Party are angry about the extent of the government's reach, but that doesn't mean they are racists. Instead, they want politicians to adopt a more conservative approach to policy making: smaller government, strict adherence to the letter of the U.S. Constitution, states' rights, and fiscal conservatism. Sniderman and Carmines (1997) have shown that conservatives are generally averse to social welfare policy – no matter if it's framed as universalistic or race specific. Perhaps the anger from public demonstrations and town hall meetings across the country attacking health care reform activated race-neutral principles and had nothing to do with race at all.

So far, my discussion of the health care debate has focused on the opposition's anger. But supporters of reform were angry as well. Their anger resulted, in part, from what they perceived as unfair criticism of Obama and his policy proposals. They considered opposition to the president's policies – particularly government bailouts of private industries – as racially motivated and outright hypocritical, given that Republicans didn't protest against former President Bush for enacting the same policies (Zernike 2010). The harsh criticism against Obama's health care reform proposal was not the only factor driving their anger. Progressives were also angry because members of Congress and the president softened their positions on specific issues in the health care reform proposal that they deeply cared about. For instance, those on the left saw their efforts to include a public option get taken off the table because of the Republicans and Tea Partiers' ability to demonize health care reform. Jacobs and Skocpol state:

[M]any public option champions on the left were enraged by the inability or unwillingness of the White House to join with progressives in Congress to deliver the public option.... Adam Green, a founder of Progressive Change, complained that Obama's Chief of Staff had a "loser mentality" that led him to be "afraid of a fight" and rely on a "very, very risk-averse" approach, urging "the President to cave instead of fighting for real change." (2010, 79–80)

In fact, Figure 1.1 illustrated that as much as 34 percent of Democrats were angry about the health care reform law. What seems apparent from the 2009–10 health care reform debate is that anger was present on both sides – albeit at a much higher rate among opponents.

AFFECTIVE INTELLIGENCE THEORY

Recently, George Marcus and his colleagues have placed anger (or aversion) as an important emotion in their theory of affective intelligence (AI hereafter). They propose a dual process model where particular emotional states trigger distinct cognitive strategies for dealing with the political environment (MacKuen et al. 2010; Marcus 2002; Marcus, Neuman, and MacKuen 2000). One of these models is the *surveillance* system, which monitors for threatening and novel stimuli and interrupts habitual routine, leading to higher cognitive engagement. Under this system, a fearful state signals that the environment is novel and threatening and prompts greater attention and cognitive engagement like searching out new information or considering alternative points of view (Brader 2006; MacKuen et al. 2010; Marcus et al. 2000). The other model is the *disposition* system where safe and familiar stimuli evoke enthusiasm and enhance reliance on habits and predispositions that have worked in the past. Under this same system, MacKuen and his colleagues also state that "[w]hen familiar averse stimuli are encountered, people rely on previously learned routines to manage these situations, just as they do for familiar rewarding circumstances" (2010, 441). That is, aversion, which includes anger, encourages reliance on previous habits that have proven effective against some adversary.

What is unclear from the AI model is which predispositions are more likely to be called on when anger is experienced. Perhaps anger does not increase reliance on any specific group or political attitude, just one that will suffice for rationalizing people's opinions on health care reform. If so, anger would have a similar effect on racial predispositions and race-neutral predispositions – enhancing reliance on both habitual routines. As a consequence, anger would bring to mind racial *and* nonracial predispositions and increase the effect of both belief systems on policy opinions. The AI model also predicts that anger and enthusiasm should have a similar effect on one's predispositions. For example, Marcus and his colleagues state that "[a]version and enthusiasm both highlight and strengthen reliance on previously learned understandings and stereotypes" (2000, 165). However, similar to anger, we do not have a clear sense about which habits people will rely on when feeling enthusiastic. Perhaps enthusiasm increases the impact of racial and nonracial predispositions on health care policy opinions. To answer such questions, this chapter examines the three affective dimensions that are central to the AI model – anger, fear, and enthusiasm.

My theory of anger and race makes specific predictions about which political attitudes are likely to be activated (and not activated) under specific emotional states. Because anger and racial attitudes are tightly linked in memory, I expect anger should make thoughts about race more accessible in the minds of both racial conservatives and racial liberals. Research has shown that opinions on health care reform are already racialized (Knowles et al. 2010; Tesler and Sears 2010). As a consequence, anger should push racial conservatives to more strongly oppose health care reform and push racial liberals to more powerfully support reform. On the other hand, I hypothesize that race-neutral considerations should be unaffected by anger. That is, anger should not boost the effect of nonracial attitudes like self-reported political ideology or preferences for small and efficient government on opinions about health care reform.

Anger was not the only emotion aroused during the 2009–10 health care reform debate. Right-wing talk show jocks, like Rush Limbaugh, incited fear when attacking health care reform, claiming it would create "death panels" and give the government the ability to determine whether people live or die. The threat of redistribution also presented itself in discussions about health care reform. For example, during the 2010 special election for the Senate in Massachusetts, Scott Brown aired an ad attacking the health care bill intending to evoke fear – claiming it would raise taxes on hardworking Americans and bankrupt the country.[9] Perhaps fear, rather than anger, increases opposition to health care reform by activating racial and nonracial considerations.

Given my contention that fear is not strongly tied to either racial or nonracial predispositions, I expect fear not to boost the effect of either predisposition on health policy opinions. Finally, I predict that enthusiasm is not strongly linked to racial considerations. The reason is that blame appraisals are an important aspect of racial conservatives and racial liberals' belief systems. Thus, enthusiasm should have a difficult time activating thoughts about race.

HEALTH CARE EXPERIMENT

The health care experiment was conducted through Knowledge Networks, an Internet survey company, from June 10 to July 6, 2010.[10] My study included 986 respondents drawn from a random sample of white adult Americans.[11] There was good variation in age (26% were 18–34; 34% 35–54; 40% 55 and over), gender (48% female), partisanship (49% Republicans), and education (41% high school degree or less; 21% some college; 30% college graduate or higher).[12] The study consists of a two-wave experimental design – consistent with the experimental studies in Chapters 2 and 3. The first wave includes measures of symbolic racism, self-reported political ideology, and preferences for limited government.[13] Several days later, respondents were recontacted to participate in the second wave that consisted of the manipulation, followed by measures of preference for health care reform.

EXPERIMENTAL MANIPULATION: EMOTION INDUCTION

Subjects were randomly assigned to one of the four conditions: an anger condition, a fear condition, an enthusiasm condition, and a relaxed condition.[14] The manipulation is identical to the one used in Chapter 2; it induces emotion in general (unrelated to politics or race).[15] The procedure asks subjects to recall and focus on events, people, or occurrences that lead them to experience a given emotion while viewing an image of a person with a facial expression corresponding to that emotion. The control condition asks subjects to focus on things that make them feel relaxed. After reading the prompt, subjects were told to take a few minutes to write down anything in general that made them feel the intended emotion. After the induction, subjects answered questions on health care reform.

THE EFFECTS OF ANGER, FEAR, AND ENTHUSIASM ON HEALTH
CARE REFORM OPINIONS

Similar to the previous chapters, I first conducted a manipulation
check to determine if the induction procedure operated as expected.
The open-ended responses to the induction task were double-coded
by two research assistants unaware of the hypotheses. They identified the intensity of several emotions expressed in the responses.[16]
The results appear in Table 4.1. As expected, participants in the anger
condition expressed significantly more intense anger than those in the
relaxed condition. They also expressed less enthusiasm, but they did
not express more fear in comparison to those in the relaxed condition. Correspondingly, respondents in the fear condition expressed
more fear and less enthusiasm, but not more anger relative to those in
the relaxed condition. Subjects in the enthusiasm condition expressed
more intense enthusiasm than those in the relaxed condition, but did
not express more fear or anger.[17] These results suggest the induction
performed as intended.[18]

My main expectation is that anger should make racial thoughts
more accessible in whites' minds, thereby increasing the impact of
racial attitudes on health care policy opinions. Because my measure
of health care reform is a dummy variable, all analyses are run using
a probit regression model. I regressed *Health Care Reform Opinion*
on treatment conditions (*Anger* and *Fear*), *Symbolic Racism*, and the
interactions between the treatment conditions and symbolic racism,
controlling for *Income, South, Employed, Own Home, Urban,* and
Political Discussion.[19] Given the complexities of nonlinear models
with interaction terms – presenting the predicted probabilities is more
meaningful (Ali and Norton 2003; Hanmer and Kalkan 2013). The
results from the probit regression model can be found in the appendix
in Table 4A.

Figure 4.1 is the converted predicted probabilities from the results
in column 1 of Table 4A.[20] The figure shows the probability of opposing health care reform at varying levels of symbolic racism conditional
on one's emotional experience. It also displays a 90 percent confidence
interval, in dotted lines, around the effect of the anger condition in
the solid black line. The long dashed line represents the fear condition
and the solid grey line represents the control (relaxed) condition. The

TABLE 4.1. *Manipulation Check*

	Intensity of Anger Expressed	Intensity of Fear Expressed	Intensity of Enthusiasm Expressed
	B (s.e.)	B (s.e.)	B (s.e.)
Anger Condition	.54***	.00	−.06***
	(.02)	(.02)	(.02)
Fear Condition	.02	.61***	−.05**
	(.02)	(.02)	(.02)
Enthusiasm Condition	.01	.01	.57***
	(.02)	(.02)	(.02)
Constant	.00	.01	.06***
	(.01)	(.01)	(.01)
N	954	954	954

Notes: * p ≤ .1; ** p ≤ .05; *** p ≤ .001 (two-tailed test). Entries are unstandardized OLS regression coefficients and the standard errors are in parentheses.

figure shows a strong effect of symbolic racism in all circumstances. For instance, there is an eighty percentage point shift in the predicted probability of opposing health care reform across values on symbolic racism for respondents in the control group. This result is not surprising given that scholars have found people's opinions on health care reform to already be racialized (Tesler 2012; Tesler and Sears 2010). For the anger condition, the figure shows that it increases this effect to about a ninety-five percentage point shift.[21] More specifically, whites high in symbolic racism in the anger condition are about eight percentage points more likely to oppose health care reform than are comparable resentful whites in the relaxed condition.[22] The difference between the anger and fear conditions is somewhat smaller (seven percentage points) for those high in symbolic racism. Looking at those low in symbolic racism, a greater difference arises between the anger condition and the relaxed condition – an increase in support of about twelve percentage points.[23] On the other hand, there is not much of a difference (four points) between the anger and fear conditions among racial liberals.

I also examine whether the anger condition boosts the effect of race-neutral principles on opposition to health care reform, in comparison

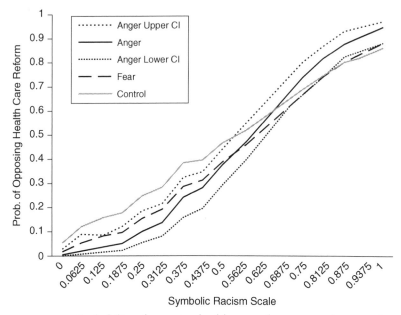

FIGURE 4.1. Probability of opposing health care reform across the anger, fear, and relaxed conditions as symbolic racism changes.

Note: These are the predicted probabilities calculated from the results in column 1 of Table 4A with 90 percent confidence intervals around the effect of anger. I calculate the probabilities by manipulating the emotion variables while holding all the other independent variables at their own values observed in the data and then averaging over all of the cases.

to the control condition. Republican leaders argued that the anger surrounding health care reform was simply triggering race-neutral conservative principles. If so, the anger condition should also make the beliefs of self-reported conservatives have a bigger effect on health opinions, relative to the control condition.[24] Figure 4.2 shows that the anger condition does not boost the effect of conservative principles on health care reform – relative to the fear and control conditions. For instance, the figure shows that the lines for the fear and control conditions are within the confidence interval for the anger condition among high conservative identifiers. On the other hand, the figure shows that the fear condition pushes political liberals to be more supportive of health care reform, relative to the anger (nine point difference) and control (six point difference) groups. The fact that Republicans threatened to

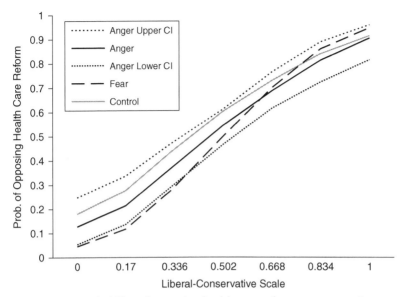

FIGURE 4.2. Probability of opposing health care reform across emotion conditions as political ideology changes.
Note: These are the predicted probabilities calculated from the results in column 2 of Table 4A with 90 percent confidence intervals around the effect of anger.

repeal the health care bill if it became a law might explain this effect. Perhaps political liberals' fear over whether the heath care law would be repealed pushed them to be more supportive of reform.[25]

When comparing Figure 4.1 to Figure 4.2, we see that the anger condition polarizes whites' opinions on health care reform more along racial lines than along race-neutral ideological lines. In the anger condition, ninety-five percentage points separate whites high in symbolic racism and whites low in symbolic racism in their opposition to health care reform. On the other hand, seventy-eight percentage points separate political conservatives and political liberals (in the anger condition) in their opposition to health care reform. As a result, the anger condition produced a difference of seventeen percentage points between racial attitudes and nonracial attitudes and their effect on health care opinions.

To ensure distinctions between symbolic racism and political ideology, I ran another model that includes both sets of interactions. I

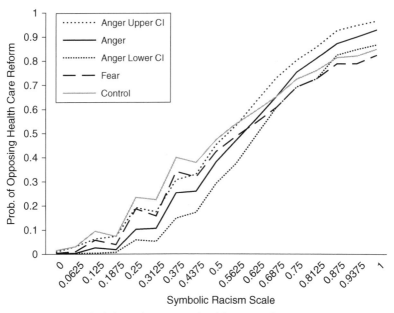

FIGURE 4.3. Probability of opposing health care reform across emotions as symbolic racism changes, controlling for race-neutral principles.

Note: These are the predicted probabilities calculated from the results in column 3 of Table 4A with 90 percent confidence intervals around the effect of anger.

estimate the interaction of each emotion condition (i.e., anger and fear) with symbolic racism and ideology simultaneously.[26] Figure 4.3 displays the interactions for the emotion conditions and symbolic racism visually and shows a similar pattern of results to Figure 4.1. There is a ninety-three percentage point shift in the predicted probability of opposing health care reform across values on symbolic racism for respondents in the anger condition. On the other hand, the control group produces an eighty-three percentage point shift. The figure shows that the anger condition boosts opposition among whites high in symbolic racism by about seven percentage points and increases support among those low in symbolic racism by about eight percentage points – relative to the control condition.[27] Moreover, the difference between the anger condition and the fear condition is even larger (about ten percentage points) among those high in symbolic racism.[28]

For racial liberals, the difference is fairly small between the anger and fear conditions.

In summary, the results show that the anger condition heightens the effect of racial attitudes on health care policy opinions – relative to the control condition. Conversely, the anger condition does not enhance the impact of race-neutral principles such as political ideology or preferences for limited government on health care reform opinions.[29] The findings indicate that anger explains why whites' support for health care reform is more divided along racial lines than along nonracial lines.

ANGER VERSUS ENTHUSIASM AND HEALTH CARE REFORM

Thus far, my findings show that anger has a strong effect on racial predispositions and no effect on nonracial predispositions. The theory of affective intelligence proposes that anger and enthusiasm should have a similar effect on one's predispositions. Specifically, Marcus and his colleagues argue that anger and enthusiasm should increase people's reliance on habits when forming a political judgment. If anger and enthusiasm have similar effects on political attitudes as AI supposes, then enthusiasm should also enhance the effect of racial predispositions on preferences for health care reform. In other words, when comparing the effect of the anger condition on racial attitudes to the enthusiasm condition, no significant differences should occur.

Moreover, this test allows me to examine whether positive emotions activate the belief system of racial liberals. Tesler and Sears contend that racial liberals' beliefs are linked to their positive feelings about blacks. "[W]e are, therefore, confident … that individuals scoring low on racial resentment are generally sympathetic – have a positive affective orientation – toward African Americans" (2010, 45). Therefore, perhaps enthusiasm also activates the belief system of racial liberals. But, as argued earlier, I predict the beliefs of whites low in symbolic racism are more tied to feelings of anger than enthusiasm. If I am correct, then the anger condition should still increase the impact of racial liberals' beliefs on support for health care reform – relative to the enthusiasm condition.

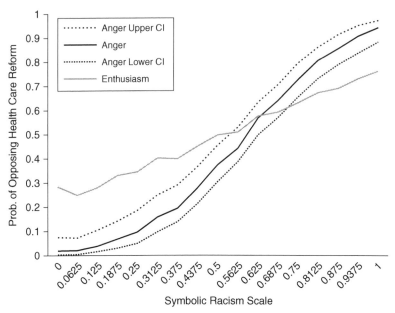

FIGURE 4.4. Probability of opposing health care reform across the anger and enthusiasm conditions as symbolic racism changes.

Note: These are the predicted probabilities calculated from the results in column 1 of Table 4B with 90 percent confidence intervals around the effect of anger.

To test these predictions, I regressed *Health Care Reform Opinion* on the *Anger* condition, *Symbolic Racism*, and the interaction between the two, controlling for *Income, Employed, South, Own Home, Urban*, and *Political Discussion* – with the enthusiasm condition now as the baseline group.[30] Figure 4.4 shows the probability of opposing health care reform at varying levels of symbolic racism conditional on experiencing anger (solid black line) and enthusiasm (solid grey line). The 90 percent confidence interval around the effect of the anger condition is displayed in dotted lines. The figure shows a forty-eight percentage point shift in the predicted probability of opposing health care reform across values on symbolic racism for respondents in the enthusiasm condition. We also see that the anger condition significantly increases this effect to about a ninety-two percentage point shift. That is, racial conservatives in the anger condition are sixteen percentage points more likely to oppose health care reform than are comparable racial

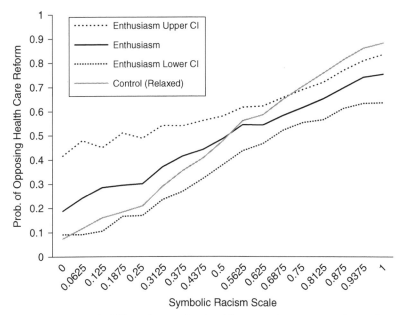

FIGURE 4.5. Probability of opposing health care reform across the enthusiasm and relaxed conditions as symbolic racism changes.
Note: These are the predicted probabilities calculated from the results in column 2 of Table 4B with 90 percent confidence intervals around the effect of enthusiasm.

conservatives in the enthusiasm condition. A bigger effect occurs for racial liberals – a difference of twenty-three percentage points between the anger group and the enthusiasm group. These results run counter to AI's predictions that both anger and enthusiasm increase reliance on one's predispositions. Moreover, they indicate that the anger condition heightens thoughts about race among those low in symbolic racism when compared to the enthusiasm condition.

Despite finding a difference between the anger and enthusiasm conditions, it might be that enthusiasm increases reliance on one's predisposition when compared to a relaxed state. Although the anger condition increases the effect of race when compared to the enthusiasm condition, we may see the enthusiasm condition heighten reliance on racial predispositions when compared to the relaxed condition. Figure 4.5 shows that this is not the case.[31] Actually, the enthusiasm condition depresses the effect of negative racial considerations on health policy opinion, relative to the relaxed condition. Thus, making racial conservatives enthusiastic causes them to rely less on their belief system – relative to a relaxed state.[32] The figure also shows a similar effect of the enthusiasm condition among those low in symbolic racism. Overall, we find that the anger and enthusiasm conditions affect whites' views about race differently. That is, the enthusiasm condition actually decreases whites' reliance on racial predispositions when compared to the relaxed condition.

CONCLUSION

What do these results tell us about the highly contentious debate on reforming the health care system? First and foremost, they reveal to us how emotions can make thoughts about race more pervasive in American society. The battle over health care reform was very emotional. Those on the right were angry about the federal government intruding into their lives, whereas those on the left were angry about the unfair criticism from the political right. My contention is that the public's anger over health care reform played an important role as to why race was such a strong predictor of people's opinions regarding health care reform.

No one would deny that the health care reform debate was filled with anger. But people vehemently disagreed over whether racism was involved. Some pundits, politicians, and scholars charged that racism fueled the rancorous town hall meetings and public demonstrations against health care reform. But leaders within the Republican Party accused the Democrats of playing the race card by calling opponents of reform racist – trying to scare off opposition. Yes, they admitted that one or two protestors held up racially offensive signs, but they represented a very small number of people in comparison to the thousands of protestors showing up at anti–health care reform rallies. However, recent research has shown that racism is a driving force in whites' opposition to health care reform (Henderson and Hillygus 2011; Knowles et al. 2010; Tesler 2012; Tesler and Sears 2010). Even so, the question remains whether anger has contributed to increasing the impact of racial prejudice on health care policy opinions. My expectation was that anger would play an important role in making race more salient in whites' minds.

The results from the health care experiment show that the anger condition enhances the impact of racism on health care policy opinions. By evoking anger in general (unrelated to politics or race), I find that racism has a larger effect in explaining whites' opposition to health care reform, compared to whites in the relaxed and fear conditions. The anger condition activates racial thoughts such that support for health care reform becomes more divided by racial attitudes. Thus, the experience of anger further polarizes racial liberals and racial conservatives by as much as fifteen percentage points relative to the relaxed condition, and ten percentage points relative to the fear condition. These results are impressive given the already high levels of racial polarization among whites on health care reform. Furthermore, my findings show that the anger condition does not prime race-neutral principles like self-reported political ideology or preferences for small, efficient government. That is, it does not increase their effect on health care policy opinion. The findings also show the fear condition has no effect on racial predispositions. The fear condition, however, does increase political liberals' support for reform, relative to the anger and control conditions. All in all, these results demonstrate that the anger condition has a strong effect on racial attitudes and no effect on non-racial attitudes.

Another purpose of this chapter was to examine whether anger and enthusiasm would have a similar effect on white racial attitudes. I find that the anger condition, relative to the enthusiasm condition, increases opposition to health care reform among those high in symbolic racism and boosts support for health policy among those low in symbolic racism. That is, the anger condition further polarizes racial liberals and racial conservatives on health care reform by about forty-four percentage points – relative to the enthusiasm condition.

The fact that anger motivates racial liberals to be more supportive of health care reform suggests that an angry public may not necessarily be detrimental for Democrats. From a strategic standpoint, Obama and his fellow Democrats should have been encouraging their constituency's anger toward the Tea Partiers rather than ignoring it. Perhaps if Democrats rallied their supporters to get angry about the Tea Party demonizing health care reform, it might have pushed more people on their side in support of the bill. But this strategy might have been easier said than done. Democrats would have needed to walk a very thin line, that is, getting their supporters angry while neutralizing anger among their opponents.

What do these results mean for the future of health care in the United States? A number of key provisions of the Patient Protection and Affordable Care Act will take effect in 2014. If the health care reform debate remains charged with anger, then race will continue to have a powerful effect on people's health care policy opinions. We might see specific provisions of the Patient Protection and Affordable Care Act garnering more support from racial conservatives if they are perceived to benefit hardworking American citizens instead of undeserving individuals. On the other hand, racial liberals might rally behind provisions of the legislative act that intend to reduce racial health disparities. As a consequence, this racial division may make achieving common ground on health care reform more difficult, especially when it comes to providing health care to minority groups.

Finally, most of the research supporting the theory of affective intelligence has demonstrated that emotions powerfully influence how people think. That is, emotions can determine how much cognitive effort people engage in – such as searching out new information or learning about politics. But the AI model doesn't make a clear prediction of *what* people think about under particular emotional states. Are they more likely to rely on their prejudiced thoughts when anger is experienced or beliefs about states' rights and individual effort? This chapter provides an answer to this question. It tells us which emotion will enhance the role of racial predispositions in determining opinions on health care reform.

APPENDIX: FACIAL EXPRESSIONS USED IN EMOTION
INDUCTION TASK

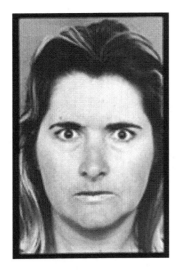

Anger Expression

Enthusiasm Expression

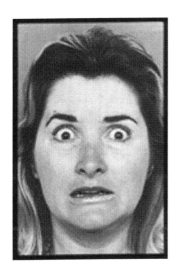

Fear Expression

APPENDIX: INDEX/SCALE CONSTRUCTION

Anger and *Fear* are dummy variables, where 1=if they are in the treatment condition and 0= if they are in the "relaxed" condition. For Table 3, the control group was the *enthusiasm* condition.

Symbolic Racism is recoded on a 0 to 1 scale where a higher value is the more racially conservative position. The specific items included: "Generations of slavery and discrimination have created conditions that make it difficult for blacks to work their way out of the lower class." "It is really a matter of some people not trying hard enough; if blacks would only try harder they could be just as well off as whites." "Irish, Italian, Jewish and many other minorities overcame prejudice and worked their way up. Blacks should do the same without any special favors." "Over the past few years, blacks have gotten less than they deserve." (Mean=.67, S.D.=.23, Min=0, Max=1).

Ideology is recoded onto a 0 to 1 scale where the highest value corresponds to identifying as extremely conservative. The specific item was: "In general, do you think of yourself as extremely liberal, liberal, slightly liberal, moderate, slightly conservative, conservative, extremely conservative?" (Mean=.54, S.D.=.23, Min=0, Max=1).

Limited government is recoded onto a 0 to 1 scale where 0=increase government spending and 1=reduce government spending. The specific item is: "Some people think the government should provide fewer services in order to reduce spending. These people are at point 1 of the scale. Other people feel it is important for the government to provide more services even if it means an increase in taxes. These people are at point 7 of the scale. Where would you place yourself on this scale, or haven't you thought much about this?" (Mean=.61, S.D.=.26, Min=0, Max=1).

Health Care Reform is a dummy variable recoded 0 to 1 with 1 equals opposition to reform. The specific item is: "As of right now, do you favor or oppose Barack Obama and the Democrats' Health Care reform bill?" The response options were yes=I favor the health care bill or no=I oppose the health care bill. (Mean=.60, S.D.=.49, Min=0, Max=1).

Employed is recoded onto a 0 to 1 scale where 0=unemployed, .5=unemployed but retired or disabled, and 1=employed. (Mean=.69, S.D.=.37, Min=0, Max=1).

Urban is a dummy variable where 1=lives in a metro area and 0=does not live in a metro area. (Mean=.79, S.D.=41, Min=0, Max=1).

South is a dummy variable, where 0=non-Southern resident and 1=Southern resident. The Southern states are Alabama, Arkansas, Delaware, Washington DC, Florida, Georgia, Kentucky, Louisiana, Maryland, Mississippi, North Carolina, Oklahoma, South Carolina, Tennessee, Texas, Virginia, and West Virginia. (Mean=.35, S.D.=.48, Min=0, Max=1).

Income is recoded onto a 0 to 1 scale where the higher value corresponds to highest income bracket. (Mean=.60, S.D.=.22, Min=0, Max=1).

Own Home is recoded onto a 0 to 1 scale where 0=does not own home and 1=own home. (Mean=.80, S.D.=.40, Min=0, Max=1).

Political Discussion is a measure of several political topics respondents mention in their open-ended responses to the emotion inductions. I had two research assistants code for whether respondents mentioned eight political or racial issues: crime, welfare, civil rights (e.g., voting rights, free speech, and freedom of religion), terrorism, education, health care, foreign policy, and economy (e.g., inflation, jobs, unemployment, recession). The Cronbach's alpha (.70) reveals a high level of reliability across the two coders. (Mean=.06, S.D.=.16, Min=0, Max=1).

APPENDIX: PROBIT REGRESSION RESULTS

TABLE 4A. *The Priming Effect of the Anger, Fear, and Relaxed Conditions on Racial and Race-Neutral Attitudes*

	Opposition to Health Care Reform (Baseline= Relaxed)	Opposition to Health Care Reform (Baseline= Relaxed)	Opposition to Health Care Reform (Baseline= Relaxed)
	B (s.e.)	B (s.e.)	B (s.e.)
Anger Condition*Symbolic Racism	1.58** (.71)		1.57* (.80)
Fear Condition*Symbolic Racism	.59 (.65)		.13 (.76)
Anger Condition*Ideology		.16 (.71)	−.35 (.76)
Fear Condition*Ideology		1.05 (.69)	.67 (.74)
Anger Condition	−1.03** (.46)	−.24 (.39)	−.89 (.61)
Fear Condition	−.50 (.45)	−.79** (.39)	−.60 (.59)
Symbolic Racism	2.48*** (.45)		2.12*** (.53)
Ideology		2.35*** (.48)	2.14*** (.51)
Income	−.40 (.31)	−.26 (.35)	−.33 (.33)
South	.17 (.13)	.20 (.13)	.14 (.14)
Employed	.35** (.17)	.40** (.18)	.47** (.18)
Political Discussion	−.69 (.46)	−.64 (.42)	−.85* (.49)
Own Home	.12 (.16)	.22 (.17)	.13 (.17)
Urban	−.50** (.16)	−.22 (.16)	−.38** (.17)
Constant	−1.04** (.37)	−1.07** (.36)	−2.16*** (.49)
N	706	719	706

Notes: * p ≤ .1; ** p ≤ .05; *** p≤ .001 (two-tailed test). Entries are probit regression coefficients and the standard errors are in parentheses. All variables are recoded onto a 0 to 1 scale, with higher values indicating more opposition to health care reform.

TABLE 4B. *The Priming Effect of the Anger Condition Relative to the Enthusiasm Condition and the Enthusiasm Condition Relative to the Control Condition on Racial Attitudes*

	Opposition to Health Care Reform (Baseline=Enthusiasm)	Opposition to Health Care Reform (Baseline=Relaxed)
	B (s.e.)	B (s.e.)
Anger Condition*Symbolic Racism	2.36*** (.73)	
Enthusiasm Condition*Symbolic Racism		−1.08 (.70)
Anger Condition	−1.50** (.50)	
Enthusiasm Condition		.56 (.49)
Symbolic Racism	1.40** (.53)	2.59*** (.46)
Income	.26 (.39)	−.17 (.38)
South	.13 (.16)	−.17 (.16)
Employed	−.16 (.21)	.05 (.20)
Political Discussion	−.44 (.52)	.56 (.61)
Own Home	−.05 (.20)	.10 (.19)
Urban	−.04 (.19)	−.28 (.18)
Constant	−.77* (.46)	−1.19** (.40)
N	465	476

Notes: * $p \leq .1$; ** $p \leq .05$; *** $p \leq .001$ (two-tailed test). Entries are probit regression coefficients and the standard errors are in parentheses. All variables are recoded onto a 0 to 1 scale, with higher values indicating more opposition to health care reform.

TABLE 4C. *The Priming Effect of Emotions on Limited Government*

	Opposition to Health Care Reform (Baseline=Relaxed) B (s.e.)
Anger Condition*Limited Government	−.13 (.60)
Fear Condition*Limited Government	.30 (.62)
Anger Condition	−.02 (.39)
Fear Condition	−.35 (.39)
Limited Government	3.10*** (.44)
Income	−.75** (.33)
South	.34** (.13)
Employed	.14 (.18)
Political Discussion	−.67 (.41)
Own Home	.22 (.17)
Urban	−.27 (.17)
Constant	−1.18*** (.34)
N	718

Notes: * p ≤ .1; ** p ≤ .05; *** p≤ .001 (two-tailed test). Entries are probit regression coefficients and the standard errors are in parentheses. All variables are recoded onto a 0 to 1 scale, with higher values indicating more opposition to health care reform.

5

The Tea Party's Angry Rhetoric and the 2010 Midterm Elections

After losing the battle over health care reform, Tea Party activists turned their efforts to the November 2010 midterm elections. Frustrated with Democrats, the GOP establishment, and government – more generally – Tea Party groups like FreedomWorks and Tea Party Express decided to endorse their own Republican candidates for Congress. The overall message of these candidates was simple – to take back America – a message that evoked passionate enthusiasm and anger from many supporters of the Tea Party movement. On the surface, some of their suggestions seemed radical and even revolutionary, but when one digs deeper, they appear merely to be new variants of long-standing conservative arguments about the role of the federal government, religion, and social welfare programs. Nonetheless, these candidates stood out from the rest in how they packaged these issues to the American public. Their attacks on Obama and his fellow Democrats were often venomous, ferocious, and confrontational. For instance, many on the left considered Sharron Angle's (candidate from Nevada backed by the Tea Party) campaign tactics as extreme and potentially dangerous. Ms. Angle aired an attack ad that linked Senate Majority Leader Harry Reid to threatening images of Latinos. The ad included photos of gang-like Latinos and warned voters that "waves of illegal aliens [stream] across our border, joining violent gangs, forcing families to live in fear" while "Reid voted to give illegal aliens social security benefits, tax breaks and college tuition."[1] Her rhetoric on religion and politics was just as intense. In an interview with a Christian radio station, Angle stated, "these programs ... that Obama has going with Reid and Pelosi ... are all entitlement programs built to make government our God."[2] These gut-level emotional appeals seemed to resonate with a movement that was far outside the mainstream of politics.

As illustrated in newspaper headlines, the blogosphere, and political talk shows, the Tea Party's contentious rhetoric appealed to a constituency thoroughly enraged about health care reform, government bailouts, a woeful economy, and most important, Barack Obama, a black man, as their president. The dominant narrative of the 2010 midterm election was that Americans were angry, but as Arianna Huffington of the *Huffington Post* said, "The Tea Party is angry! Really, *really* angry."[3] For example, in a *NY Times*/CBS poll conducted in April 2010, respondents were asked how they felt about the way things were going in Washington. Ninety-four percent of Tea Party supporters described feeling angry and dissatisfied.[4] One example of this deep-seated anger is when thousands of Tea Partiers descended on the U.S. Capitol, right before the midterm elections, to express their anger toward government. Not only were they angry about "ObamaCare," as Tea Partiers called it, but also government spending, illegal immigration, and the building of a mosque near Ground Zero. For example, angry protestors at a rally, organized by FreedomWorks, held up signs that read "Redistribute My Work Ethic," "Uncle Sam wants you to speak English," and "Obama Creates Jobs at Ground Zero" over a picture of a mosque.[5] Those on the left suggested that these offensive signs indicated that the Tea Party's contentious rhetoric was inciting bigotry.

For example, the National Association for the Advancement of Colored People (NAACP) released a report – shortly before the midterm elections – that accused the Tea Party of using racially charged language. More specifically, it stated that Tea Party groups "have given a platform to anti-Semites, racists and bigots" and "unleashed a still inchoate political movement who are in the numerical majority, angry middle-class white people who believe their country, their nation, has been taken from them."[6] But are the NAACP's accusations correct? Was the Tea Party heightening white racist attitudes? And if so, what about their rhetoric stimulated racial animosity? This chapter examines if the anger from the Tea Party's harsh and extreme campaign rhetoric increased the role racial considerations played in whites' voting decisions. One way to test this proposition is by examining whether racial predispositions were more likely to be amplified in congressional races with a Tea Party candidate than in races with no such candidate, and to see if increases in the prominence of racial considerations can be linked to anger. Thus, the main priority of this chapter is to investigate if anger exacerbates the impact of racial attitudes on congressional vote choice – but in Tea Party races as opposed to congressional races with no Tea Party candidate.[7]

TEA PARTY MOVEMENT: SELLING AND DRINKING THE TEA

Sharron Angle was not the only Tea Party candidate whose campaign antics were considered gut wrenching and emotionally charged. A significant number of other candidates backed by the Tea Party used similar strategies to appeal to their conservative base. Renee Ellmers, a registered nurse from North Carolina, was a first-time Tea Party candidate hoping to change the political culture in Washington DC. Angry over the new health care law and the impact it would have on her and her husband's medical practice, she decided to challenge the long-time Democratic incumbent, Bob Etheridge, for North Carolina's 2nd District congressional seat. With Etheridge typically winning his district by more than 60 percent of the vote, journalists close to the election believed that Ellmers faced a tough uphill battle. In an attempt to appeal to Tea Party supporters, she aired a controversial attack ad that linked Etheridge to the building of an Islamic community center near Ground Zero. The ad states, "After Muslims conquered Jerusalem, and Cordoba, and Constantinople they built victory mosques.... And, now, they want to build a mosque by Ground Zero. Where does Bob Etheridge stand? He won't say. Won't speak out. Won't take a stand." Then Ellmers appears on the screen and states, "the terrorists haven't won and we should tell them in plain English, no, there will never be a mosque near Ground Zero."[8] Her offensive attack on Etheridge was intended to question his patriotism and to arouse disdain for his alleged support of terrorists. In the end, Ellmers defeated Etheridge by the narrowest of margins – 1 percent of the vote.

Rick Barber, a Tea Party-backed candidate running for Alabama's 2nd District congressional seat, used similar emotionally loaded language and imagery to attack the Islamic community center. In one ad, Barber criticized the Obama administration for calling 9/11 "a man-caused disaster." With a look of anger and disgust on his face, Barber stated about the opening of the Islamic center: "[T]his is unacceptable. There is a difference between tolerance and surrendering ... if we don't start electing leaders that are able to recognize the enemy, call them by name, and stand up against them – then surrendering is exactly what we are doing." Barber's hot, fiery rhetoric was most notable in his racially charged ad that equated Obama's economic policies to slavery. Speaking about the evils of taxation, he stated, "Hey, Abe, if someone's forced to work for months to pay taxes so a total stranger can get a free meal, medical procedure or a bailout, what's that called? What's it called when one man is forced to work for another?" The screen then zooms in on a Lincoln impersonator who says, "Slavery." The ad was an attempt to align Obama and his policies with enslaving whites. Although this racially inflammatory rhetoric was not the norm among Tea Party candidates, it illustrated that a segment of them was willing to use explicitly racial messages to motivate their base. This extreme rhetoric proved unsuccessful; Barber lost his runoff race to Republican Martha Roby. Other Tea Party candidates took a more subtle approach, one that resonated with many Tea Party members – us versus them.

Theda Skocpol and Vanessa Williamson came to a similar opinion in their impressive book entitled *The Tea Party and the Remaking of Republican Conservatism.* They argue the reason that Tea Partiers support large-scale government spending programs like social security and not "ObamaCare" is because the former is seen as going to people who have earned these benefits (Tea Partiers) while the latter is considered as going to freeloaders who have placed an unfair burden on taxpayers. "A well-marked distinction between workers and nonworkers – between productive citizens and freeloaders – is central to the Tea Party worldview and conception of America" (2012, 65). Many Republican candidates backed by the Tea Party presented this same view to voters by attacking "ObamaCare" and by criticizing the federal government's intrusion into their lives. Paul Gosar, a Tea Party-backed candidate running for Congress in Arizona, told a reporter, if elected, he would adhere "to the words of the founding fathers [which] means putting the government role in health care ... on the table for a constitutional examination." Rand Paul, a Republican Senate candidate backed by the Tea Party, made waves stating that private companies should not be required to comply with civil rights laws. Although he asserted that institutional racism was wrong, he felt that the federal government overreached and impinged on the rights of private owners in the Civil Rights Act of 1964 and the American Disabilities Act of 1990.

This kind of rhetoric seized on the passion of Tea Partiers – who favored smaller government and turning back the clock in America – to the days of Samuel Adams, Benjamin Franklin, and George Washington. But what do Tea Partiers really mean by taking America back to the days of our founding fathers? Basically, they mean restoring the country to when whites had all the privileges and minority groups like blacks were second-class citizens. Because it's against the racial norm to espouse racial animosity, Tea Partiers hide behind issues like the size of government to camouflage their racist convictions. For instance, they are quick to demonize "ObamaCare" – criticizing its high costs to taxpayers – but favor social security, which makes up 20 percent of the federal budget.[9] A large number of Tea Partiers support policies, such as social security, that protect their in-group (whites) and want to eliminate public programs intended to help the out-group (people of color), such as health care. Nick Winter agrees, stating "the framing of Social Security in political discourse has associated it symbolically with race. The linkages are subtle and symbolic, and they serve to associate Social Security with *whiteness* in a mirror image of the association of welfare with blackness. In turn, these associations have racialized white opinion on the program" (2006, 400).

Delaware Senate Tea Party-backed candidate Christine O'Donnell received a lot of attention for her extreme rhetoric, particularly on mixing religion and politics. Even before her 2010 Senate bid, O'Donnell was known for her strict religious beliefs. For example, in an MTV documentary, she said, "it's not enough to be abstinent with other people, you should also have to be abstinent alone. The Bible says that lust in your heart is committing adultery, so you can't masturbate without lust."[10] In a bitter debate at Widener University Law School, she attacked her democratic opponent, Chris Coons, for opposing the teaching of creationism in public schools – repeatedly asking Coons, "where in the constitution is separation of church and state?"[11] Although O'Donnell aroused passionate enthusiasm from ultraconservative groups, some from the GOP establishment feared that she was doing more harm than good. Karl Rove, an oft-acclaimed GOP mastermind, criticized Christine O'Donnell's outlandish comments and questionable background, which he felt would ultimately hurt the Republican's chances of winning the Delaware Senate seat.[12] Instead of Tea Party candidates being fixated on displaying their anger at the Obama administration, some Republicans felt, they should have devoted their attention to maximizing the number of Republicans in Congress. Essentially, the Republican establishment criticized the Tea Party movement for not being more strategic. But Cho, Gimpel, and Shaw (2012) argue that the movement's expressive (not strategic) nature demonstrates that it's not just an "AstroTurf" phenomenon. In other words, neither billionaire Tea Party backers like the Koch brothers, disgruntled Republican elites, nor Fox News executives are pulling the strings of this grassroots movement. Instead, Cho and her colleagues suggest, it is a real grassroots rebellion. For instance, looking at the geography of Tea Party events, they find that expressive factors (e.g., rate of home foreclosures) are a more consistent predictor of Tea Party activism than strategic ones (e.g., open House or Senate seat).

Since the movement began, pundits and scholars have vigorously debated the composition of the Tea Party. The left often portrays Tea Partiers as old white racists. On the other hand, the movement itself claims only to be concerned with libertarian principles – smaller government and fiscal responsibility. Recent evidence demonstrates that supporters of the Tea Party embody both characteristics. In the Multi-State Survey on Race and Politics (MSSRP), Parker and Barreto (2013) find that Americans who are older, white, Republican, conservative, highly religious, favor smaller government, and hold racist attitudes tend to support the Tea Party. Using the 2010 American National Election Study (ANES), Abramowitz (2011) finds that supporters of the Tea Party differ from Republicans in dramatic ways. Tea Partiers are more likely to identify strongly with the Republican Party, hold conservative political views, have a strong dislike for Obama and his policies, and score higher on the symbolic racism scale than the average Republican. Because the Tea Party is an ultraright-wing element of the Republican Party, it's not surprising that Tea Party candidates would use such extreme and emotionally packed rhetoric to motivate their base.

As Election Day 2010 ended, Americans woke up the next morning to find that Republicans had made historic gains in the midterm congressional elections. They captured sixty-three seats in the House – giving control back to Republicans – and gained five seats in the Senate. It is usually a given that the president's party will lose seats in the midterm elections. But this loss was the largest by the in-party in more than seven decades (Busch 2010). No one can deny that the energetic Tea Party movement greatly contributed to a Republican victory. Of the sixty-three House seats Republicans won, thirty-two of them were won by Tea Party-backed candidates. In the Senate, Tea Party-backed candidates won in Florida, Kentucky, Pennsylvania, Utah, and Wisconsin. Karpowitz and colleagues (2011) examined the impact the Tea Party had on the 2010 midterm elections and found that a Tea Party endorsement did lead to an increase in the Republican vote share. Overall, it seems that the Tea Party greatly contributed to Republicans' victory in the 2010 midterm elections.

An important question is whether the steady diet of angry rhetoric by Tea Party candidates increased the role of race in voters' decision making. Did Rick Barber's highly emotional claims – like telling voters to "gather your armies" – create the right conditions for race to bubble to the surface? The argument put forward in this book is that anger is the emotional underpinning of contemporary racial attitudes. So when anger is experienced, it should increase the use of race as a criterion in evaluating relevant policy and candidate preferences. Thus, I expect that the angry campaign rhetoric from Tea Party candidates created an atmosphere for racial considerations to loom large in many whites' voting decisions.

In this chapter, I examine how emotions (i.e., anger and fear) influence whites' racial predispositions in congressional races where a Tea Party candidate is running for office versus races with no such candidate. I hypothesize that when a Tea Party candidate is on the ballot anger should increase support for Republicans among racially prejudiced whites. On the other hand, when a Tea Party candidate is not on the ballot, I do not expect to find anger to have a strong effect on whites' negative racial attitudes. Furthermore, I expect anger to boost support for Democrats among racial liberals residing in congressional districts (or states) with a Tea Party candidate. And again when there is no Tea Party candidate running for office, anger should have no effect on racial liberals. As a result, in Tea Party races, anger should enhance racial conservatives' support for Republican candidates and increase racial liberals' support for Democratic candidates.

But why should anger enhance the impact of racial considerations in Tea Party races and not in non-Tea Party races? The reason is that the confrontational rhetoric of Tea Party candidates racialized people's voting decisions. We often saw the rhetoric of Tea Party candidates couched in the language of us versus them. Their goal was to protect the interest of hardworking Americans (i.e., whites) and fight policies perceived to benefit undeserving individuals (i.e., minorities). Given that I expect anger to increase the impact of racial attitudes on relevant political opinions – such as racialized candidate evaluations – we should only see the role of race becoming more important in Tea Party races.

Conversely, I expect fear to have no effect on race predispositions in either Tea Party races or non-Tea Party races. This effect occurs because fear is not strongly tied to whites' beliefs about race. Some might argue that the Tea Party candidates' angry rhetoric was simply promoting race-neutral conservative principles like smaller government, fiscal responsibility, and states' rights. If so, anger should also increase support for Republican candidates among self-identified conservatives (or Republicans) in races with a Tea Party candidate. Because I argue that no particular emotion is strongly linked to race-neutral principles, my prediction is that none of the emotions should boost the impact of this belief system on congressional vote choice.

2010 ANES OF EVALUATIONS OF GOVERNMENT AND SOCIETY STUDY

To determine if anger enhances the effect of racial attitudes on congressional vote choice in Tea Party races, I use data from the October wave of the 2010 American National Election Study of the Evaluation of Government and Society Study (EGSS). The sample includes 1,151 American voting-aged citizens and 863 whites. The October survey is one of several cross-sectional studies the ANES conducted in 2010, 2011, and 2012. The survey was conducted through Knowledge

Networks, an Internet survey company, from October 8 to October 19, 2010. Respondents are members of the Knowledge Network panel and are recruited by telephone through random digit dialing. Those who do not have access to the Internet are provided access through Web TV, free of charge.

Measures

My dependent variable is congressional vote choice. The specific question for House elections asked: "Who did you vote for in the election for the U.S. House of Representatives?" With regards to the Senate, the question asked: "Who did you vote for in the election for the U.S. Senate?" Both variables were recoded where 1=voted for the Republican candidate and 0=voted for the Democratic candidate.[13] The 2010 ANES (EGSS) is ideal because it includes my main explanatory variables such as self-report measures of emotion (e.g., anger and fear), symbolic racism, political ideology, and party identification. To measure emotion, I used the following question, "Generally speaking, how do you feel about the way things are going in the country these days? How angry/afraid/worried?"[14] The response options included "extremely," "very," "moderately," "a little or not at all."[15] Ideally, emotion measures about the congressional candidates or the campaign would have been better. Remember, my argument is that the angry campaign rhetoric from Tea Party candidates should increase the role of race in whites' voting decisions. Thus, these general measures of emotion present a very conservative test of my hypotheses. To measure symbolic racism, I used Kinder and Sander's standard four-item battery. I also included party identification and political ideology in my model.

At the time of the midterm elections, most Americans were still feeling the effect of a woeful economy; therefore, I control for voters' perception of the status of our economy. The specific question is: "Now thinking about the economy in the country as a whole, would you say that as compared to one year ago, the nation's economy is now better, about the same, or worse?" The variable was recoded where 1=worse, .5=the same, and 0=better.[16] I also include competitiveness as a control variable. My suspicion is that Tea Party races are more contentious than other contests, and another possible predictor of contentiousness is competitiveness. That is, one might expect more confrontational campaign rhetoric to occur in very close races.[17] The other control variables for my model of vote choice include education, income, age, Southern resident, gender, and Internet access.[18]

The 2010 ANES (EGSS) also collected information on the state and congressional district that respondents resided in. This information allows me to identify those congressional races where a Tea Party candidate is running for office. One can use several sources to identify Tea Party candidates. I chose to use the *NY Times* report.[19] Although any list identifying Tea Party candidates would undoubtedly be inexact, the *NY Times* report was the most explicit in the criteria it used to identify a Tea Party candidate.[20] The *NY Times* indexed Tea Party candidates based on several criteria such as: if the candidate entered politics through the Tea Party movement, is receiving support from local Tea Party groups, or shares the ideology of the movement. Most Tea Party candidates were endorsed by national groups like FreedomWorks, Tea Party Express, and Tea Party Nation or by conservative activist Sarah Palin. In total, the *NY Times* identified Tea Party candidates in one hundred twenty-nine House races and nine Senate races.

SENATE RESULTS

My main expectation is that the confrontational rhetoric by Tea Party candidates provided a venue for anger to augment the role race played in white support for congressional candidates. I predict that anger should increase the impact of racial attitudes on vote choice in Tea Party races as opposed to non-Tea Party races. More specifically, anger should increase support for Republican candidates among racially prejudiced whites. Furthermore, in these same electoral contests, anger should increase support for Democratic candidates among those low in symbolic racism. When it comes to non-Tea Party races, anger should not affect racial attitudes. My first set of analyses examines whites' support for Senate Republican candidates. Because vote choice is a dummy variable, all analyses are run using a probit regression model. I regressed *Senate Vote Choice* on *Anger, Fear, Symbolic Racism*, and the interactions between these specific emotions and racial attitude, controlling for *Ideology, Party Identification, Income, Age, South, Gender, Education, Internet Access, Worse Economy*, and

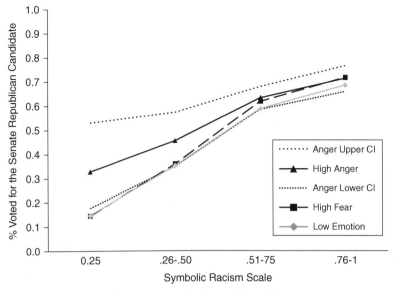

FIGURE 5.1. Probability of voting for Senate Republicans across emotions as symbolic racism changes for the overall sample of whites.

Note: These are the predicted probabilities calculated from the results in column 1 of Table 5A with 90 percent confidence intervals around the effect of anger. I calculate the probabilities by manipulating the emotion variables while holding all the other independent variables at their own values observed in the data and then averaging over all of the cases.

Competitiveness. Before turning to races with a Tea Party-endorsed candidate, I first look at the effect of emotion on racial attitudes for the whole sample of whites. This allows me to see if anger heightens racial attitudes regardless if there is a Tea Party candidate seeking office. The probit regression coefficients are reported in column 1 of Table 5A in the appendix. Because of the fact that these are nonlinear models with interaction terms, presenting the predicted probabilities is much more informative.

Figure 5.1 is the converted predicted probabilities from the results in column 1 of Table 5A. The figure shows the probability of voting for a Republican Senate candidate at varying levels of symbolic racism conditional on emotional intensity. The thick solid black line represents those who experience a high level of anger. The figure also displays a 90 percent confidence interval, in dotted lines, around the effect of anger. The

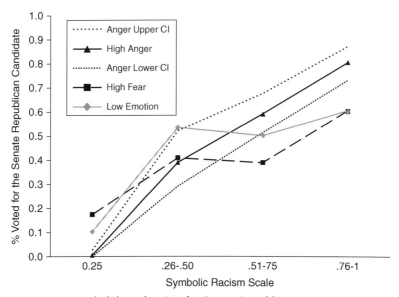

FIGURE 5.2. Probability of voting for Senate Republicans across emotions as symbolic racism changes in Tea Party races.

Note: These are the predicted probabilities calculated from the results in column 2 of Table 5A with 90 percent confidence intervals around the effect of anger.

long dashed black line represents those who experience a high level of fear, and the thick solid grey line represents people who experience a low level of fear and anger (low emotion hereafter).[21] The figure shows that whites high in symbolic racism and extremely angry are not more likely to vote for Republicans than comparable whites who experience high levels of fear or low emotion. For those low in symbolic racism, I find that anger makes them less supportive of Democrats in comparison to racial liberals who experience high levels of fear and low emotion. Overall, the figure demonstrates that anger doesn't enhance the effect of racial attitudes on Senate vote choice for the overall sample.

On the other hand, Figure 5.2 (Tea Party races) shows strong support for my hypotheses. We see that whites high in symbolic racism and extremely angry (black line) are about twenty-one percentage points more likely to have voted Republican than comparable whites who experience high levels of fear (long dashed line) or low levels of emotion (grey line). The figure shows that the effect of anger on whites

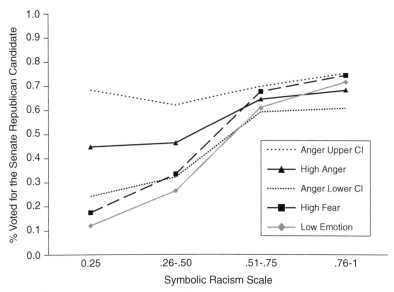

FIGURE 5.3. Probability of voting for Senate Republicans across emotions as symbolic racism changes in non-Tea Party races.

Note: These are the predicted probabilities calculated from the results in column 3 of Table 5A with 90 percent confidence intervals around the effect of anger.

high in symbolic racism is statistically different from fear and low emotion.[22] Moving to whites low in symbolic racism and extremely angry, we see they are seventeen percentage points more likely to have voted Democratic than those experiencing high levels of fear. When comparing racial liberals who are extremely angry to those reporting low levels of emotion, a smaller difference appears – ten percentage points.[23] Overall, the figure shows that eighty-one percentage points separate strong racial conservatives and strong racial liberals in their support for Republican candidates. And this difference is almost twice as large as the racial polarization effect produced by high levels of fear and low levels of emotion.[24]

Figure 5.3 shows the results for the non-Tea Party races. We see that the line for anger is relatively flat. It shows that the effect of anger on Senate vote choice is not statistically different from fear and low emotion among racially prejudiced whites. That is, angry racial conservatives are not more likely to have voted Republican than comparable whites who experience fear or low emotion. The figure also demonstrates that high levels of anger decrease racial liberals' support for Democrats when compared to similar whites reporting high levels of fear and low emotion. However, the large confidence interval around the effect of anger suggests that this estimate may be somewhat imprecise. In sum, the Senate results provided strong evidence that anger exacerbated the impact of racial attitudes on vote choice in Tea Party races as opposed to non-Tea Party races.

HOUSE RESULTS

We now move to the House electoral contests. We begin by looking at the overall sample of whites.[25] Figure 5.4 converts the probit coefficients in column 1 of Table 5B in the appendix into predicted probabilities. The thick solid black line represents high levels of anger. The 90 percent confidence interval around the effect of anger is represented

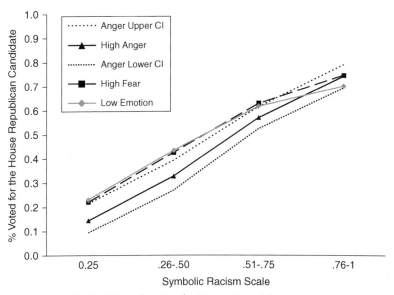

FIGURE 5.4. Probability of voting for House Republicans across emotions as symbolic racism changes for the overall sample of whites.

Note: These are the predicted probabilities calculated from the results in column 1 of Table 5B with 90 percent confidence intervals around the effect of anger.

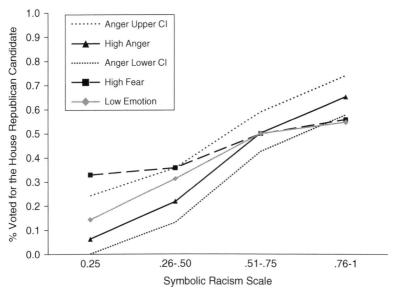

FIGURE 5.5. Probability of voting for House Republicans across emotions as symbolic racism changes in Tea Party races.

Note: These are the predicted probabilities calculated from the results in column 2 of Table 5B with 90 percent confidence intervals around the effect of anger.

in dotted lines. The long dashed line represents high levels of fear, and the thick solid grey line represents low levels of emotion. The figure displays the interactions visually and shows that the effect of anger is not statistically different from fear and low emotion at high levels of symbolic racism. However, the figure shows that extreme anger increases support for Democratic candidates among racial liberals, and this effect is statistically different from low emotion.[26] Thus, regardless if racial liberals reside in a district with a Tea Party candidate, anger pushes them to vote for House Democrats.

My main prediction is that anger should enhance the effect of racial attitudes on vote choice in Tea Party races as opposed to non-Tea Party races. Figure 5.5 provides support for this hypothesis. The figure shows that whites high in symbolic racism and extremely angry are ten percentage points more likely to support the Republican candidate than comparable whites who experienced high levels of fear or low levels of emotion. For those low in symbolic racism and angry, they are eight

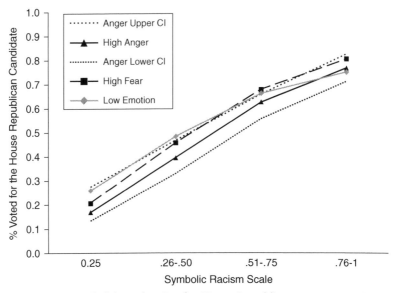

FIGURE 5.6. Probability of voting for House Republicans across emotions as symbolic racism changes in non-Tea Party races.
Note: These are the predicted probabilities calculated from the results in column 3 of Table 5B with 90 percent confidence intervals around the effect of anger.

points more likely to support the Democratic candidate than are racial liberal whites who experience low emotion. The difference between anger and fear among racial liberals is even greater. In sum, these results show that among extremely angry whites changing from least to most racially resentful increases preference for House Republicans by sixty-five percentage points. This effect is twice as large as the effect produced by fear and about twenty percentage points larger than the effect produced by low emotion. Moving to non-Tea Party races in Figure 5.6, we don't find that anger increases the impact of racial predispositions on vote choice. The figure shows that the effect of anger doesn't differ from fear and low emotion for either racial conservatives or racial liberals.

Perhaps anger not only increases the impact of racial predispositions on vote choice in Tea Party races, but also has a similar effect on nonracial predispositions. To determine if the effect of anger is unique to racial attitudes, I also examine its impact on political ideology.[27]

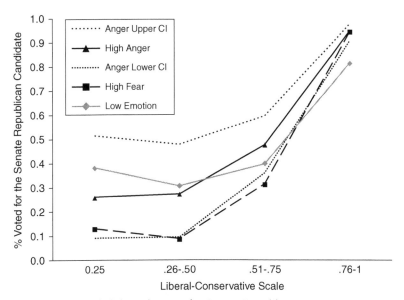

FIGURE 5.7. Probability of voting for Senate Republicans across emotions as political ideology changes in Tea Party races.
Note: These are the predicted probabilities calculated from the results in column 2 of Table 5C with 90 percent confidence intervals around the effect of anger.

The probit regression coefficients are presented in the appendix in Table 5C. Figure 5.7 displays the Senate results. The first thing that stands out is how high support for Republicans is among strong conservatives regardless of their emotional intensity. Looking closer at the figure, we see that political conservatives experiencing extreme anger or fear are more supportive of Republicans than those who experience low emotion. Looking at the House in Figure 5.8, I find similar results. That is, political conservatives who experience extreme fear or anger are more likely to support Republican candidates than comparable conservatives who experience low levels of anger and fear. Therefore, negative affect, rather than anger itself, increases conservatives' willingness to vote for Republican candidates.

In summary, the findings show that anger brings racial attitudes to bear on vote choice in Tea Party races. In other words, it pushes racial liberals and racial conservatives further apart in their vote choices. On the other hand, in non-Tea Party races, anger doesn't produce this

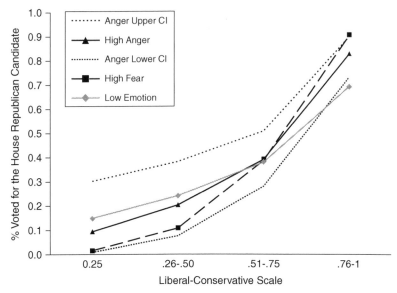

FIGURE 5.8. Probability of voting for House Republicans across emotions as political ideology changes in Tea Party races.

Note: These are the predicted probabilities calculated from the results in column 1 of Table 5C with 90 percent confidence intervals around the effect of anger.

racial polarization effect. Furthermore, fear has no effect on racial predispositions whatsoever in either Tea Party races or non-Tea party races. The results also show that negative affect (i.e., fear and anger) increases the effect of nonracial predispositions on vote choice in Tea Party races.

RALLYING THE TROOPS

During the 2010 midterm elections, Tea Partiers mobilized thousands of Americans to rally in front of the U.S. Capitol to protest against health care reform and government bailouts. Conservatives who traveled to the capitol wanted their voices heard. They distrusted the federal government and felt immediate action was needed. Thus far, I have demonstrated that anger increases the role of race in whites' evaluation of congressional candidates in Tea Party races. Still, did the angry rhetoric from Tea Party candidates also mobilize people to participate in politics? And if so, who was most likely affected? Research has shown that anger plays an important role in mobilization (Valentino et al. 2011). Furthermore, scholars have shown that anger helps explain why people with strong group attachments are more likely to participate than individuals without such strong attachments (Groenendyk and Banks 2013; Mackie, Devos, and Smith 2000).

As a result, I am interested in whether anger boosts participation among racial conservatives. At Tea Party rallies across the country, protestors held up racially offensive signs. Perhaps the angry rhetoric from Tea Party candidates mobilized racial conservatives to attend political rallies and express their dissatisfaction with the federal government. To test this prediction, I examine one form of participation – *attending a rally*.[28] The specific question asks respondents "During the past twelve months, have you gone to a political speech, march, rally or demonstration, or have you not done this in the past twelve months?"[29] The results are presented in Figure 5.9.[30] The figure shows anger increases the probability of attending a rally by 18 percent among

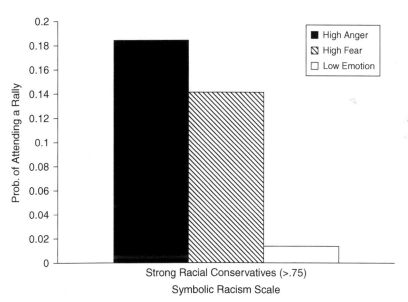

FIGURE 5.9. Probability of attending a rally across emotions among racial conservatives in Tea Party races.

Note: These are the predicted probabilities calculated from the results in column 1 of Table 5D.

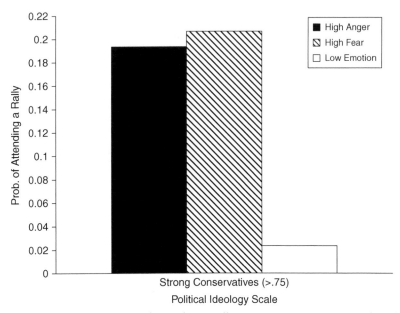

FIGURE 5.10. Probability of attending a rally across emotions among political conservatives in Tea Party races.

Note: These are the predicted probabilities calculated from the results in column 2 of Table 5D.

those high in symbolic racism. Given that the probability of attending a rally among racial conservatives experiencing low levels of emotion (anger and fear) is only 1 percent, the effect of anger is substantively large. That is, angry racial conservatives are about 17 percent more likely to attend a rally than are racial conservatives who experience low levels of emotion. Looking at the figure, we see that extreme fear also increases the probability of attending a rally (14%). This effect is consistent with research showing fear can also increase people's level of participation.[31] Nonetheless, anger has a slightly larger effect (four point difference) on attending a rally than fear.

Anger may not have only mobilized racial conservatives to participate, but political conservatives as well. Figure 5.10 supports this prediction.[32] Anger increases political conservatives' probability of attending a rally by 19 percent. A similar effect occurs for fear, increasing the probability by 20 percent. All in all, I find that anger and fear boost the probability of racial conservatives and political conservatives attending a political rally.[33] These results suggest that the Tea Party's emotional rhetoric was effective in getting its base to participate in politics.

CONCLUSION

Throughout the 2010 midterm elections, a bitter debate occurred among pundits, politicians, and groups such as the NAACP as to whether the Tea Party was fostering racism or merely expressing libertarian principles. Those on the left accused the leaders within the movement of using racially charged language to appeal to their ultra-right constituency. Supporters of the Tea Party disagreed in the strongest possible terms, arguing that their main priorities were limiting the role of the federal government and advocating for fiscal responsibility. This chapter set out to test these competing perspectives by examining the impact of emotions on racial predispositions and nonracial predispositions in Tea Party races. The results showed that when racial conservatives were extremely angry, they were more likely to vote for Republican congressional candidates than those who experienced fear or low levels of emotion. Likewise, racial liberals that were extremely angry were more supportive of Democratic candidates than those who experienced fear or low levels of emotion (in the case of the Senate). On the other hand, fear did not enhance the effect of racial attitudes on vote choice. Thus, in Tea Party races, anger racially polarized white support for congressional candidates by as much as forty percentage points in comparison to those who experienced fear or low levels of anger and fear. In congressional races with no Tea Party-backed candidate, the effect of anger on whites' racial predispositions did not differ from fear and low emotion.

Overall, the findings from this chapter demonstrate that anger brings race to bear on whites' voting decisions in Tea Party races. It is not that anger increases the effect of racial attitudes on any type of political judgment. For example, in Chapter 2, anger didn't increase the impact of symbolic racism on support for the Iraq War. This effect indicates that the policy or candidate under evaluation has to be linked to race (explicitly or implicitly) for anger to increase the effect of racial considerations on political evaluations. This would explain why race played a substantial role in whites' voting decisions in Tea

Party races, rather than non-Tea Party races, because the atmosphere in these contests was racially charged – explicitly and implicitly.

The results also revealed that race-neutral principles were strongly affected by negative emotions. For instance, strong conservative identifiers who expressed an extreme level of anger and fear were more likely to have voted for Senate Republicans than those who experienced a low level of emotion. Similarly, in terms of the House, high levels of fear and anger had a larger effect on conservatives than low emotion. What is clear from these findings is that negative emotions strongly benefited Republican candidates in Tea Party races. Not only did negative emotions increase support for Republican candidates (among political conservatives), but they also mobilized racial conservatives and political conservatives to participate in politics.

.The issue of busing is another example of Americans submersed in an emotionally and racially charged environment. The main purpose of busing was to assign and transport children (white and black) to schools in such a manner as to redress racially segregated schools. During the 1970s, school districts across the country implemented busing programs, which created a firestorm of opposition from parents and other members of the community. The most notable resistance to busing was in Boston from a group called Restore Our Alienated Rights (ROAR). In 1974, while a group of black students was being bused to South Boston High School (a predominantly white school), protestors greeted the group with racial epithets and hurled bottles and rocks at the bus – breaking the bus's windows. Outside of the school, a rowdy crowd of five hundred had gathered – yelling "Go Home Nigger" and "Turn the Bus Over."[34] This deep-seated anger, overshadowing Boston on the issue of busing, created conditions for racism to flourish. Therefore, when the political environment evokes passion and race, we can expect anger to increase the relationship between whites' racial attitudes and race-related political opinions and their willingness to act on these beliefs.

Besides the Tea Party's gut-wrenching emotional appeals, some of its rhetoric was pretty explicit. For instance, there was Rick Barber's ad that linked Obama's economic policies to slavery – implying that the president intended to enslave whites. The findings from Chapter 3 would suggest that anger from an explicit racial appeal should dampen the effect of race. As a result, how might the findings from this chapter be reconciled with those from Chapter 3? One explanation is that race may have played a larger role in whites' vote choice because of Barber's explicit racial language. Hutchings and his colleagues (2010) argue that explicit racial appeals are effective in certain areas like the South because this region has not yet fully embraced the norm of racial equality. Perhaps Rick Barber's explicit racial appeal was effective at drawing out racism because his constituency resided in the Deep South (Alabama), a region known to have an ugly history on race. Under these conditions, we might see anger from an explicit racial appeal activate whites' racial predispositions. Still, Barber's strategy to explicitly evoke race was ineffective because he lost the Republican primary.

MEASUREMENT APPENDIX

Party identification is measured with the standard seven-point party identification scale. This measure is captured with a three-item, skip pattern design: (1) "Generally speaking, do you usually think of yourself as a Republican, a Democrat, and Independent, or what?" (2) [If R answers Rep or Dem] "Would you call yourself a strong Republican/Democrat or a not very strong Republican/Democrat?" [3] [If R answers Independent] "Do you think of yourself as closer to the Republican Party or the Democratic Party? The variable is coded onto a 0 to 1 scale, where the highest value equals strong Republican. (Mean=.48, S.D.=35, Min=0, Max=1).

Ideology is measured with the standard seven-point liberal-conservative scale. The specific question asked, "When it comes to politics, how would you describe yourself?" The response options ranged from "very liberal" to "very conservative." (Mean=.55, S.D.=.28, Min=0, Max=1).

Gender is a dummy variable, where 0=female and 1=male. (Mean=.48, S.D.=.50, Min=0, Max=1).

South is a dummy variable, where 0=non-Southern resident and 1=Southern resident. The Southern states are Alabama, Arkansas, Delaware, Washington DC, Florida, Georgia, Kentucky, Louisiana, Maryland, Mississippi, North Carolina, Oklahoma, South Carolina,

Tennessee, Texas, Virginia, and West Virginia. (Mean=.37, S.D.=.48, Min=0, Max=1).

Education is coded onto a 0 to 1 scale, where the higher value corresponds to a postgraduate degree. (Mean=.72, S.D.=.15, Min=0, Max=1).

Age is a continuous variable and ranges from eighteen to one hundred years old. (Mean=49, S.D.=17)

Income is coded onto a 0 to 1 scale, where the higher value corresponds to the highest income bracket, which. (Mean=.57, S.D.=.23, Min=0, Max=1).

Internet Access is recoded where 1=the household has Internet and 0=it does. (Mean=.76, S.D.=.43).

APPENDIX: RESULTS

TABLE 5A. *The Impact of Emotion and Symbolic Racism on Preference for Senate Republicans*

	Republican Vote Choice	Republican Vote Choice: (Tea Party Candidate)	Republican Vote Choice: (No Tea Party Candidate)
	B (s.e.)	B (s.e.)	B (s.e.)
Anger*Symbolic Racism	−1.30 (1.15)	7.64** (2.52)	−3.08** (1.32)
Fear*Symbolic Racism	.77 (1.39)	−3.01 (2.64)	1.09 (1.64)
Anger	1.15 (.79)	−3.92** (1.63)	2.20** (.95)
Fear	−.51 (.97)	.57 (1.68)	−.47 (1.09)
Symbolic Racism	.32 (.88)	−2.52 (1.63)	1.25 (.84)
Ideology	1.19*** (.36)	2.34** (.79)	.97** (.43)

	Republican Vote Choice	Republican Vote Choice: (Tea Party Candidate)	Republican Vote Choice: (No Tea Party Candidate)
	B (s.e.)	B (s.e.)	B (s.e.)
Party Identification	2.64*** (.29)	3.45*** (.52)	2.65*** (.36)
Income	1.15** (.43)	.84 (.89)	1.27** (.50)
Age	.000 (.004)	−.013 (.009)	−.004 (.005)
South	.09 (.19)	−.79* (.45)	.16 (.24)
Gender	−.13 (.16)	−.22 (.29)	−.07 (.19)
Education	−.05 (.59)	−1.59 (1.20)	.19 (.71)
Worse Economy	1.06** (.35)	1.47** (.69)	1.07** (.41)
Internet Access	−.29 (.21)	−.55 (.45)	−.36 (.24)
Competitiveness	−.34** (.17)	−.98** (.43)	−.30 (.19)
Constant	−1.30** (1.15)	−2.64 (1.76)	−3.65*** (.19)
N	595	160	435

Notes: * p ≤ .1; ** p ≤ .05; *** p ≤ .001 (two-tailed test). Entries are probit regression coefficients and the standard errors are in parentheses. All variables are recoded onto a 0 to 1 scale, with higher values indicating respondent voted for Senate Republicans.

TABLE 5B. *The Impact of Emotion and Symbolic Racism on Preference for House Republicans*

	Republican Vote Choice	Republican Vote Choice: (Tea Party Candidate)	Republican Vote Choice: (No Tea Party Candidate)
	B (**s.e.**)	**B** (**s.e.**)	**B** (**s.e.**)
Anger*Symbolic Racism	1.50 (1.03)	3.83* (2.27)	.66 (.99)
Fear*Symbolic Racism	.07 (1.08)	−2.18 (2.30)	.87 (1.25)
Anger	−1.27* (.75)	−2.60 (1.64)	−.76 (.73)
Fear	.14 (.76)	1.47 (1.71)	−.34 (.87)
Symbolic Racism	−.44 (.71)	−.53 (1.39)	−.32 (.75)
Ideology	1.49*** (.36)	1.15* (.69)	1.60*** (.43)
Party Identification	2.74*** (.27)	3.08*** (.47)	2.68*** (.31)
Income	−.07 (.39)	−.41 (.66)	−.12 (.47)
Age	.000 (.004)	−.004 (.008)	.000 (.005)
South	.34** (.17)	.15 (.32)	.34* (.19)
Gender	−.02 (.15)	.02 (.26)	−.02 (.17)
Education	.32 (.49)	.81 (.90)	.33 (.59)
Worse Economy	1.07*** (.33)	.81 (.69)	1.26*** (.36)
Internet Access	−.51*** (.15)	−.10 (.34)	−.25 (.22)
Competitiveness	−.19 (.19)	−.26 (.25)	−.62** (.22)
Constant	−2.39** (.79)	−2.56 (1.77)	−2.44** (.83)
N	743	212	531

Notes: * $p \le .1$; ** $p \le .05$; *** $p \le .001$ (two-tailed test). Entries are probit regression coefficients and the standard errors are in parentheses. All variables are recoded onto a 0 to 1 scale, with higher values indicating respondent voted for House Republicans.

TABLE 5C. *The Impact of Emotion and Political Ideology on Preference for Republicans in Tea Party Races*

	Republican Vote Choice (House)	Republican Vote Choice: (Senate)
	B (s.e.)	**B** (s.e.)
Anger*Ideology	.38 (1.81)	1.42 (1.78)
Fear*Ideology	2.91* (1.74)	3.18* (1.87)
Anger	−.24 (1.22)	.01 (1.24)
Fear	−1.61 (1.22)	−2.62** (1.16)
Party Identification	3.03*** (.49)	3.47*** (.50)
Symbolic Racism	−05 (.62)	−.25 (.81)
Ideology	−63 (1.42)	−.40 (1.16)
Income	−.07 (.68)	.21 (.90)
Age	−.004 (.009)	.015 (.009)
South	−.03 (.33)	−.36 (.43)
Gender	−.03 (.26)	−.11 (.28)
Education	.92 (.92)	−.48 (1.15)
Worse Economy	.69 (.66)	1.03 (.76)
Internet Access	−.13 (.37)	−.46 (.46)
Competitiveness	−.20 (.26)	−.81* (.42)
Constant	−2.04 (1.57)	−1.30 (1.33)
N	212	160

Notes: * $p \leq .1$; ** $p \leq .05$; *** $p \leq .001$ (two-tailed test). Entries are probit regression coefficients and the standard errors are in parentheses. All variables are recoded onto a 0 to 1 scale, with higher values indicating respondent voted Republican.

TABLE 5D. *The Impact of Emotion and Racial and Nonracial Attitudes on Attending a Rally in Tea Party Races*

	Attend Rally	Attend Rally
	B (s.e.)	B (s.e.)
Anger*Symbolic Racism	3.65** (1.45)	
Fear*Symbolic Racism	−1.00 (1.29)	
Anger*Ideology		1.66* (1.00)
Fear*Ideology		.59 (.97)
Anger	−2.11** (.97)	−.75 (.65)
Fear	1.13 (.88)	.11 (.58)
Symbolic Racism	−1.55 (1.01)	.03 (.58)
Ideology	.36 (.50)	−1.11* (.68)
Party Identification	.47 (.39)	.44 (.38)
Income	.36 (.52)	.48 (.53)
Age	.003 (.005)	.001 (.005)
South	−.27 (.22)	−.33 (.23)
Gender	−.14 (.20)	−.10 (.20)
Education	1.18 (.75)	1.26* (.76)
Worse Economy	−.56 (.48)	−.62 (.49)
Internet Access	.28 (.26)	.23 (.26)
Competitiveness	−.13 (.22)	−.16 (.22)
Constant	−2.23** (.89)	−2.26** (.86)
N	414	414

Notes: * $p \leq .1$; ** $p \leq .05$; *** $p \leq .001$ (two-tailed test). Entries are probit regression coefficients and the standard errors are in parentheses. All variables are recoded onto a 0 to 1 scale, with higher values indicating respondent attended a rally. The sample is whites who reside in Senate and House races with a Tea Party candidate on the ballot.

Conclusion

In this final chapter, I begin by summarizing the findings on emotions and racial politics. Then, I discuss when anger should make race more salient in people's political decision making and when it should not. Afterward, this chapter explores how anger and out-group prejudice operate politically in places outside of the United States. Finally, the chapter explores the implications of the findings.

A poorly understood aspect of American public opinion is how emotions shape our political decisions on matters of race. We know issues such as affirmative action, reparations for blacks, busing, and health care reform stimulate strong emotions. We are less clear about whether emotions influence the application of racial attitudes in these policy domains. My theory of emotion and race proposes that anger (not other negative emotions) is strongly linked to contemporary racial attitudes in memory for many white Americans, and evoking this emotion should bring these attitudes to mind. As a consequence of this process, political opinions related to race should be more strongly predicted by the primed racial predisposition. In fact, I contend that anger and racial schemas form such a strong bond that the emotion may bring the racial attitude to the top of the head even when triggered by an event unrelated to race or politics.

The data reported here demonstrate that evoking anger independent of any racial or political content, via exposure to a racialized campaign ad, and toward politics in general increases the effect of racial attitudes on a diverse set of racial policy opinions and candidate evaluations. Putting an end to affirmative action; repealing health care reform; hanging the Confederate flag high; voting for Tea Party-backed candidates: in all of these cases, anger plays an important role in enhancing the impact of race on one's political judgment. On the other hand, old-fashioned attitudes, such as the belief that blacks are a biologically inferior race, are mainly activated by feelings of disgust. Over the years, scholars have disagreed about the distinctiveness of contemporary racism and old-fashioned racism. But the fact that these attitude dimensions are activated by different emotional states is evidence that these concepts are indeed distinct. Scholars have also had a difficult time agreeing on whether symbolic racism is in fact distinct from race-neutral principles (e.g., individual initiative and political ideology). As shown throughout this book, anger, time and again, is linked to and can in fact prime racial prejudice while having no such effect on race-neutral principles. Anger is not only the emotional substrate of antiblack attitudes but also out-group prejudice more broadly. For instance, the results demonstrate that anger increases the effect of ethnocentrism on racial and immigration policy preferences across a large and diverse group of Americans – broadening the reach of my basic hypothesis.

Not only does anger make thoughts about race more accessible in the minds of racial conservatives, but racial liberals as well. For example, in Chapter 4, we saw that the anger condition pushed racial liberals to more strongly support health care reform – relative to the control condition. Even so, the findings throughout this book clearly demonstrate that anger is more strongly tied to the beliefs of racial conservatives than to the beliefs of racial liberals. For instance, in most cases, the differences between the anger condition and the fear condition were small and statistically insignificant for racial liberals while substantively large and significant for racial conservatives. Moreover, the anger condition did not consistently increase support for racial policies and candidates perceived as racially sympathetic among racial liberals. For example, the emotion induction experiment (Chapter 2) showed that the anger condition failed to increase support for racial policies among those scoring low in symbolic racism, compared to those in the control condition. Conversely, in later chapters (3–5), we saw that the anger condition heightened the effect of racial liberals' beliefs on race-related political decisions – relative to the control condition. What might explain this discrepancy in results? One possible explanation is the criticism Obama experienced after capturing the White House. Perhaps racial liberals believed the election of Barack Obama would begin to remove the negative character traits that have been associated with blacks for so long. To them, Obama is a symbol of what African Americans can become as a group when racism is removed from American society. Consequently, when racial liberals believed the political right (most notably the Tea Party) was unfairly criticizing Obama and his policies, they reacted with strong feelings of anger. The rise in anger may have caused race to play a bigger role in racial liberals' political evaluations. The difference in time periods of data collection between Chapter 2 (during the 2008 primary season) and Chapters 3 through 5 (after Obama won the presidency) seems to support this proposition. All in all, the conclusion to be drawn from the data is that anger causes contemporary ideas about race to enter into American public opinion.

In some cases, anger alone was not responsible for bringing ideas about race to mind. For example, absent anger (control group), we still saw that symbolic racism had a strong effect on racial policy opinions (Chapters 2 and 3) and opinions about health care reform (Chapter 4). It seems that when race is highly salient in a policy domain, anger simply increases the existing relationship between racial attitudes and policy opinions. On the other hand, when race is less conspicuous such as during the 1988 presidential election or the 2010 midterm election, anger determines if racial predispositions will matter in whites' voting decisions.[1] These findings demonstrate that ignoring the specific emotional underpinnings of racial attitudes has led scholars to underestimate the impact of race on American public opinion.

It is also important to point out that the effect of race-neutral principles (e.g., political ideology and limited government) on policy and candidate opinions was also significant in the control condition (Chapters 2 and 4) – even when controlling for racial predispositions. Thus, racial considerations are not the only force driving public opinion on matters of race. Consistent with the racial politics literature, race-related policy and candidate decisions are also predicted by non-racial considerations.

The circumstances under which anger does not prime racial considerations are as informative as the circumstances that do. An example of this failure was during the 2010 midterm elections in non-Tea Party congressional races. In these congressional elections, anger failed to enhance the effect of racial attitudes on vote choice. In Chapter 5, I attributed this effect to the fact that people's voting decisions were not as racialized as they were in Tea Party races. Tea Party candidates deliberately framed the midterm election as us versus them. Their campaign message was to enact legislation that protected the interest of hardworking Americans (e.g., whites) and repeal legislation considered to help undeserving freeloaders (e.g., blacks). Because code words like *hardworking* and *undeserving* have racial undertones, it is not surprising that people's voting decisions became racialized. On the other hand, this confrontational rhetoric was less likely to be present in congressional races with no Tea Party candidate. This difference in campaign rhetoric tells us that when the candidate (or policy) is not linked to race, anger should not bring race to bear on political evaluations. In fact in Chapter 2, the anger condition failed to increase the role of race in people's support for the Iraq War – a policy domain that is not linked to race. Thus, the political object under evaluation has to be associated with race for anger to enhance the effect of racial attitudes on people's opinions about politics.

Another circumstance when anger may not activate thoughts about race is among immigrants who have recently come to the United States. The link between anger and racial prejudice may work less well among these people because they have not learned to associate anger with their racial attitudes. Although the 2008 American National Election Study (ANES) includes an oversample of Latinos, it does not allow me to test if the link between anger and racial attitudes is weaker among immigrants. The sample only includes a handful of Latinos who have become U.S. citizens or moved to the country recently (i.e., past ten years). Nonetheless, I believe future research needs to examine if groups not implicated in the history of U.S. race relations are less subject to associate anger with their views on matters of race.

EMOTIONS AND PREJUDICE ABROAD

My analysis has shown that anger plays a powerful role in activating out-group prejudice among different groups and in different contexts in the United States. Aside from the United States, out-group prejudice is an important determinant of out-group attitudes abroad. Over the past fifty years, European countries (e.g., Germany, Spain, France, Greece, and Italy) have experienced a substantial growth in their immigrant populations, particularly from groups whose cultural background is distinct from that of the host nations. For instance, as of 2002, fifty-six million immigrants live in Europe compared to forty-two million living in North America (Zick, Pettigrew, and Wagner 2008). With an increase in the immigrant population in Western Europe, racial and ethnic minorities have been the target of discrimination and violence (Pettigrew, Wagner, and Christ 2007; Wagner, Christ, and Heitmeyer 2010). Still, Pettigrew contends that the experiences of racial and ethnic minorities in Europe differ drastically from those of African Americans in the United States. "African Americans endured two centuries of slavery and another of legal segregation. They still face intense racial barriers.... Nonetheless, African Americans 'belong' in the United States.... Not even racists question their citizenship" (1998, 78). On the other hand, the new immigrant groups, from countries such as Nigeria or Pakistan, are considered strange and not "belonging." And several scholars have found that white Europeans' negative attitudes toward immigrants are a strong predictor of anti-immigrant policies (Esses et al. 2001; Jackson et al. 2001; Pettigrew et al. 2007; Pettigrew and Meertens 1995).

Scholars have offered group conflict theory as one explanation for anti-immigrant sentiment in Europe. With the massive migration of immigrant groups into Western Europe, Quillian (1995) finds that group threat is important.[2] Moreover, Jackson and his colleagues (2001) show that group threat, along with blatant racism, increases support for sending immigrants back to their home countries. In places outside the United States, other emotions, such as fear, may play a larger role in driving support for anti-immigrant policies. Perhaps the negative rhetoric on out-groups in Europe focuses more on people's concern about ethnic competition over scarce resources, such as jobs, than in the United States. For example, since the 2009 global economic crisis, the European Union has been deeply worried about immigration. In fact, Rachel Donadio, a *New York Times* reporter, states, "fear of immigrants, fanned by right-wing parties and voter discontent over economic malaise, have deepened already profound divisions within

Europe."[3] Therefore, in places abroad, fear might matter more in driving out-group animosity.

Nevertheless, research also suggests that scapegoating is an important component of anti-immigrant attitudes. Wagner, Christ, and Heitmeyer state, in reference to immigrants in Europe, "due to their status of not belonging to the ingroup and their political powerlessness, immigrants can be easily used as scapegoats for nearly any undeserved development within societies, be it unemployment, deficits in the health system, problems in education, and so on, which in turn, leads to bias against immigrants" (2010, 368). Perhaps during a financial crisis, Europeans blame immigrant groups for their countries' economic and social problems. An example is the 2009 debt crisis that adversely impacted almost every nation in the European Union. Countries like Greece were hit extremely hard by the economic crisis. The *New York Times* sums up the economic turmoil in Greece: "Over the last decade, Greece went on a debt binge that came crashing to an end in late 2009, provoking an economic crisis that has decimated the country's economy, brought down its government, unleashed increasing social unrest and threatened the future of the euro."[4]

With Greece on the brink of financial ruin, many of its citizens reacted with anger over the austerity measures that involved significant spending cuts, tax increases, and pension reforms. According to a news report from *The Guardian*, twenty thousand protestors, in the summer of 2010, marched through Athens disapproving of the International Monetary Fund's (IMF) austerity measures. During the protest, angry Greeks shouted, "Capitalists, not workers, should pay for this crisis" and "IMF – get out of Greece."[5] Their anger over the austerity measures soon turned to blaming immigrant groups for the country's economic woes. In fact, Sutherland and Malmstrom (2012) state, "to place blame for this on immigrants is wrong, and exacerbates the problem. We are all at fault. By not taking responsibility, we allowed immigration to become the scapegoat for a host of other unrelated problems."[6]

Far-right groups in Greece, such as the Golden Dawn party (winning eighteen seats in the Greek Parliament), fed on Greeks' deep feelings of anger for their political benefit. And the Golden Dawn has used this anger to promote an anti-immigrant ideology of racism and intimidation. A legal Pakistani immigrant reported of the

Golden Dawn: "[T]hey said: You're the cause of Greece's problems. You have seven days to close or we'll burn your shop – and we'll burn you."[7] Stavroula Logothettis, a journalist for *Maclean's* magazine, also vividly captures how Greeks' anger has heightened anti-immigrant bigotry. For example, while riding a commuter train to Athens, a Greek, in his twenties, overheard a young Nigerian talking about looking for work and angrily stated, "Why should you monkeys have work when I don't? I've been unemployed for a year. This is my country and if anyone should have work, it should be me."[8] As a result of the public's anger, violence toward immigrant groups is also more common in Greece than in years past. The Human Rights Watch group released a report stating, "racist violence in Athens has increased over the last two or three years, reaching alarming proportions in 2011."[9] One example of this violence is when a young Iraqi was brutally stabbed to death in the streets of Athens.[10] Some journalists and human rights groups attribute the increase in racist violence to the Golden Dawn's fiery anti-immigrant rhetoric. And research suggests that the angry rhetoric from the Golden Dawn may have contributed to this violence. For instance, Kalmoe (2013) shows that angry individuals are more likely to support state violence, acts such as painful interrogation of terrorists, than non-angry individuals. Perhaps anger does not only operate as a vehicle that brings out-group prejudice to the surface, but also motivates violent actions toward members of the out-group.

Unfortunately Greece is not the only European nation experiencing an increase in anti-immigrant rhetoric. With anger swelling over austerity measures in other countries in Europe, ultranationalist groups like the National Front in France, the Northern League in Italy, and the Jobbik in Hungary have gained an increase in public support. According to David Frum of CNN, Maine Le Pen, leader of the National Front Party, "is giving expression to public distress that is going unexpressed by the mainline parties."[11] Her public expression, however, has been antagonistic toward immigrants – claiming that "Muslims using the streets to pray because mosques were overflowing was an occupation of French territory."[12] Le Pen's anti-immigrant rhetoric has gotten so bad that she faces criminal charges from the European Parliamentary Committee for igniting racism. All of these events suggest that anger may play a large role in heightening racial bigotry and violence in places outside the United States. Thus, I encourage scholars to investigate how emotion and out-group prejudice interact in other settings like Europe.

A comparative analysis would also expand our understanding of how differences in culture and history could lead to different emotions increasing the role of prejudice in politics. The United States and European nations like Greece and France have a different history of interracial and interethnic relations (Pettigrew 1998). This difference in intergroup relations may cause one type of emotion to be linked to out-group prejudice in one society and not in another.

IMPLICATIONS

Is anger detrimental to achieving racial equality? Given the findings presented in this book, it would seem so. Anger operates as a switch that amplifies (or turns on) racist thinking – exacerbating America's racial problem. It pushes prejudiced whites to oppose policies and candidates perceived as alleviating racial inequality. Anger about blacks cheating the welfare system is not only responsible for triggering racial bigotry among many whites, but also anger over issues that seemingly have nothing to do with race. For example, whites' nonracial anger causes racism to play a larger role in opinions on race-related policies. Therefore, although anger is not directed at blacks, it could still have a detrimental effect on policies perceived to benefit them. So when the political environment fills with anger (nonracial), legislation or policies intending to reduce racial inequality may face harsher opposition from racial conservatives. Sears and Citrin (1982) argue that political symbols, such as higher taxes, can elicit racism. As a result, race can enter into politics even when political elites avoid using group cues. My findings demonstrate that anger is another factor that racializes American public opinion even when the political debate has little manifest racial content.

Not only does anger make racism more pervasive in American society, but it also causes whites' views to be more racially polarized. Racial polarization poses considerable challenges to the democratic process. This racial bias makes reaching common ground in solving America's racial problem extremely difficult. When in a state of anger, people are less willing to compromise and seek out the point of view of others

(MacKuen et al. 2010; Valentino et al. 2009). In addition, anger causes people to pay less attention to the quality of the argument (systematic processing) and more on superficial cues (heuristic processing) (Tiedens and Lerner 2001). As a result, under states of anger, racial conservatives and racial liberals will move further apart in solving America's racial problem and remain steadfast in their positions. According to democratic theorists like Guttmann and Thompson, deliberation is the lifeblood of democracy.

> Deliberation increases the chances of arriving at justifiable policies. More than other kinds of political processes, deliberative democracy contains the means of its own correction. Through the give-and-take of argument citizens and their accountable representatives can learn from one another, come to recognize their individual and collective mistakes, and develop new views and policies that are more widely justifiable. (1996, 43)

From this perspective, for America to move forward on race, deliberation from both sides is needed. Guttmann and Thompson suggest that only through deliberation will policies justifiable to both parties emerge.[13] One solution to America's racial problem may be minimizing the angry rhetoric within the racial debate. By doing so, people from both sides may be willing to compromise on policies intended to reduce inequality between whites and blacks.

In addition to reducing the angry rhetoric in the contemporary debate on race, other emotions, such as shame and guilt, may play a significant role in solving America's racial problem. During the civil rights movement, many Americans watched on their television screens the evil of Jim Crow. As blacks protested against segregation in places like Selma, Alabama, they were often met with racial slurs and racist violence. These horrific images of police dogs attacking nonviolent young black men and women evoked strong feelings of shame and guilt among many white Americans. In fact, Martin Luther King Jr. recognized the power of guilt by adopting a strategy that took segregationists' hate and responded with love. In his speech "Loving Your Enemies," he states, "they react with bitterness because they're mad because you love them like that. They react with guilt feelings and sometimes they'll hate you a little more at the transition period, but just keep loving them." He further states, in his speech at a march in Detroit, "but if he puts you in jail, you go in this jail and transform it from a dungeon of shame to a haven of freedom and human dignity." By causing many whites to feel guilty and shameful about the injustices blacks experienced, King and other civil rights leaders were able to put pressure on the federal government to pass the Civil Rights Act of 1964 and the Voting Rights Act of 1965. Research on emotion shows that guilt leads people to make amends for the harm they cause others. Lazarus states "[g]uilt is felt when we believe we have acted in a morally deficient way, all the more so if in doing we have wronged or harmed an innocent other" (1991, 240). Rather than blaming others, as in the case of anger, a person who experiences guilt blames oneself for the moral transgression. And he/she copes with this feeling by apologizing or atoning for his/her past mistakes.

Shelby Steele has written extensively on white guilt and its impact on race relations in America. He argues that black leaders have used white guilt as a strategy to persuade whites to support racial policies, such as affirmative action. He believes racial oppression no longer exists in this country, and black leaders unfairly use guilt as political leverage to get policies enacted that benefits their group.

But after America entered the age of white guilt in the mid-sixties, racism began to go underground even diminish. Just as white guilt began to make white racism into an opportunity for blacks – an occasion for "demands" – it became harder to provoke the racist theater that the South had so willingly offered up for early civil rights leaders. For black leaders in the age of white guilt the problem was how to seize all they could from white guilt without having to show actual events of racism. (2006, 36)

Steele's argument, regrettably, misses the fact that racial discrimination still exists in this country. Despite civil rights legislation making discrimination illegal, it did not eliminate discriminatory behavior from society. For instance, research shows strong evidence of racial discrimination in the job market (Bertrand and Mullanianthan 2004) and politics (Butler and Brookman 2011). Although I disagree with Steele about the presence of racial bigotry in America, he might be correct that evoking guilt in whites will lead them to support policies that reduce racial inequality. Research, however, has shown that people who should feel the most guilt about race do not. That is, Swim and Miller (1999) find that whites scoring high in today's subtle form of prejudice report less guilt than those scoring low in prejudice. Perhaps the belief that blacks lack motivation is not considered by society as morally wrong like the view that blacks are biologically inferior. As a result, whites harboring this subtle belief system do not experience strong feelings of guilt.

Martin Luther King Jr. realized that Americans needed to see with their own eyes that racism and discrimination are wrong. Only then will they feel guilt and shame for supporting such beliefs and actions. But Allport contends that prejudiced people are inclined to deal with their guilt by denying it or placing blame on the out-group. He states there is "among prejudiced people a marked tendency to regard others (but not oneself) as blameworthy" (1954, 378). According to Allport, they evade guilt by projecting their feelings on those they have wronged (e.g., blacks). But, Chris Lebron, in *The Color of Our Shame*, argues that for society to solve America's racial problem we ought to respond to inequality with shame. "[S]hame allows our moral sense to tune into the beacon of goodness and justice. That is why the problem of race is the color of our shame – the color of a person's skin remains an obstacle in being the society we believe ourselves to value and hold true" (2013, 13). Therefore, we need to increase the public's awareness that racism, even subtle forms of it, is morally wrong and supporting this belief system should create a strong feeling of guilt and shame. In fact, scholars have found that when whites feel guilty and shameful, they are more likely to support programs that intend alleviate to racial inequality (Harvey and Oswald 2000). While my findings show that anger causes racism to have a larger impact on public opinion, perhaps guilt and shame are the emotional conditions that can attenuate its effect on American society.

Notes

Introduction

1 "The Big Tax Revolt," *Newsweek*, June 19, 1978.
2 "Proposition Man; Howard Jarvis, the Taxed Man, Is Riding High on Number 13," *Washington Post*, June 20, 1978.
3 "Conservatives Seek to Shift Blame for Crisis onto Minority Housing Law," *Huffington Post*, October, 1, 2008.
4 On *NBC Nightly News* with Brian Williams, former President Jimmy Carter argued that racism was behind opposition to Obama and his policies.
5 Former Republican National Committee (RNC) chairman Michael Steele disagreed with Carter and others' accusation of racism. He firmly believed that opposition to health care reform was strictly about the government encroaching on the lives of Americans.
6 They show that over time (1980–2004) people express more anger than fear toward the presidential candidates. There was only one year (1980) when people reacted with more fear than anger, but the difference was fairly small.
7 To create such minimal conditions, subjects never interacted with other group members or knew who was in their group. In addition, there was no conflict of interest between groups because subjects were allowed to allocate resources to both groups. Self-interest was also removed because participants could only allocate resources to others. Because participants never heard of or belonged to these groups beforehand, previous hostility was eliminated.
8 Marilynn Brewer's position on SIT diverges from Tajfel's original theory in that in-group/out-group differentiation reflects more in-group bias than out-group prejudice. Specifically, she questions the widespread assumption

that in-group favoritism and out-group hate are reciprocally related. Put differently, she contends that preference for positivity toward the in-group does not necessarily imply hostility toward the out-group. Brewer's (1999) extension of SIT demonstrates that in-group identification is a necessary but not sufficient cause of out-group prejudice.

1 A Theory of Anger and Contemporary White Racial Attitudes

1   This is from a *CNN Politics* news article, "Protesters Hurl Slurs and Spit at Democrats," March 20, 2010, accessed online at http://politicalticker. blogs.cnn.com/2010/03/20/protesters-hurl-slurs-and-spit-at-democrats/.

2   This is from the *Sun* newspaper's "Letter to the Editor" edition on May 24, 1961, p. 18.

3   Specifically, about 90 percent of the white sample report feeling angry about welfare. A possible explanation for the high percentage is question wording. Respondents are asked to indicate how angry they feel about someone "who collects welfare because he is too lazy to get a job."

4   This relationship is even stronger among the college educated.

5   "Anger Fuels Anti-Health Care Rally," *CBS News*, November 5, 2009.

6   Besides members of the public expressing anger about health care, they were also anxious. Nonetheless, the Kaiser poll showed that white Republicans reported more anger than anxiety regarding health care reform – an average difference of 6 percent (and as great as 11 percent).

7   Feeling thermometers are the main instrument used to capture antiblack affect (Bobo and Taun 2006; Kinder and Sanders 1996; Sears and Henry 2003; Sniderman and Piazza 1993), which measure general evaluations of blacks and other objects on a warm-cold scale. An obvious weakness of this measurement strategy is that it does not take into account the unique influences of specific emotions on whites' racial predispositions.

8   Another view is that this change may have been more gradual. Prior to the civil rights movement, whites were starting to abandon segregationist beliefs and slowly embracing the principle of racial equality (Schuman et al. 1997).

9   Furthermore, Iyengar (1990) finds that black poverty is understood in terms of individualistic treatment responsibility – it is the responsibility of the individual to get himself or herself out of poverty – while white poverty is comprehended in terms of societal treatment responsibility – societal intervention is needed.

10 Racial liberals' anger might not be as intense as the anger racial conservatives feel, because blaming blacks, as opposed to discrimination, for blacks' misfortunes has been more prominent in the contemporary debate on race.

11 The severe beating of Rodney King in 1991 by several Los Angeles police officers is an example of an anger-inducing event for racial liberals. This incident is an example of blacks, like Rodney King, subject to racist

actions by whites, which is considered unfair and unjust by racial liberals and the black community at large.

12 Fear may have been the dominant emotional response among whites right after the Civil War. At this time, there was a strong sense of uncertainty among many white Americans about blacks' freedom (Wood 1968).

2 The Emotional Foundation of White Racial Attitudes

1 Recently, Carmines, Sniderman, and Easter (2011) suggested that symbolic racism reflects racial policy opinions. In other words, the reason for the strong relationship between the two is that symbolic racism is primarily a measure of racial policy opinions.

2 Of course, the *laziness* stereotype may overlap both old-fashioned racism and symbolic racism belief systems, because some might believe dispositional differences between blacks and whites are innate. Consistent with this is Huddy and Feldman's (2009) argument that symbolic racism is a mixture of internal and external attributions.

3 The study was conducted during the tail end of the primary season when Barack Obama led in delegates. The timing of my study makes this a conservative test of my hypotheses. If Obama activated race for everyone, there should be no differences between conditions. To be confident that the effects of the treatment conditions were not correlated with the effect of the campaign (Obama), I controlled for when subjects participated in the experiment. The results are essentially the same when the variable "interview date" is included in the models.

4 Seven subjects were dropped from the analysis because they failed to follow instructions. None of the results change substantively if these respondents are included.

5 White Southerners were more likely to be racially conservative than white Northerners.

6 I do not employ weights, because the goal is to estimate the effect of the manipulation. Weights are randomly distributed across cells, and inferences are unchanged when they are used.

7 If some respondents were turned off by the measures of racial attitudes in the pretest, they might opt out of the second wave. This could dampen effects. Fortunately, mortality was equivalent across cells of the design. There was a recontact success rate of 60 percent, and no biases appeared across conditions on variables such as partisanship, education, and gender.

8 The facial images were of the same middle-aged white woman. The pictures, displayed in the appendix, are drawn from Ekman's archive of emotional expressions (Ekman and Friesen 1976).

9 For the relaxed condition, there was no image because Ekman's archive of emotional expressions did not include a facial expression of a relaxed person. The text for this condition was exactly the same as for the

other conditions except the emotional label was replaced with the word "relaxed." Full description is in the appendix.

10 The scale for the variable ranged from 0 to 1; 0=no emotion, .5=some emotion, and 1=extreme emotion. The reliability of our coders was high: Cronbach's alpha for anger=.85, fear=.93, and disgust=.87.

11 Subjects reported the target emotion more at moderate-high levels of intensity than at low levels of intensity. That is, 15 percent of subjects in the anger condition experienced no anger, while 70 percent experienced moderate levels of anger and 15 percent felt high levels of anger. For respondents in the fear condition, 27 percent of them experienced no emotion, whereas 55 percent experienced moderate levels and 18 percent experienced high levels of fear. For the disgust condition, 31 percent of subjects felt no emotion, and 49 percent felt moderate levels, while 20 percent felt high levels of disgust.

12 *Political discussion* is a measure of political topics subjects mentioned in their open-ended responses to the emotion induction. Controlling for whether subjects mention political issues or racial issues in response to the emotion induction I believe is important. I argue that anger itself (not anger toward politics or race) should make race more accessible in people's minds. To be confident that my effects are not driven by what people wrote (that is, political issues or racial issues), I control for political discussion.

13 These four items were additively scaled to create the symbolic racism scale.

14 The items scale nicely (Cronbach's alpha=.75).

15 The priming effect for anger is statistically larger than that for either disgust or fear. The difference is (F, 1, 168, 2.62) significant at the .1 level between anger*symbolic racism and fear*symbolic racism (two-tailed test). For anger*symbolic racism and disgust*symbolic racism the difference (F, 1, 168, 2.58) is significant at the .11 level (two-tailed test).

16 In another model, I included symbolic racism, old-fashioned racism, and race-neutral values (limited government) and interacted each attitude with anger, fear, and disgust conditions. Results were similar to those reported here.

17 I also examined these effects by region, gender, age, and education. The interaction between the anger condition and symbolic racism was strongest in the North (B=.42, p ≤ .05), among men (B=.43, p ≤ .05), the older population (B=.50, p ≤ .05), and those who did not earn a college degree (B=.63, p ≤ .05). The interaction between the disgust condition and old-fashioned racism was strongest in the South (B=.80, p ≤ .05) and among the older population (B=.49, p ≤ .1). These findings suggest that symbolic racism is more powerfully linked to anger among men, the elderly, and those without a college degree living in the North while

old-fashioned racism is linked more strongly to disgust among older Southerners.

18 I also investigated to see if whites high in symbolic racism who reported anger (in the emotion induction task) across conditions were more likely to oppose racial policies than those who did not report anger. The findings still supported my expectations about the role of anger and contemporary racism. To be specific, the interaction between reported anger and symbolic racism (B=.21, p ≤ .1) was positive and statistically significant.

19 Even though Barack Obama was grabbing media headlines as the eventual Democratic nominee at the time of the study, only one subject mentioned Obama in his/her open-ended response. This result indicates that Obama wasn't on the mind of participants, at least consciously.

20 References to gender include words such as *women* or *men*, while references to class include *poor*, *middle class*, or *upper class*.

21 I ran a simple t-test to see if these differences were statistically significant. Relative to the control group, the test showed that each of the three treatment groups discussed race at a significantly higher rate. There was also a significant difference between the anger condition and the fear condition (t=2.83, p ≤ .01), as well as the disgust condition and fear condition (t=2.32, p ≤ .05).

22 Items asked how "preferential treatment to blacks," "changes in race relations," and "presidential candidate Mondale/Reagan" makes the respondent feel. Exact question wording is located in the appendix.

23 The results are similar when I only look at the emotion measures toward the presidential candidates (Mondale/Reagan).

24 This finding makes some sense given that research has shown that conservatives fear uncertainty and changing the status quo (Wilson 1973).

25 A total of 2,322 respondents took the preelection survey, and 2,102 respondents took the postelection survey.

26 Another benefit of the survey is that it has an oversample of black and Latino respondents, which allows me to examine if anger activates prejudice for other groups.

27 The ethnocentrism measure runs from −.8 to .8 where higher values indicate an endorsement of ethnocentrism (Mean=.11, S.D.=.18).

28 Anger's Mean=.27, S.D.=22, Min=0, Max=1. Fear's Mean=.24, S.D.=.23, Min=0, Max=1.

29 Mean=.64, S.D.=.28, Min=0, Max=1.

30 Mean=.64, S.D.=.22, Min=0, Max=1.

31 Research shows that the media coverage of immigration has focused more on Hispanics than on other immigrant groups like Asians, Africans, or Muslims (Valentino, Brader, and Jardina, 2013). Because of this, I only exclude Hispanics from the analysis. However, when I exclude both Asians and Hispanics, the results are essentially the same.

3 The Emotional Content in Racialized Campaign Ads Primes White Racial Attitudes

1 Al Gore, in the Democratic primary, was the first to capitalize on the Horton story. He attempted to align Dukakis with black criminals, although he didn't explicitly mention Horton.

2 Contrary to the racial priming literature, Huber and Lapinski (2006) find that racial messages, either implicit or explicit, have no effect on racial predispositions. Scholars have also found that explicit appeals are effective under more finite circumstances. For instance, Hutchings, Walton, and Benjamin (2010) find that explicit appeals are most effective among Southern men and women. McConnaughy, White, and Laird (2010) find similar results in regard to the effectiveness of explicit appeals on certain groups of the population.

3 The racial priming theory suggests that this process is automatic. That is, a subtle racial message primes racial predispositions when the racial meaning is outside of conscious awareness. The work on emotional priming suggests that the activation of objects learned under a specific emotional state can be an automatic process as well. The connection between an emotion and attitude object could be so strong that evoking the emotion could bring the object to people's minds outside of their awareness.

4 A total of one hundred ninety participants took part in wave 1, and one hundred thirteen participants participated in wave 2. The response rate was 59 percent.

5 The study's mortality rate was equivalent across the two waves – no biases occurred between waves 1 and 2 on the symbolic racism variable.

6 I increased the monetary incentive to ten dollars toward the tail end of the study because of my concern regarding a low recontact response rate. On November 17, 2009, respondents were informed via e-mail that they would now receive ten dollars for their participation in the second survey. No significant differences appeared on racial attitude and social demographic variables between respondents paid five dollars and those paid ten dollars.

7 The control group viewed a Starbucks advertisement. The product was a double shot espresso drink considered to brighten up your day. In the ad, a man drinks a double shot espresso while going through his morning routine before heading to work – with a band playing "Eye of the Tiger" in the background. The duration of the ad was fifty-nine seconds.

8 Andrew Fellows was uncontested in the mayoral race. So I created a fictitious candidate named Brian Alexander as his opponent. Most of the sample was unaware of the election, and only five students could identify that the race was uncontested. I dropped those individuals from the analysis. When they are included, the results are essentially the same. The ad lasted fifty-one seconds.

9 Although Brader (2006) does not differentiate the sound effects for anger and fear, I suspect police sirens lead to fear more than anger.

10 Some research suggests that self-report measures of emotion can be problematic (Larsen and Fredrickson 1999). One potential problem is that respondents might not be willing to report their emotions. However, respondents wrote on average fifty-two words describing how the ad made them feel. This result indicates subjects were very willing to express their emotions. Another potential problem is when respondents are given multiple emotion items; the emotional state of interest may be altered as a result. My emotion measure avoids this problem because each condition asks about their emotional state in response to the stimulus rather than via an adjective checklist.

11 The scale for the variable ranged from 0 to 1; 0=no emotion, .5=some emotion and 1=extreme emotion. The Cronbach's alpha reveals a high level of reliability across the two coders – fear (.89) and anger (.85).

12 Respondents in the anger condition were also more likely to experience anger at moderate-high levels of intensity (69 percent) than to not experience the emotion at all (31 percent). For participants in the fear condition, 40 percent of them experienced no fear, whereas 60 percent of them felt moderate-high levels of fear.

13 The items scale nicely (Cronbach's alpha=.63). In addition, the mean level of support for racial policies does not differ across conditions (Anger Condition =.50; Fear Condition=.49; Control Condition=.51).

14 When I take out the control variables, the direction and magnitude of the coefficients are essentially the same. All variables are coded on a 0 to 1 scale; higher values indicate a more conservative response. A detailed description of the coding procedures is in the appendix.

15 Recent research by Sears and colleagues has demonstrated that symbolic racism may be a broader concept of prejudice than previously considered, in that it not only reflects racial prejudice among whites, but also captures nonwhite ethnic groups' negative attitudes toward blacks (Henry and Sears 2002; Sears, Haley, and Henry 2008; Tesler and Sears 2010). Banks and Bell (2013) include other racial and ethnic groups in their analysis and find similar results.

16 I also examined the effects by gender. Perhaps women are more persuaded by the subtle racial fear appeal than are men. The results didn't support this proposition. The interaction between the fear condition and symbolic racism was still insignificant for women.

17 Given the relatively small sample size, I used bootstrapping to reestimate the standard errors from column 1 of Table 3.2. The bootstrapping technique takes a new sample from the original using sampling with replacement so that it is not identical to the original "real" sample. I drew five hundred replacements. This approach produced results comparable to the OLS regression model.

18 Like in Chapter 2, I also examined whether reported anger or fear (across experimental conditions) boosted the impact of racial attitudes on racial policy opinions. I found that the interaction between reported anger and symbolic racism was positive and significant (β=.53 p $\geq$ .05) while the effect of reported anger (racial liberals) on opposition to racial policies was negative and significant (β=–.21 p $\geq$ .05). On the other hand, reported fear had no effect on racial attitudes.

19 The difference (chi-square, 1.96) between the anger condition*symbolic racism and the fear condition*symbolic racism is significant at the .08 level (one-tailed test).

20 Using survey data, Krosnick and Kinder (1990) perform a similar test for priming effects.

21 To increase confidence that feelings toward Dukakis capture some sentiment toward Horton, I examined respondents' open-ended responses to the question of why they would vote against Dukakis. If perceptions of Horton drive negative feelings toward Dukakis, I suspect that mentioning crime in the open-ended response, over other issues, should be a strong predictor of feelings toward Dukakis. Based on a 1988 Gallup poll (No. 277), three issues dominated the campaign: economy, crime, and national security. Using a logit model, I regressed *anger toward Dukakis* (or *fear toward Dukakis*) on *crime, national security, economy, ideology, party identification, education, income, South, gender,* and *age*. In terms of fear toward Dukakis, I only find crime to have a significant and positive effect (β=.69 p $\geq$ .001). In terms of anger toward Dukakis, crime (β=.97 p $\geq$ .001) and national security (β=.47 p $\geq$ .05) have a significant effect. Calculating the predicted probabilities, I find that 53 percent of whites who mention crime as a reason they don't support Dukakis feel angry toward him, in comparison to 40 percent of whites who mention national security – a 13 percent difference. In sum, crime, as opposed to the economy and national security, was a major determinant in driving whites' negative emotional reaction to Dukakis.

22 Unfortunately, I do not have any way to gauge what respondents were actually exposed to across the different phases of the campaign. Nevertheless, I looked at whether respondents' levels of emotion (anger or fear toward Dukakis), symbolic racism, partisanship, ideology, education, and income differed across the three phases. The ordered logit model did not produce any differences across the three phases on these variables.

23 Coding procedures for all variables from the 1988 ANES are described in the appendix.

24 Another way to capture people's feelings toward Horton is to combine anger at Dukakis (or fear of Dukakis) with whether people mentioned crime as a reason they voted against Dukakis. The results with these emotion measures were essentially the same as those reported in Table 3.3. That is, the interactive effect between anger (combination

of anger at Dukakis and mentioning crime) and symbolic racism was positive and significant (β=.29 p $\geq$ .05) in the high-exposure implicit phase.

25 Fear may have an impact on women, given that some people believe blacks desire to take advantage of white women. As a result, I ran separate models for men and women. The results show that white men are mostly driving the effect of anger. There is a positive and significant interaction (β=.42 p $\geq$ .1) between anger and symbolic racism for white men. On the other hand, neither anger nor fear has a significant effect on white women.

26 The difference is (F, 1, 272, 2.91 statistic) significant at the .09 level between anger*symbolic racism and fear*symbolic racism (two-tailed test).

27 When I substitute feelings toward Bush for feelings toward Dukakis, I don't find that anger increases reliance on symbolic racism.

28 Other models were run to see if anger or fear from any of the phases boosted the impact of race-neutral principles (i.e., political ideology and party identification). I found that none of the emotions enhanced the impact of nonracial considerations on support for Bush. This result is consistent with the finding from the crime experiment that anger uniquely primes racial predispositions and has no effect on nonracial predispositions.

29 For the high-exposure implicit phase, I ran another model that includes interaction terms of anger and fear with symbolic racism and political ideology simultaneously. The results show that the interaction between anger and symbolic racism is even larger while the coefficients for anger*ideology and fear*ideology are insignificant. The findings are presented in the appendix in Table 3A.

4 The Public's Anger: Racial Polarization and Opinions about Health Care Reform

1 Other work, specifically that by Brader (2006), shows that emotions from campaign messages can persuade the American electorate. He finds that fear campaign appeals cause citizens to defect from prior habits and consider contemporary issue and character information. As a result, fear appeals can persuade voters to alter their vote preferences.

2 On the other hand, Fiorina and his colleagues (2006) argue that polarization is an elite phenomenon unlikely to resonate among the American mass public.

3 "Obama, 3 Years Ago: 'I will judge my first term as president based on' whether we delivered health care," *Think Progress*, March 23, 2010.

4 "Specter Town Hall Crowd Gets Rough and Rowdy," *Huffington Post*, September 11, 2009.

5   Although self-report measures of emotion are malleable to situational cues, the Kaiser Family Foundation Health Tracking Poll (Figure 1.1) shows that people's anger concerning health care reform was fairly consistent from 2009 to 2011.

6   The interview can be found at: http://www.msnbc.msn.com/id/3032619/ns/nightly_news#32867107.

7   "Obama as a Witch Doctor: Racist or Satirical?" *CNN Politics*, September 18, 2009 (updated version). http://www.cnn.com/2009/POLITICS/09/17/obama.witchdoctor.teaparty/.

8   "'Tea Party' Protestors Accused of Spitting on Lawmaker, Using Slurs," *Washington Post*, March 20, 2010.

9   The ad can be found at: http://www.youtube.com/watch?v=-3F1KlESnzs.

10 Participants in the Knowledge Network panel are recruited by telephone through random digit dialing. Respondents who do not have access to Internet are provided access through Web TV, free of charge. The response rate for wave 1 was 71 percent and 78 percent for wave 2.

11 Several subjects were dropped from the analysis because they failed to follow proper instructions. The results are similar substantively and statistically if these respondents are included.

12 I use weights because my goal is to estimate the effect of the manipulation for the entire population under study.

13 The mortality rate was equivalent across the two waves – no biases occurred between waves 1 and 2 on the symbolic racism variable.

14 The random assignment of subjects to conditions was successful. No significant differences appeared across conditions in terms of the means/proportions across sociodemographic or partisan variables. The means are virtually the same across conditions (*Income*: Anger M=.61, Fear M=.59, Enthusiasm M=.60, Relaxed M=.61; *Education*: Anger M=.47, Fear M=.45, Enthusiasm M=.45, Relaxed M=.48; *Age*: Anger M=49, Fear M=50, Enthusiasm M=50, Relaxed M=50; *Party ID*: Anger M=.52, Fear M=.53, Enthusiasm M=.54, Relaxed M=.50; *Ideology*: Anger M=.54, Fear M=.55, Enthusiasm M=.55, Relaxed M=.54).

15 For the enthusiasm condition, subjects were asked via the computer to respond to the following prompt: "Here is a picture of someone who is **ENTHUSIASTIC**. We would like you to describe in general things that make you feel like the person in the picture. It is okay if you don't remember all the details, just be specific about what exactly it is that makes you **ENTHUSIASTIC** and what it feels like to be **ENTHUSIASTIC**. Please describe the events that make you feel the **MOST ENTHUSIASTIC**; these experiences could have occurred in the past or will happen in the future. If you can, write your description so that someone reading it might even feel **ENTHUSIASTIC**."

16 The coding procedure is identical to the one used in Chapter 2. The reliability of the coders was high: Cronbach's alpha for anger=.90, fear=.93 and enthusiasm=.91.

17 Subjects were also more likely to experience the target emotion at moderate-high levels of intensity. That is, 19 percent of subjects in the anger condition experienced no anger, while 51 percent experienced moderate levels of anger and 30 percent felt high levels of anger. For the fear condition, 16 percent of participants experienced no emotion, whereas 46 percent experienced moderate levels and 38 percent experienced high levels of fear. I found a similar pattern of results for subjects in the enthusiasm condition.

18 The output across conditions in the emotion induction task was nearly identical. Subjects in the anger condition wrote an average of thirty words in comparison to thirty-three words for the fear condition, twenty-eight words for the enthusiasm condition, and twenty-seven words for the relaxed condition. Altogether, participants discussed events in their personal lives that reflected the intended emotion.

19 When I take out the control variables, the direction and magnitude of the coefficients are essentially the same. The control variables are described in the appendix.

20 I calculate the predicted probabilities by manipulating the emotion variables while holding all the other independent variables at their own values observed in the data and then averaging over all of the cases. (See Hanmer and Kalkan 2013 for a more detailed description of this approach.)

21 The slope difference between the anger condition and relaxed condition is statistically significant at the .05 level (two-tailed test). To calculate the difference in slope, I took the difference between the anger slope and relaxed slope and calculated the 95 percent confidence interval for that difference. The confidence interval doesn't overlap with zero (ranges from .01 to .31).

22 To determine if these differences were statistically significant, I ran a direct test of the differences in the estimated probabilities of those scoring high in symbolic racism for the anger and control conditions. The test shows that the effect of the anger group is statistically different from that of the control group for whites at the very high end of the symbolic racism scale. The difference between the two groups is .09 with a confidence interval between .002 and .178. Because the confidence interval does not overlap with zero, I can conclude that the effect is statistically significant at the 90 percent confidence interval (two-tailed).

23 Similar to the difference test for those high in symbolic racism, I find that the effect of the anger condition is statistically different from that of the control condition (-.12) among those low in symbolic racism. This effect has a confidence interval between -.246 and -.024. Because this effect

doesn't overlap with zero, it is statistically significant at the 90 percent confidence interval (two-tailed).

24 The probit regression coefficients are in column 2 of Table 4A.

25 I also replicated these analyses using another race-neutral principle – preference for limited government – and found similar results. These results can be found in Table 4C in the appendix.

26 The probit regression coefficients from this analysis are in column 3 of Table 4A.

27 The difference between the anger condition and the control condition for those at the very high end of the symbolic racism scale is significant at the 87 percent confidence interval (two-tailed). The slope difference between the anger condition and the relaxed condition is significant at the 88 percent confidence interval (two-tailed).

28 The difference between the anger condition and the fear condition for those high in symbolic racism is significant at the 90 percent confidence interval (two-tailed). In addition, the slope difference between the anger condition and the fear condition is significant at the 90 percent confidence interval (two-tailed).

29 When I controlled for partisanship in these models, the results were essentially the same.

30 The probit regression coefficients are in the appendix in column 1 of Table 4B.

31 The probit coefficients are in the appendix in column 2 of Table 4B.

32 I ran one model that substituted political ideology for symbolic racism. The predicted probabilities showed that the effect of the enthusiasm condition on ideology did not differ from the relaxed condition. In another model, I included both symbolic racism and ideology. The results are essentially the same. The coefficient on enthusiasm*symbolic racism is negative ($\beta = -1.28$ $p \leq .13$), and the coefficient on enthusiasm*ideology is essentially zero ($\beta = .02$ $p \leq .98$). This evidence reinforces that enthusiasm doesn't increase people's reliance on habits such as political ideology or racial attitudes when making health policy decisions.

5 The Tea Party's Angry Rhetoric and the 2010 Midterm Elections

1 "Sharron Angle Ad Attacks Harry Reid While Vilifying Latinos," *Huffington Post*, October 26, 2010.

2 "Sharron Angle: Obama and Reid are Making Government Our False 'GOD,'" *Washington Post*, August 4, 2010.

3 "Dear Angry American, Joining the Tea Party is NOT Your Only Option," *Huffington Post*, September 22, 2010.

4 Sixty-seven percent of all respondents in the survey described a strong level of anger and dissatisfaction.

5 "Tea Partiers Bring Cause to Washington," *New York Times*, September 12, 2010.

6 "N.A.A.C.P Report Raises Concerns about Racism within Tea Party Groups," *New York Times*, October 20, 2010.

7 Tea Party races refer to congressional races where a Republican candidate backed by the Tea Party is running for congressional office.

8 "Renee Ellmers, GOP Congressional Candidate, Links Opponent to Park 51 'Victory Mosque,'" *Huffington Post*, September 23, 2010.

9 This percentage is based on the 2010 fiscal year. The Center on Budget and Policy Priorities conducted the report. It can be found at: http://www.cbpp.org/cms/index.cfm?fa=view&id=1258.

10 "The 14 Craziest Things Tea Party Candidates Believe In," *Business Insider*, September 24, 2010.

11 "Christine O'Donnell vs. Chris Coons: Gloves Come off in a Bitter Debate," *CBS News*, October 19, 2010.

12 "Karl Rove: Christine O'Donnell Says 'Nutty Things,' O'Donnell Fires Back," *CBS NEWS*, September 15, 2010.

13 The House variable's Mean=.49 and S.D.=.50 and the Senate variable's Mean=.51 and S.D.=.50.

14 As is common in the political science literature, I combined *afraid* and *worry* to create a variable that captures fear (Marcus et al. 2000).

15 The emotion variables were recoded to reflect emotional intensity (extremely and very =1, moderately = .5, and a little or not at all =0). Given that a small number of respondents experienced no emotion, I combined the "a little" and "not at all" categories. This measure of emotion poses a conservative test of my hypotheses. For example, instead of comparing anger to no anger, it compares extreme anger to low levels of anger. (Anger's Mean=.50, S.D.=.42, Min=0, Max=1) (Fear's Mean=.55, S.D.=.37, Min=0, Max=1).

16 Mean=.62, S.D.=.26, Min=0, Max=1.

17 A race is considered competitive if the vote margin from the election results is 10 percent or less. I recoded competiveness into a dummy variable where 1=competitive and 0=noncompetitive. The election results were obtained from: http://elections.nytimes.com/2010/results/house/big-board (House competitive variable's Mean=.21, S.D.=.41, Min=0, Max=1 and Senate competitive variable's Mean=.27, S.D.=.44, Min=0, Max=1).

18 The exact question wording for these variables is described in the appendix.

19 Alexandra Moe, from NBC, also compiled a list of Tea Party candidates. This list slightly differed from the *NY Times* list. It identified one hundred thirty Tea Party candidates running for the House and ten for the Senate. The results do not differ if the NBC list is used. The NBC list can

be found at http://firstread.msnbc.msn.com/_news/2010/11/03/5403120-just-32-of-tea-party-candidates-win.

20 Kate Zernike, Kitty Bennett, Ford Fessenden, Kevin Quealy, Amy Schonenfeld, Archie Tse, and Derick Willis conducted the report. The *NY Times* list of candidates is available at http://www.nytimes.com/interactive/2010/10/15/us/politics/tea-party-graphic.html?ref=politics.

21 I calculate the predicted probabilities by manipulating the emotion variables while holding all the other independent variables at their own values observed in the data and then averaging over all of the cases.

22 I ran a difference test (the same as in Chapter 4) for those high in symbolic racism. The confidence interval (CI) for the difference between anger and low emotion did not overlap with zero (CI is between .05 and .35). The same can be said between anger and fear (CI is between .07 and .31). Because these effects do not overlap with zero, they are statistically significant at the 90 percent CI (two-tailed).

23 The difference between anger and low emotion for those low in symbolic racism (CI is between -.01 and -.47) is significant at the 90 percent CI (two-tailed).

24 As in Chapter 4, I calculated whether the difference in the slopes between high anger and low emotion was statistically significant. The difference between the anger slope and low emotion slope is significant at the .05 level (i.e., the 95% CI ranges from .04 to .88). In addition, the high anger slope is statistically different from the high fear slope at the .05 level (two-tailed).

25 The probit regression coefficients for the House are reported in the appendix in Table 4B.

26 The difference between anger and low emotion for those low in symbolic racism (CI is between -.02 and -.26) is significant at the 90 percent CI (two-tailed).

27 The results were nearly identical when anger and fear were interacted with partisanship. I also ran a model that interacted each emotion with racial attitudes and nonracial attitudes (ideology and partisanship) simultaneously. The results were essentially the same.

28 For the whole sample, 12 percent of respondents reported that they had attended a speech, march, rally, or demonstration in the previous twelve months.

29 The variable was a dummy variable 1=Have done this in the past twelve months and 0=Have not done this in the past twelve months.

30 I regressed *Attending a Rally* on *Anger, Fear, Symbolic Racism,* and the interactions between these specific emotions and racial attitude, controlling for *Ideology, Party Identification, Income, Age, South, Gender, Education, Internet Access, Worse Economy,* and *Competitiveness.* The model only examines respondents in Tea Party races. The probit coefficients are in column 1 of Table 5D.

31 Scholars have found mixed results for whether fear increases participation. In some cases, researchers have found fear does increase participation (Marcus et al. 2000), while others have found it to have mixed effects. For instance, Valentino and his colleagues (2011) find that fear is more likely to increase "cheap" forms of participation such as wearing a campaign button but not "costly" forms of participation such as donating money.

32 The probit regression coefficients are in column 2 of Table 5D.

33 For racial liberals (scoring from 0-.25), I find that fear has the biggest effect on attending a rally while anger has a small effect. Fear increases racial liberals' probability of attending a rally by about 39 percent. Similarly, fear (13%) is more likely to mobilize political liberals to participate than anger (5%).

34 "Violence Mars Busing in Boston: Mayor Restricts Gatherings to Prevent Recurrence of Stonings," *New York Times*, September 13, 1974.

Conclusion

1 Tea Party candidates varied in how explicit or implicit their campaign rhetoric was on race. Some candidates (e.g., Rick Barber) were very explicit about race while other candidates were more implicit in discussing race.

2 In the case of group threat in the United States, Green, Strolovitch, and Wong (1998) demonstrate that hate crimes against minorities in NYC are more frequent in predominantly white areas where the minority population has increased.

3 "Fear about Immigrants Deepen Divisions in Europe," *New York Times*, April 12, 2011.

4 "Greece," *New York Times*, Oct. 17, 2012.

5 "Greek Anger over Austerity Measures Spills on to Athens Streets," *The Guardian*, June 29, 2010.

6 "Europe's Immigration Challenge," *The Guardian*, July 24, 2012.

7 "Greek Far Right Hangs a Target on Immigrants," *New York Times*, July 10, 2012.

8 Greece Takes It Out on Immigrants: Bloody Attacks against Minorities Have Spiked as Golden Dawn Rises," *Macleans*, October 10, 2012.

9 "Greece: Rare Hate Crime Trial Opens," *Human Rights Watch* (Press Release), December 12, 2011.

10 "Racist Attacks on the Rise in Greece-Migrants Group," Reuters, August 14, 2012.

11 "Euro Crisis Invites Political Extremism in French Vote," CNN, April 16, 2012.

12 "French Far-Right Leader Loses Immunity, Faces Charges," *BBC News Europe*, June 1, 2013.

13 Lynn Sanders (1997), however, points out that deliberation does not necessarily enhance democracy. Although people get together to deliberate, it

does not mean they will mutually respect each other's opinions – because not everyone is on equal footing. Perhaps taking anger out of the racial equation will not necessarily increase the likelihood of better policy outcomes for blacks, because racial conservatism and racial liberalism may not be on equal footing in this country. If one perspective has more public support (e.g., racial conservatism), deliberation still might lead certain ideas to matter more in the type of policies enacted.

Bibliography

Aboud, Frances E. 2005. "The Development of Prejudice in Childhood and Adolescence." In John F. Dovidio, Peter Glick, and Laurie A. Rudman (eds.) *On the Nature of Prejudice: Fifty Years after Allport* (pp. 310–326). Massachusetts: Blackwell Publishing.

Abramowitz, Alan I. 2011. "Partisan Polarization and the Rise of the Tea Party Movement." Typescript. Emory University.

Abramowitz, Alan I. and Kyle L. Saunders. 2008. "Is Polarization a Myth?" *Journal of Politics*, 70: 542–555.

Adorno, T. W., Else Frenkel-Brunswk, Daniel J. Levinson, and R. Nevitt Sanford. 1950. *The Authoritarian Personality*. New York: Harper & Row.

Ai, Chunrong and Edward C. Norton. 2003. "Interaction Terms in Logit and Probit Models." *Economic Letters*, 80: 123–129.

Alderman, Liz. 2012. "Greek Far Right Hangs a Target on Immigrants." The *New York Times* on the Web. http://www.nytimes.com/2012/07/11/world/europe/as-golden-dawn-rises-in-greece-anti-immigrant-violence-follows.html?pagewanted=all.

Allport, Gordon W. 1954. *The Nature of Prejudice*. Addison-Wesley Publishing Company.

Arsenault, Raymond. 2006. *Freedom Riders: 1961 and the Struggle for Racial Justice*. New York: Oxford University Press.

Averill, James R. 1982. *Anger and Aggression: An Essay on Emotion*. New York: Springer-Verlag.

    1983. "Studies of Anger and Aggression: Implication for Theories of Emotion." *American Psychologist*, 38: 1145–1160.

Bang Peterson, Michael. 2010. "Distinct Emotions, Distinct Domains: Anger, Anxiety and Perceptions of Intentionality." *Journal of Politics*, 72: 357–365.

Banks, Antoine J. and M. A. Bell. 2013. "Racialized Campaign Ads: The Emotional Content in Implicit Racial Appeals Primes White Racial Attitudes." *Public Opinion Quarterly*, 77: 549–560.

Banks, Antoine J. and Nicholas A. Valentino. 2012. "Emotional Substrates of White Racial Attitudes." *American Journal of Political Science*, 56: 286–297.

Baron, Reuben M. and David A. Kenny. 1986. "The Moderator-Mediator Variable Distinction in Social Psychological Research: Conceptual, Strategic, and Statistical Considerations." *Journal of Personality and Social Psychology*, 51: 1173–1182.

Berinsky, Adam J. 2009. *In Time of War: Understanding American Public Opinion from World War II to Iraq*. Chicago: University of Chicago Press.

Berinsky, Adam J., Vincent L. Hutchings, Tali Mendelberg, Lee Shaker, and Nicholas A. Valentino. 2011. "Sex and Race: Are Black Candidates More Likely to be Disadvantaged by Sex Scandals?" *Political Behavior*, 33: 179–202.

Bertrand, Marianne and Sendhil Mullanianthan. 2004. "Are Emily and Greg More Employable than Lakisha and Jamal? A Field Experiment on Labor Market Discrimination." *American Economic Review*, 94: 991–1013.

Blake, Robert and Wayne Dennis. 1943. "The Development of Stereotypes Concerning the Negro." *Journal of Abnormal and Social Psychology*, 38: 525–531.

Blumer, Herbert G. 1955. "Reflections on Theory of Race Relations." In Andrew Lind (ed.) *Race Relation in World Perspective* (pp. 3–24). Honolulu: University of Hawaii Press.

    1958. "Race Prejudice as a Sense of Group Position." *Pacific Sociological Review*, 1: 3–7.

Bobo, Lawrence D. 1983. "Whites' Opposition to Busing: Symbolic Racism or Realistic Group Conflict?" *Journal of Personality and Social Psychology*, 45: 1196–1210.

    1988. "Group Conflict, Prejudice, and the Paradox of Contemporary Racial Attitudes." In Phyllis Katz and Dalmas Taylor (eds.) *Eliminating Racism: Profiles in Controversy* (pp. 85–109). New York: Plenum Press.

    2000. "Race and Beliefs about Affirmative Action: Assessing the Effects of Interest, Group Threat, Ideology, and Racism." In David Sears, Jim Sidanius, and Lawrence Bobo (eds.) *Racialized Politics: The Debate about Racism in America* (pp. 137–164). Chicago: University of Chicago Press.

Bobo, Lawrence D. and Vincent L. Hutchings. 1996. "Perceptions of Racial Group Competition: Extending Blumer's Theory of Group Position to a Multiracial Social Context." *American Sociological Review*, 61: 951–972.

Bobo, Lawrence D. and James R. Kluegel. 1997. "Status, Ideology, and Dimensions of Whites' Racial Beliefs and Attitudes: Progress and Stagnation." In Steven A. Tuch and Jack K. Martin (eds.) *Racial Attitudes in the 1990s: Continuity and Change* (pp. 93–120). Westport, CT: Praeger Press.

Bobo, Lawrence D. and Mia Tuan. 2006. *Prejudice in Politics: Group Position, Public Opinion, and the Wisconsin Treaty Rights Dispute.* Cambridge, MA: Harvard University Press.

Bower, Gordon. H. 1981. "Mood and Memory." *American Psychologist*, 36: 129–148.

Bower, Gordon H. and Joseph P. Forgas. 2001. "Mood and Social Memory." In J. P. Forgas (ed.) *The Handbook of Affect and Social Cognition* (pp. 95–120). Mahwah, NJ: Lawrence Erlbaum Associates.

Bower, Gordon. H., Kenneth P. Monteiro, and Stephen G. Gilligan. 1978. "Emotional Mood as a Context for Learning and Recall." *Journal of Verbal Learning and Verbal Behavior* 17: 573–585.

Brader, Ted. 2005. "Striking a Responsive Chord: How Political Ads Motivate and Persuade Voters by Appealing to Emotions." *American Journal of Political Science* 49: 388–405.

2006. *Campaigning for Hearts and Minds: How Emotional Appeals in Political Ads Work.* Chicago: University of Chicago Press.

Brader, Ted, Eric W. Groenendyk, and Nicholas A. Valentino. 2011. "Fight or Flight? When Political Threats Arouse Public Anger and Fear." University of Michigan Typescript.

Brader, Ted, Nicholas A. Valentino, and Elizabeth Suhay. 2008. "What Triggers Public Opposition to Immigration? Anxiety, Group Cues, and Immigration Threat." *American Journal of Political Science*, 52: 959–978.

Brewer, Marilynn B. 1999. "The Psychology of Prejudice: Ingroup Love or Outgroup Hate?" *Journal of Social Issues*, 55: 429–444.

Brewer, Marilynn B. and Donald T. Campbell. 1976. *Ethnocentrism and Intergroup Attitudes: East African Evidence.* Beverly Hills, CA: Sage.

Busch, Andrew E. "The 2010 Midterm Elections: An Overview." *The Forum*, 8: 1–15.

Butler, Daniel M. and David E. Broockman 2011. "Do Politicians Racially Discriminate against Constituents? A Field Experiment on State Legislators." *American Journal of Political Science*, 55: 463–477.

Campbell, Angus, Philip E. Converse, Warren E. Miller, and Donald E. Stokes. 1960. *The American Voter.* Chicago: University of Chicago Press.

Carmines, Edward G., Paul Sniderman, and Beth C. Easter. 2011. "On the Meaning, Measurement, and Implications of Racial Resentment." *ANNALS of the American Academy of Political and Social Science*, 634: 98–116.

Cho, Wendy K. Tam, James G. Gimpel, and Daron R. Shaw. 2012. "The Tea Party Movement and the Geography of Collective Action." *Quarterly Journal of Political Science*, 7: 105–133.

Clore, Gerald L. and David B. Centerbar. 2004. "Analyzing Anger: How to Make People Mad." *Emotion*, 4: 139–144.

Converse, Phillip E. 1964. "The Nature of Belief Systems in Mass Publics." In D. E. Apter (ed.), *Ideology and Discontent* (pp. 206–261). New York: Free Press.

Crandall, Christian S. 1994. "Prejudice against Fat People: Ideology and Self-Interest." *Journal of Personality and Social Psychology*, 66: 882–894.

Cuddy Amy J. C., Susan T. Fiske, and Peter Glick. 2007. "The BIAS Map: Behaviors from Intergroup Affect and Stereotypes." *Journal of Personality and Social Psychology*, 92: 631–648.

Damasio, Antonio R. 1994. *Descartes' Error: Emotion, Reason and the Human Brain*. New York: Putnam and Sons.

DeSteno, David, Nilanjana Dasgupta, Monica Y. Bartlett, and Aida Cajdric. 2004. "Prejudice from Thin Air: The Effect of Emotion on Automatic Intergroup Attitudes." *Psychological Science*, 15: 319–324.

Devine, Patricia G., E. Ashby Plant, and Kristen Harrison. 1999. "The Problem of 'US' Versus 'Them' and Aids Stigma." *American Behavioral Scientist*, 42: 1212–1228.

Druckman, James N. 2004. Priming the Vote: Campaign Effects in a U.S. Senate Election. *Political Psychology*, 25: 577–594.

Ekman, Paul. 1993. "Facial Expression and Emotion." *American Psychologist*, 48: 384–392.

Ekman, Paul and Wallace W. Friesen. 1976. "Pictures of Facial Affect." *Human Interaction Laboratory*. San Francisco: University of California Medical Center.

Epstein, Ralph and S. S. Komorita. 1966. "Prejudice among Negro Children as Related to Parental Ethnocentrism and Punitiveness." *Journal of Personality and Social Psychology*, 4: 643–647.

Edsall, Thomas B. and Mary D. Edsall. 1991. *Chain Reaction: The Impact of Race, Rights, and Taxes on American Politics*. New York: W. W. Norton & Company.

Esses, Victoria M., John F. Dovidio, Lynne M. Jackson, and Tamara L. Armstrong. 2001. "The Immigration Dilemma: The Role of Perceived Group Competition, Ethnic Prejudice, and National Identity." *Journal of Social Issues*, 57: 389–412.

Farley, Reynolds. 1984. *Blacks and Whites: Narrowing the Gap?* Cambridge, MA: Harvard University Press.

Federico, Christopher M. 2005. "Racial Perceptions and Evaluative Responses to Welfare: Does Education Attenuate Race-of-Target Effects?" *Political Psychology*, 26: 683–698.

Fazio, Russell H. 1990, " A Practical Guide to the Use of Response Latency in Social Psychological Research." In Clyde Hendrick and Margaret Clark (eds.) *Research Methods in Personality and Social Psychology: Review of Personality and Social Psychology Volume 11* (pp. 74–97). Newbury Park, CA: Sage.

Feldman, Stanley and Leonie Huddy. 2005. "Racial Resentment and White Opposition to Race-Conscious Programs: Principles or Prejudice?" *American Journal of Political Science*, 49: 168–183.

Fiorina, Morris P., with Samuel J. Abrams and Jeremy C. Pope. 2006. *Culture War? The Myth of a Polarized America*. 2nd ed. New York: Pearson Longman.

Forgas, Joseph P. 1995. "Mood and Judgment: The Affect Infusion Model (AIM)." *Psychological Bulletin*, 117: 39–66.

Fredrickson, George M. 1971. *The Black Image in the White Mind: The Debate on Afro-American Character and Destiny, 1817–1914*. New York: Harper and Row.

2002. *Racism: A Short History*. Princeton, NJ: Princeton University Press.

Frijda, Nico H., Peter Kulpers, and Elisabeth ter Schure. 1989. "Relations among Emotion, Appraisal, and Emotional Action Readiness." *Journal of Personality and Social Psychology*, 57: 212–228.

Gamson, William A. and A Modigliana. 1987. "The Changing Culture of Affirmative Action." In *Research in Political Sociology*, vol. 3, ed. Richard D. Braungart. Greenwich, CT: JAI Press.

Gaertner, Samuel L. and John F. Dovidio. 1986. "The Aversive Form of Racism." In John F. Dovidio and Samuel L. Gaertner (eds.) *Prejudice, Discrimination, and Racism* (pp. 61–89). Orlando, FL: Academic Press.

Germond, Jack W. and Jules Witcover. 1989. *Whose Broad Stripes and Bright Stars? The Trivial Pursuit of the Presidency 1988*. New York: Warner Books.

Gilens, Martin. 1995. "Racial Attitudes and Opposition to Welfare." *Journal of Politics*, 57: 994–1014.

1999. *Why Americans Hate Welfare: Race, Media, and the Politics of Antipoverty Policy*. Chicago: University of Chicago Press.

Gilliam Frank D. Jr. and Shanto Iyengar. 2000. "Prime Suspects: The Influence of Local Television News on the Viewing Public." *American Journal of Political Science*, 44: 560–573.

Glick, Peter. 2005. "Choice of Scapegoats." In John F. Dovidio, Peter Glick, and Laurie A. Rudman (eds.) *On the Nature of Prejudice: Fifty Years after Allport* (pp. 245–261). Massachusetts: Blackwell Publishing.

Goldberg, Julie H., Jennifer S. Lerner, and Philip E. Tetlock. 1999. "Rage and Reason: The Psychology of the Intuitive Prosecutor." *European Journal of Social Psychology*, 29: 781–795.

Gray, Jeffrey A. 1987. *The Psychology of Fear and Stress*. New York: Cambridge University Press.

Green, Donald P., Dara Z. Strolovitch, and Janelle S. Wong. 1998. Defended Neighborhoods, Integration, and Racially Motivated Crime. *American Journal of Sociology*, 104: 372–403.

Griffin, John D. and Brian Newman. 2008. *Minority Report: Evaluating Political Equality in America*. Chicago: University of Chicago Press.

Groenendyk, Eric W. and Antoine J. Banks. (2013) "Emotional Rescue: How Affect Helps Partisans Overcome Collective Action Problems." Political Psychology (published online).

Gurin, Patricia, Arthur H. Miller, and Gerald Gurin. 1980. "Stratum Identification and Consciousness." *Social Psychology Quarterly*, 43: 30–47.

Guttmann, Amy and Dennis Thompson. 1996. *Democracy and Disagreement*. Cambridge, MA: Harvard University Press.

Hancock, Angie Marie. 2004. *The Politics of Disgust and the Public Identity of the "Welfare Queen."* New York: New York University Press.

Hanmer, Michael J. and Kerem O. Kalkan. 2013. "Behind the Curve: Clarifying the Best Approach to Calculating Predicted Probabilities and Marginal Effects from Limited Dependent Variable Models." *American Journal of Political Science*, 57: 263–277.

Harding, John, Harold Proshansky, Benard Kutner, and Isidor Chein. 1969. "Prejudice and Ethnic Relations." In G. Lindzey and E. Aronson (eds.) *The Handbook of Social Psychology* (Vol. 5). (pp. 1–76). Reading, MA: Addison-Wesley.

Harvey, Richard D. and Debra L. Oswald. 2000. "Collective Guilt and Shame as Motivation for White Support of Black Programs." *Journal of Applied Social Psychology*, 30: 1790–1811.

Henderson, Michael and D. Sunshine Hillygus. 2011. "The Dynamics of Health Care Opinion, 2008–2010: Partisanship, Self-Interest, and Racial Resentment." *Journal of Health Politics, Policy, and Law*, 36: 945–960.

Henry, P. J. and David O. Sears. 2002. "The Symbolic Racism 2000 Scale." *Political Psychology*, 23: 253–283.

Huber, Gregory A. and John S. Lapinski. 2006. "The 'Race Card' Revisited: Assessing Racial Priming in Policy Contests." *American Journal of Political Science*, 50: 421–440.

Huddy, Leonie, and Stanley Feldman. 2009. "On Assessing the Political Effects of Racial Prejudice." *Annual Review of Political Science*, 12: 423–447.

Huddy, Leonie, Stanley Feldman, and Erin Cassese. 2007. "On the Distinct Political Effects of Anxiety and Anger." In W. Russell Neuman, George E. Marcus, Ann N. Crigler, and Michael MacKuen (eds.) *The Affect Effect: Dynamics of Emotion and Political Thinking and Behavior* (pp. 202–230). Chicago: University of Chicago Press.

Huddy, Leonie, Stanley Feldman, Charles Tabler, and Gallaya Lahav. 2005. "Threat, Anxiety, and Support of Antiterrorism Politics." *American Journal of Political Science* 49: 593–608.

Hutchings, Vincent L. 2009. "Change or More of the Same? Evaluating Racial Attitudes in the Obama Era." *Public Opinion Quarterly*, 73: 917–942.

Hutchings, Vincent L. and Ashley E. Jardina. 2009. "Experiments on Racial Priming in Political Campaigns." *Annual Review of Political Science*, 12: 397–402.

Hutchings, Vincent L., Nicholas A. Valentino, Tasha Philpot, and Ismail White. 2006. "Racial Cues in Campaign News: The Effects of Candidate Issue Distance on Emotional Responses, Political Attentiveness." In David Redlawsk (ed.) *Feeling Politics* (pp. 165–186). New York: Palgrave Macmillan.

Hutchings, Vincent L., Hanes Walton Jr., and Andrea Benjamin. 2010. "The Impact of Explicit Racial Cues on Gender Differences in Support for Confederate Symbols and Partisanship." *Journal of Politics*, 72: 1175–1188.

Hurwitz, Jon and Mark Peffley. 2005. "Playing the Race Card in the Post-Willie Horton Era." *Public Opinion Quarterly*, 69: 99–112.

Iyengar, Shanto. 1989. "How Citizens Think about National Issues: A Matter of Responsibility." *American Journal of Political Science*, 33: 878–900.

1990. "Framing Responsibility for Political Issues: The Case of Poverty." *Political Behavior*, 12: 19–40.

1996. "Framing Responsibility for Political Issues." *Annals of the American Academy of Political and Social Science*, 546: 59–70.

Iyengar, Shanto and Donald R. Kinder. 1987. *News that Matters: Television and American Public Opinion*. Chicago: University of Chicago Press.

Jackson, James S., Kendrick T. Brown, Tony N. Brown, and Bryant Marks. 2001. "Contemporary Immigration Policy Orientation among Dominant-Group Members in Western Europe." *Journal of Social Issues*, 57: 431–456.

Jackson, Walter A. 1990. *Gunnar Myrdal and America's Conscience: Social Engineering and Racial Liberalism, 1938–1987*. Chapel Hill: University of North Carolina Press.

Jacobs, Lawrence R. and Theda Skocpol. 2010. *Health Care Reform and American Politics: What Everyone Needs to Know*. New York: Oxford University Press.

Jamieson, Kathleen Hall. 1992. *Dirty Politics: Deception, Distraction and Democracy*. Oxford: Oxford University Press.

Johnson, Alex M. "Tennessee ad ignites internal GOP squabbling." NBC News. Oct. 25, 2006. http://www.nbcnews.com/id/15403071/#.UsRSkXmQf8s.

Kalmoe, Nathan P. 2013. From Fistfights to Firefights: Trait Aggression and Support for State Violence." *Political Behavior*, 35: 311–330.

Kam, Cindy D. and Donald R. Kinder. 2007. "Terror and Ethnocentrism: Foundations of American Support for the War on Terrorism." *Journal of Politics*, 69: 320–338.

Karpowitz, Christopher, J. Quin Monson, Kelly D. Patterson, and Jeremy C. Pope. 2011. "Tea Time in America? The Impact of the Tea Party Movement on the 2010 Midterm Elections." *PS: Political Science and Politics*, 44: 303–309.

Karlins, Marvin, Thomas L. Coffman, and Gary Walters. 1969. "On the Fading of Social Stereotypes: Studies in the Three Generation of College Students." *Journal of Personality and Social Psychology*, 13: 1–16.

Katz, Daniel and Kenneth Braly. 1933. "Racial Stereotypes of One Hundred College Students." *Journal of Abnormal and Social Psychology*, 28: 280–290.

Kaufmann, Karen M. 2004. *The Urban Voter: Group Conflict and Mayoral Voting Behavior in American Cities*. Ann Arbor: University of Michigan Press.

Key, V. O., Jr. 1949. *Southern Politics in State and Nation*. New York: Knopf.

Keltner, Dacher, Phoebe C. Ellsworth, and Kari Edwards. 1993. "Beyond Simple Pessimism: Effects of Sadness and Anger on Social Perception." *Journal of Personality and Social Psychology*, 64: 740–752.

Kinder, Donald R. and Cindy D. Kam. 2009. *Us against Them: Ethnocentric Foundations of American Opinion*. Chicago: University of Chicago Press.

Kinder, Donald R. and Thomas Palfrey. 1993. "On Behalf of an Experimental Political Science." In D. R. Kinder and T. Palfrey (eds.), *Experimental Foundations of Political Science* (pp. 1–42). Ann Arbor: University of Michigan Press.

Kinder, Donald R. and Lynn M. Sanders. 1996. *Divided by Color: Racial Politics and Democratic Ideals*. Chicago: University of Chicago Press.

Kinder, Donald R. and David O. Sears. 1981. "Prejudice and Politics: Symbolic Racism Versus Racial Threats to the Good Life." *Journal of Personality and Social Psychology*, 40: 414–431.

Knowles, Eric. D. Brian, S. Lowery, and Rebecca L. Schaumberg. 2010. "Racial Prejudice Predicts Opposition to Obama and His Health Care Reform Plan." *Journal of Experimental Social Psychology*, 46: 420–423.

Krosnick, Jon A. and Donald R. Kinder. 1990. "Altering the Foundations of Support for the President through Priming." *American Political Science Review*, 84: 497–512.

Kuklinski, James H., Paul M. Sniderman, Kathleen Knight, Thomas Piazza, Philip E. Tetlock, Gordon R. Lawrence, and Barbara Mellers. 1997. "Racial Prejudice and Attitudes toward Affirmative Action." *American Journal of Political Science*, 41: 402–419.

Lane, Robert E. 1962. *Political Ideology: Why the American Common Man Believes What He Does*. New York: Free Press

Larsen, Randy J. and Barbara L. Fredrickson. 1999. Measurement Issues in Emotion Research. In D. Kahneman, E. Diener, and N. Schwarz (eds.)

Well-being: Foundation of Hedonic Psychology (pp. 40–60) New York: Russell Sage.

Layman, Geoffrey C. and Thomas M. Carsey. 2002. "Party Polarization and 'Conflict Extension' in the American Electorate." *American Journal of Political Science* 46: 786–802.

Lazarus, Richard S. 1991. *Emotion and Adaptation*. New York: Oxford University Press.

Lebron, Christopher J. 2013. *The Color of Our Shame: Race and Justice in Our Time*. New York: Oxford University Press.

Lee, Taeku. 2002. *Mobilizing Public Opinion: Black Insurgency and Racial Attitudes in the Civil Rights Era*. Chicago: University of Chicago Press.

Lerner, Jennifer S. and Dacher Keltner. 2001. "Fear, Anger and Risk." *Journal of Personality and Social Psychology*, 81: 146–159.

Lerner, Jennifer S. and Larissa Z. Tiedens. 2006. "Portrait of Angry Decision Maker: How Appraisal Tendencies Shape Anger's Influence on Cognition." *Journal of Behavioral Decision Making*, 19: 115–137.

Lerner, Jennifer S. Julie H. Goldberg and Philip E. Tetlock. 1998. "Sober Second Thought: The Effect of Accountability, Anger, and Authoritarianism on Attributions of Responsibility." *Personality and Social Psychology Bulletin*, 24: 563–574.

Lerner, Jennifer S., Roxana M. Gonzalez, Deborah A. Small, and Baruch Fischhoff. 2003. "Effects of Fear and Anger on Perceived Risks of Terrorism: A National Field Experiment." *Psychological Science*, 14: 144–150.

Lewis, John with Michael D'Orso. 1998. *Walking with the Wind: A Memoir of the Movement*. New York: Simon and Schuster.

Mackie, Diane M., Thierry Devos, and Eliot R. Smith. 2000. "Intergroup Emotions: Explaining Offensive Action Tendencies in an Intergroup Context." *Journal of Personality and Social Psychology*, 79: 602–616.

MacKuen, Michael, Jennifer Wolak, Luke Keele, and George E. Marcus. 2010. "Civic Engagements: Resolute Partisanship or Reflective Deliberation." *American Journal of Political Science*, 54: 440–458.

Marcus, George E. 2002. *The Sentimental Citizen: Emotion in Democratic Politics*. University Park: Pennsylvania State University Press.

Marcus, George E., W. Russell Neuman, and Michael MacKuen. 2000. *Affective Intelligence and Political Judgment*. Chicago: University of Chicago Press.

Mayer, Jeremy D. 2002. *Running on Race: Racial Politics in Presidential Campaigns, 1960–2000*. New York: Random House.

McClosky, Herbert, and John Zaller. 1984. *The American Ethos: Public Attitudes toward Capitalism and Democracy*. Cambridge, MA: Harvard University Press.

McConahay, John B. 1986. "Modern Racism, Ambivalence, and the Modern Racism Scale. In Samuel Gaertner and John Dovidio (eds.) Prejudice,

Discrimination, and Racism: Theory Research (pp. 91–125). San Diego, CA: Academic Press.

McConahay, John B. and Joseph C. Hough Jr. 1976. "Symbolic Racism." *Journal of Social Issues*, 32: 23–45.

McConnaughy, Corrine, Ismail K. White, and Chryl Laird. 2010. "Racial Politics Complicated: The Work of Gendered Race Cues in American Politics." Typescript. Ohio State University.

McGinniss, Joe. 1969. *The Selling of the President of 1968.* New York: Trident Press.

Mendelberg, Tali. 1997. "Executing Hortons: Racial Crime in the 1988 Presidential Campaign." *Public Opinion Quarterly*, 61: 134–157.

   2001. *The Race Card: Campaign Strategy, Implicit Messages, and the Norm of Equality.* Princeton, NJ: Princeton University Press.

   2008. "Racial Priming Revived." *Perspectives on Politics*, 6: 109–123.

Merolla, Jennifer L. and Elizabeth Zechmeister. 2009. *Democracy at Risk: How Terrorist Threat Affect the Public.* Chicago: University of Chicago Press.

Miller, Arthur H., Patricia Gurin, Gerald Gurin, and Oksana Malanchuk. 1981. "Group Consciousness and Political Participation." *American Journal of Political Science*, 25: 494–511.

Miller, Steven D. and David O. Sears. 1986. "Stability and Change in Social Tolerance: A Test of the Persistence Hypothesis." *American Journal of Political Science*, 30: 214–236.

Mosher, Donald L. and Alvin Scodel. 1960. "Relationships between Ethnocentrism in Children and the Ethnocentrism and Authoritarian Rearing Practices of their Mothers." *Child Development*, 31: 369–376.

Myrdal, Gunnar. 1944. *An American Dilemma: The Negro Problem and Modern Democracy.* New York: Harper and Row.

Nelson, Thomas E., Rosalee A. Clawson, and Zoe Oxley. 1997. "Media Framing of a Civil Liberties Controversy and Its Effect on Tolerance." *American Political Science Review*, 91: 567–583.

Olbermann, Keith. "Beware fear's racist temptation: Don't blame your fear of the future on Obama's skin color." MSNBC. Feb. 15, 2010. http://www.msnbc.msn.com/id/35413401/.

Oliver, Eric. 2005. *Fat Politics: The Real Story behind America's Obesity Epidemic.* New York: Oxford University Press.

Oliver, Melvin L. and Thomas M. Shapiro. 2006. *Black Wealth/White Wealth: A New Perspective on Racial Inequality.* New York: Routledge Taylor and Francis Group

Orfield, Gary. 1988. "Race and the Liberal Agenda: The Loss of the Integrationist Dream, 1965–1974." In Margaret Weir, Ann Shola Orloff, and Theda Skocpol (eds.) *The Politics of Social Policy in the United States* (pp. 313–355). Princeton, NJ: Princeton University Press.

Owen, Diana and Jack Dennis. 1987. "Preadult Development of Political Tolerance." *Political Psychology*, 8: 547–561.

Parker, Christopher S. and Matt A. Barreto. 2011. "Exploring the Causes and Consequences of Tea Party Support." Typescript. University of Washington.

    2013. *Change They Can't Believe In: The Tea Party and Reactionary Politics in America*. Princeton, NJ: Princeton University Press.

Pettigrew, Thomas F. 1979. "The Ultimate Attribution Error: Extending Allport's Cognitive Analysis of Prejudice." *Personality and Social Psychological Bulletin*, 5: 461–476.

    1998. "Reaction toward the New Minorities of Western Europe." *Annual Review of Sociology*, 24: 77–103.

Pettigrew, Thomas F. and R. W. Meertens. 1995. "Subtle and Blatant Prejudice in Western Europe." *European Journal of Social Psychology*, 25: 57–75.

Pettigrew, Thomas F., Ulrich Wagner, and Oliver Christ. 2007. "Who Opposes Immigration? Comparing German with North American Findings." *Du Bois Review* 4: 19–39.

Phillips, Kate. 2009. Carter's Racism Charge Sparks War of Words. New York Times on the Web, September 16. http://thecaucus.blogs.nytimes.com/2009/09/16/carters-racism-charge-sparks-war-of-words/.

Piston, Spencer. 2010. "How Explicit Racial Prejudice Hurt Obama in the 2008 Election." *Political Behavior* 32: 431–451.

Quillian, Lincoln. 1995. "Prejudice as a Response to Perceived Group Threat: Population Composition and Anti-Immigrant and Racial Prejudice in Europe." *American Sociological Review*, 60: 586–611.

Reeves, Keith. 1997. *Voting Hopes or Fears?: White Voter, Black Candidates and Racial Politics in America*. Oxford: Oxford University Press.

Rosenstone, Steven J., Roy L. Behr, and Edward H. Lazarus. 1984. *Third Parties in America: Citizen Response to Major Party Failure*. Princeton, NJ: Princeton University Press.

Rozin Paul and April E. Fallon. 1987. "A Perspective on Disgust." *Psychological Review*, 94: 23–41.

Salmond, John A. 1997. *My Mind Set on Freedom: A History of the Civil Rights Movement, 1954–1968*. Chicago: The American Ways Series.

Sanders, Lynn M. 1997. "Against Deliberation." *Political Theory*, 25: 347–376.

Schuman, Howard and Maria Krysan. 1999. "A Historical Note on Whites' Beliefs about Racial Inequality." *American Sociological Review*, 64: 847–855.

Schuman, Howard, Charlotte Steeh, Lawrence Bobo, and Maria Krysan. 1997. *Racial Attitudes in American: Trends and Interpretations*. Revised Edition. Cambridge, MA: Harvard University Press.

Searing, Donald, Gerald Wright, and George Rabinowitz. 1976. "The Primacy Principle: Attitude Change and Political Socialization." *British Journal of Political Science*, 6: 83–113.

Sears, David O. 1988. "Symbolic Racism." In Phyllis Katz and Dalmas Taylor (eds.) *Eliminating Racism: Profiles in Controversy* (pp. 53–84). New York: Plenum Press.

1990. "Whither Political Socialization Research? The Question of Persistence." In O. Ichilov (ed.) *Political Socialization, Citizenship Education, and Democracy*, (pp. 69–97). New York: Teachers College Press.

Sears, David O. and Jack Citrin. 1982. *Tax Revolt: Something for Nothing in California*. Cambridge, MA: Harvard University Press.

Sears, David O. and P. J. Henry. 2003. "The Origins of Symbolic Racism." *Journal of Personality and Social Psychology*, 85: 259–275.

Sears, David O., Carl P. Hensler, and Leslie K. Speer. 1979. "Whites' Opposition to 'Busing': Self-Interest or Symbolic Politics?" *American Political Science Review*, 73: 369–384.

Sears, David O. and Donald Kinder. 1971. "Racial Tensions and Voting in Los Angeles." In W. Hirsch (ed.) *Los Angeles: Viability and Prospects for Metropolitan Leadership* (pp. 51–88). New York: Praeger.

Sears, David O. and John B. McConahay. 1973. *The Politics of Violence: The New Urban Blacks and the Watts Riot*. Boston, MA: Houghton Mifflin Company.

Sears, David O. Hilary Haley, and P. J. Henry. 2008. "Cultural Diversity and Sociopolitical Attitudes at College Entry." In Jim Sidanius, Shana Levin, Colette van Larr, and David O. Sears (eds.) *The Diversity Challenge: Social Identity and Intergroup Relations on the College Campus* (pp. 65–99). New York: Russell Sage Foundation.

Sears, David O., John J. Hetts, Jim Sidanius, and Lawrence D. Bobo. 2000. "Race in American Political Framing the Debates." In David O. Sears, Jim Sidanius, and Lawrence D. Bobo (eds.) *Racialized Politics: The Debate about Racism in America*. (pp. 1–43). Chicago: University of Chicago Press.

Sears, David O. Colette Van Laar, Mary Carrillo, and Rick Kosterman. 1997. "Is it Really Racism?: The Origins of White Americans' Opposition to Race-Targeted Policies." *Public Opinion Quarterly*, 61: 16–53.

Seelye, Katherine Q. " Fighting Health Care Overhaul, and Proud of it." *NY Times*. Sugust 30, 2009. http://www.nytimes.com/2009/08/31/us/politics/31demint.html.

Shadish, William R., Thomas D. Cook, and Donald T. Campbell. 1979. *Experimental and Quasi-Experimental Designs for Generalized Causal Inference*. Boston, MA: Houghton Mifflin.

Sidanius, Jim and Felicia Pratto. 1999. *Social Dominance: An Intergroup Theory of Social Hierarchy and Oppression*. New York: Cambridge University Press.

Skocpol, Theda and Vanessa Williamson. 2012. *The Tea Party and the Remaking of Republican Conservatism*. Oxford: Oxford University Press.

Smedley, Brian D. and John E. McDonough. 2011. "Repeal Would Dash Hopes to Reduce Disparities." *Baltimore Sun*, January 18.

Smith, Craig A. and Phoebe C. Ellsworth. 1985. "Patterns of Cognitive Appraisal in Emotion." *Journal of Personality and Social Psychology*, 48: 813–838.

Smith, Craig A., Kelly N. Haynes, Richard S. Lazarus, and Lois K. Pope. 1993. "In Search of the 'Hot' Cognitions: Attributions, Appraisals, and Their Relation to Emotion." *Journal of Personality and Social Psychology*, 65: 916–929.

Smith, Eliot R. 1993. "Social Identity and Social Emotions: Toward New Conceptualization of Prejudice." In D. Mackie and D. Hamilton (eds.) *Affect, Cognition, and Stereotyping: Interactive Processes in Group Perception* (pp. 297–315). New York: Academic Press.

Smith, Kevin B., Douglas R. Oxley, Mathew V. Hibbing, John R. Alford, and John R. Hibbing. (n.d.) "The Ick Factor: Physiological Sensitivity to Disgust as a Predictor of Political Attitudes." Typescript. University of Nebraska at Lincoln.

Sniderman, Paul M. and Edward G. Carmines. 1997. *Reaching beyond Race.* Cambridge, MA: Harvard University Press.

Sniderman, Paul M. and Thomas Piazza. 1993. *The Scar of Race.* Cambridge, MA: Harvard University Press.

Sniderman, Paul M. and Philip E. Tetlock. 1986. "Reflections on American Racism." *Journal of Social Issues*, 42: 173–187.

Sniderman, Paul M., G. C. Crosby, and W. G. Howell. 2000. "The Politics of Race." In David Sears, Jim Sidanius, and Lawrence Bobo (eds.) *Racialized Politics: The Debate about Racism in America.* (pp. 263–279) Chicago: University of Chicago Press.

Steele, Shelby 2006. *White Guilt: How Blacks and Whites Together Destroyed the Promise of the Civil Rights Era.* New York: Harper Collins.

Stephan, Walter. G., Kurt A. Boniecki, Oscar Ybarra, Ann Bettencourt, Kelly S. Ervin, Linda A. Jackson, Penny S. McNatt, and C. L. Renfro. 2002. "The Role of Threats in the Racial Attitudes of Blacks and Whites." *Personality and Social Psychology Bulletin*, 28: 1242–1254.

Sutherland, Peter D. and Cecilia Malmstrom. 2012. Europe's Immigration Challenge. The Guardian on the Web. http://www.guardian.co.uk/business/economics–blog/2012/jul/24/europe–immigration–challenge.

Suthammanont, Christina, David A. M. Peterson, Chris T. Owens, and Jane E. Leighley. 2010. "Taking Threat Seriously: Prejudice, Principle, and Attitudes toward Racial Policies." *Political Behavior*, 32: 231–253.

Swim, Janet K. and Deborah L. Miller 1999. "White Guilt: Its Antecedents and Consequences for Attitudes toward Affirmative Action." *Personality and Social Psychology Bulletin*, 25: 500–514.

Tajfel, Henri. 1981. *Human Groups and Social Categories.* Cambridge: Cambridge University Press.

Taylor, Donald M. and Vaishna Jaggi. 1974. "Ethnocentrism and Causal Attribution on a South Indian Context." *Journal of Cross-Cultural Psychology*, 5: 162–171.

Tesler, Michael. 2012. "The Spillover of Racialization into Health Care: How President Obama Polarized Public Opinion by Race and Racial Attitudes and Race." *American Journal of Political Science*, 56: 690–704.

Tesler, Michael and David O. Sears. 2010. *Obama's Race: The 2008 Election and the Dream of a Post-Racial America*. Chicago: University of Chicago Press.

Thernstrom, Abigail. 1987. *Whose Votes Count? Affirmative Action and Minority Voting Rights*. Cambridge, MA: Harvard University Press.

2010. Racial Epithets and the Tea Partiers, cont'd. http://www.nationalre-view.com/corner/197423/racial-epithets-and-tea-partiers-contd/abigail-thernstrom.

Thernstrom, Stephan and Abigail Thernstrom. 1997. *America in Black and White: One Nation, Indivisible*. New York: Simon & Schuster.

Tiedens, Larissa Z. and Susan Linton. 2001. "Judgment under Emotional Certainty and Uncertainty: The Effects of Specific Emotions on Information Processing." *Journal of Personality and Social Psychology*, 81: 973–988.

Toner, Robin. 2006. "Ad Seen as Playing to Racial Fears." New York Times on the Web October 26. http://www.nytimes.com/2006/10/26/us/politics/26tennessee.html.

Ture, Kwame and Charles V. Hamilton 1992. *Black Power: The Politics of Liberation*. New York: Vintage Books.

Tyler, Tom R. and Renee Weber. 1982. "Support for the Death Penalty; Instrumental Response to Crime or Symbolic Attitude." *Law and Society Review*, 17: 21–46.

Valentino, Nicholas A. 1999. "Crime News and the Priming of Racial Attitudes during Evaluations of the President." *Public Opinion Quarterly*, 63: 293–320.

Valentino, Nicholas A., and David O. Sears. 2005. "Old Times There Are Not Forgotten: Race and Partisan Realignment in the Contemporary South." *American Journal of Political Science*, 49: 672–688.

Valentino, Nicholas A., Antoine J. Banks, Vincent L. Hutchings, and Anne K. Davis. 2009. "Selective Exposure in the Internet Age: The Interaction between Anxiety and Information Utility." *Political Psychology* 30: 591–613.

Valentino, Nicholas A., Ted Brader, Eric W. Groenendyk, Krysha Gregorowicz, and Vincent L. Hutchings. 2011. "Election Night's Alright for Fighting: The Role of Emotions in Political Participation." *Journal of Politics*, 73: 156–170.

Valentino, Nicholas A., Ted Brader, and Ashley E. Jardina. 2013. "Immigration Opposition among U.S. Whites: General Ethnocentrism or Media Priming of Attitudes about Latinos?" *Political Psychology*, 34: 149–166.

Valentino, Nicholas A., Krysha Gregorowicz, and Eric W. Groenendyk. 2009. "Efficacy, Emotions and the Habit of Participation." *Political Behavior* 31: 307–330.

Valentino, Nicholas A., Vincent L. Hutchings, Antoine J. Banks, and Anne K. Davis. 2008. "Is a Worried Citizen a Good Citizen? Emotions, Political Information Seeking, and Learning via the Internet." *Political Psychology*, 29: 247–273.

Valentino, Nicholas A., Vincent L. Hutchings, and Ismail K. White. 2002. "Cues That Matter: How Political Ads Prime Racial Attitudes during Campaigns." *American Political Science Review*, 96: 75–90.

Wagner Ulrich, Oliver Christ, and Wilhelm Heitmeyer. 2010. "Anti-Immigration Bias." In John F. Dovidio, M. Hewstone, Peter Glick, and V. M. Esses (eds.) *Handbook of Prejudice, Stereotyping, and Discrimination* (pp. 361–376). Thousand Oaks, CA: Sage.

Ward, Dana. 1985. "Generation and the Expression of Symbolic Racism." *Political Psychology*, 6: 1–18.

Weiner, Bernard. 1986. *An Attributional Theory of Motivation and Emotion.* New York: Springer-Verlag.

White, Ismail K. 2007. "When Race Matters and When It Doesn't: Racial Group Differences in Response to Racial Cues." *American Political Science Review*, 02: 339–354.

Williamson, Vanessa, Theda Skocpol, and John Coggin. 2011. "The Tea Party and the Remaking of Republican Conservatism." *Perspectives on Politics*, 9: 25–43.

Wilson, Glenn D. 1973. *The Psychology of Conservatism.* New York: Academic Press.

Winter, Nick. 2006. "Beyond Welfare: Framing and the Racialization of White Opinion on Social Security." *American Journal of Political Science*, 50: 400–420.

Wood, Forrest G. 1968. *Black Scare: The Racist Response to Emancipation and Reconstruction.* Berkeley: University of California Press.

Zaller, John R. 1992. *The Nature and Origins of Mass Opinion.* Cambridge: Cambridge University Press.

Zeleny, Jeff. 2009. "Thousands Rally in Capital to Protest Big Government." New York Times on the Web, September 12. http://www.nytimes.com/2009/09/13/us/politics/13protestweb.html.

Zellman, Gail L. and David O. Sears. 1971. "Childhood Origins of Tolerance for Dissent." *Journal of Social Issues*, 27: 109–135.

Zernike, Kate. 2010. *Boiling Mad: Inside Tea Party America.* New York: Times Books.

Zick, Andreas, Thomas F. Pettigrew, and Ulrich Wagner. 2008. "Ethnic Prejudice and Discrimination in Europe." *Journal of Social Issues*, 64: 233–251.

Index

ABC News/*Washington Post* poll
  2009, 2
affective intelligence, 111–112, 124
  anger vs. enthusiasm, 119
  aversion, 111
  disposition system, 111
  enthusiasm, 112
  surveillance system, 111
affirmative action, 3, 8, 14–15, 17, 34–35,
  35 f. 1.4, 42, 47–48, 56, 59, 62, 64,
  68, 82, 159–160, 168. *See also* issues
Affordable Care Act, 105, 124.
  See also health care reform
African Americans, 8–9, 22, 34, 40, 108,
  119, 161, 163. *See also* civil rights
  legislation; civil rights movement;
  racism; segregation; slavery
Alabama, 12–13, 22, 80, 133, 153, 167
Allport, Gordon, 4–5, 6, 26, 29, 169
American Community Survey
  2009, 33
American National Election Studies
  (ANES), 38, 47, 93
  1985, 10, 35, 59–60
  1988, 10, 93–94, 95, 98
  2008, 10, 27, 62–64, 68, 162
  2010, 11, 136, 138–140
ANES. *See* American National Election
  Studies (ANES)
anger
  affective intelligence, 112
  affirmative action, 9, 35
  appraisal theories of emotion, 20

  attending a rally, 149–151
  austerity measures in Europe, 165
  contemporary racism, 3–4
  economic recession, 2
  emotion induction task, 45
  ethnocentrism, 10, 68, 160
  explicit appeals, 85
  health care reform, 2, 108, 111, 122,
    160, 166
  Horton, William, 78
  House vote choice in 2010, 144–146
  ideology, 42, 146–147
  implicit appeals, 84
  link to racial attitudes, 18, 31–32, 159
  link to symbolic racism, 9, 26–27,
    41–42, 61, 67, 68. (*see also* symbolic
    racism)
  nonracial, 2
  prejudice, 5, 8
  presidential candidates, 3
  racial liberals, 28, 84, 161
  racial polarization, 166
  racial socialization.
    (*see also* socialization)
  risk assessments, 21
  Senate vote choice in 2010, 141–144
  supporters of health care, 110
  Tea Party candidates, 137–138, 151
  Tea Party movement, 13, 16, 110, 132
  Tea Party rallies, 149
  toward government, 14
  welfare. (*see* welfare)
Angle, Sharron, 131–132, 133

203

Book 1-2 Feb Tickets

Made in the USA
Columbia, SC
24 January 2018